low-carb
meals in minutes

linda gassenheimer

Kyle Cathie Limited

low-carb
meals in minutes

a three-stage plan for permanent weight loss

linda gassenheimer

Kyle Cathie Limited

To Harold – for his love, support and advice.

Published in Great Britain 2002 by
Kyle Cathie Limited
122 Arlington Road
London NW1 7HP
www.kylecathie.com
general.enquiries@kyle-cathie.com

Reprinted in 2002

First published in USA in 2000 as *Low-carb Meals in Minutes:*
The Busy Person's Guide to Low-carbohydrate Meals in as Little as Ten Minutes
by Bay Books, San Francisco, USA

ISBN 1 85626 452 1

Text © 2000 Linda Gassenheimer
Photography © 2001 Juliet Piddington

UK Edition
Senior Editor: Helen Woodhall
Editorial Assistant: Esme West
Anglicisation: Dee Jones
Designer: Mark Buckingham
Production: Lorraine Baird and Sha Huxtable

Linda Gassenheimer is hereby identified as the author of this work
in accordance with Section 77 of the Copyright, Designs and Patents Act 1988.

A Cataloguing In Publication record for this title is available from the British Library.

Colour separations by Scanhouse Ltd.
Printed and bound by Kyodo

contents

introduction

Why are millions of people giving up their bagels, sandwiches and pasta meals? After unsuccessful attempts at weight loss from low-fat, high-carb diets, they're finally getting the results they want from a low-carb lifestyle.

My experience began five years ago. My husband told me he was going to try a low-carbohydrate diet. My first reaction was, 'Why? We have always eaten well-balanced meals, and most diets are just fads.' But he was determined. He had never had a weight problem before, but he found the few pounds gained during a holiday weren't coming off. In addition, he had just come from the cardiologist, where he learned his triglycerides were at an all-time high and his cholesterol was creeping into an area of concern.

As I watched him struggle to put together low-carb meals, I realised that this was going to be a challenge for both of us. Bagels for breakfast and cans of sugary soft drinks after tennis were out. No more baked potato with his steak. And what could he substitute for crackers and crisps with drinks?

I read all of the available books on the subject and set out to create low-carb recipes and menus that suited our fast-paced lives. As I became more involved, I worked with several cardiologists, endocrinologists and nutritionists working in the field. What I found was that the doctors and nutritionists could readily explain why this approach worked, but they could not tell me how to adapt it to my busy life. In fact, when I attended medical lectures, the reception for the diet was highly enthusiastic, but the questions at the end – even from the doctors in the audience – were 'How do I do it? What do I eat?' I began writing articles, giving lectures and teaching cooking classes. As I heard from readers and worked with participants in my classes, I was astounded by their weight-loss results. However, they were starved for additional recipes, techniques and guidelines.

I was lost when I first tried to make low-carbohydrate meals. I had to fundamentally rethink my approach to shopping and cooking. I started by restocking the pantry and refrigerator. The changes were dramatic.

off the list were:

- Low-fat processed foods, such as fat-free biscuits, cakes and other sugary desserts.
- Fat-free mayonnaise, salad dressings, cream cheese and soured cream.
- Condiments, sauces and salsas where sugar is one of the first five ingredients.
- Pancakes, bagels and waffles.
- Jams and jellies.
- Pizza and platefuls of pasta as a main course.
- Garnished baked potato as a meal.
- Sugary soft drinks and fruit juices.
- Crisps, pretzels and popcorn.

on the list were:

- Eggs, as many as four a week. We hadn't eaten them for breakfast in 10 years.
- Egg substitute (which is basically egg whites), as a good source of protein.
- A well-stocked vegetable drawer, with cucumbers, lettuce, celery, peppers, mushrooms and tomatoes.
- Low-fat deli meats, such as turkey breast, chicken, ham and lean roast beef.
- Brown rice and wholemeal pasta, in place of the lower fibre, less nutritious white varieties.
- High-fibre, whole-grain breads that are relatively low in carbohydrate.
- No-sugar-added tomato sauce and salad dressings.
- Real mayonnaise made with soya bean or olive oil
- High-fibre, no-sugar-added, bran breakfast cereal.
- Olive and rapeseed oil.
- Walnuts, pecans, almonds and peanuts.
- Eight glasses or 1.8 litres (3 pints) of water per day.

With this list of dos and don'ts, I created recipes that are fast, fun and delicious. My husband's response was enthusiastic: he lowered his cholesterol and triglyceride counts to healthy levels, lost his extra weight and has kept it off for five years.

Why is this lifestyle becoming mainstream? What are the principles behind it, and why is it working for so many people?

The theory behind low-carbohydrate, high-protein diets is this: eating lots of carbohydrates could over-stimulate insulin production, causing peaks and valleys in blood sugar levels that might, in turn, create hunger pangs. On the other hand, protein is digested more slowly, promoting more even blood sugar levels. Eating more protein, fewer carbs and more mono-unsaturated fat promotes weight loss by decreasing fat storage, increasing fat burning and delaying the onset of hunger pangs.

The major low-carbohydrate books, such as *The Zone*, *Protein Power*, *Sugar Busters*, *Dr. Atkins' New Diet Revolution* and *The Carbohydrate Addict's Diet*, differ in their approaches, but their central idea is the use of diet to moderate insulin levels. All the recipes in this book conform to the guidelines outlined in these books.

Several cardiologists steered me away from diets that call for high levels of saturated fat. My experience has also been that many diets are based on gimmicks. My husband and I, as well as my readers, like to go out and enjoy our meals. We don't want to be oddities at the dinner table, especially in business situations. We want to be part of the mainstream, and we've found that special timing and food combination requirements are unnecessary. They're difficult to follow and stick to over a long period, and they're not necessary for a successful low-carb lifestyle.

So how do you get started? *Low-Carb Meals in Minutes* follows my 'Dinner in Minutes' promise: attractive, delicious, fun, healthy, complete meals that are quick and easy to make.

The menus are designed to fit our fast-paced lives. After many years of juggling my family, career and a desire for good food, I've learned to use classic techniques and familiar combinations to produce delicious results while cutting cooking time.

For many days of the week we eat breakfast on the run, if at all, and lunch at our desks or at a fast food restaurant, while dinner is takeaway, home-delivered or restaurant fare. So, I've included some recipes based on assembling prepared foods, as well as a guide to eating out and ordering in.

You will find a wide variety of meals that sample many ethnic flavours. Wherever I travel throughout the world, I go to street markets with chefs, taste their foods and bring back their flavours to add to the repertoire of simple, low-carb recipes.

Low Carb Meals in Minutes covers all aspects of food, from preparing to purchasing ingredients. It streamlines the organisation of your kitchen. An efficient kitchen with equipment in easy reach, uncluttered work surfaces and a clean sink can save 10 to 15 minutes of preparation time. The recipes use products you can readily buy with one-stop shopping in your local supermarket, and there's no need to think about how to cook a dish or what goes with it.

Lastly, presentation is as important as preparation. If a dish doesn't look attractive, nothing else matters.

Consider 'Dinner in Minutes' an approach you can use for everyday meals, or dressed up for parties and special events. Each recipe works as a blueprint you can adapt to suit both your taste and the occasion:

- You can buy the freshest looking fish available rather than the variety called for in a recipe.

- You can use the best sirloin or fillet steak, or more economical cuts like flank and skirt steaks.

- Branching out to use the freshest and best ingredients, like a gourmet infused olive oil or aged balsamic vinegar, will add even more flavour.

- You can use the ingredients called for or change them within the blueprint guidelines.

- This flexible approach lets you choose whatever is in season, on sale or just fits your mood.

shopping list

Each recipe contains a shopping list based on how most people buy food.

- The shopping list saves you both time and money since you buy only what you need.

- Ingredients are listed by supermarket sections to help you navigate the aisles with ease.

- I've included tips on how to get in and out of the supermarket fast and how to take advantage of today's timesaving prepared foods.

- Quick shopping is as important as quick cooking. You won't have to think about how many mushrooms to buy. I've given you the amount.

- The staples list helps you organise your cupboards, so that they are not filled with extraneous items. You will already have many of the ingredients for the recipes and will only need to buy a few fresh items.

helpful hints and countdown

Each meal contains helpful hints on shopping, cooking and substitutions, as well as a countdown for getting the whole meal on the table at the same time.

- You can hit the kitchen on the run without having to plan or think about each step.

- In my home the dinner preparation starts the minute I turn on the light in the kitchen, and it does not end until the plates are brought to the table.

- The helpful hints tell you what to buy, how to buy it and what you can substitute. They include tips on the best preparation method and quick-cooking techniques, as well as time-saving clean-up tips.

3-step low-carb eating plan

Low-carbohydrate programs are normally divided into three phases: an initial phase of significant carbohydrate reduction, an intermediate phase for reintroduction of carbs and a maintenance phase of balanced eating.

1 quick start: reducing carbohydrate intake for maximum weight loss

The first step to successful eating in this plan calls for a reduction of carbohydrates. While differences exist, most proponents of lower carb levels advise an intake of about 30 to 40 grams of carbs a day. My Quick Start section maintains that level through healthy recipes containing vegetables and lean proteins. My students tell me breakfast presents the greatest challenge to adapting to low-carb eating. This 14-day meal plan gives you a variety of easy recipes, including some simple recipes for breakfast on the run, and others that can be completed in 15–20 minutes. Salads and wraps fit the bill for lunches. Try the Mozzarella Tomato Tower or Smoked Trout Salad. Many are available on restaurant menus, and you can use the recipes for proportion guidelines. Dinner can be Pecan-Crusted Fish or Pacific Rim Pork, both taking only minutes to make.

2 which carbs: reintroducing carbohydrates while continuing to lose weight

Two things usually happen at this point. You're losing weight and feel good, so you stay on the first phase until you get bored, or tempted. Or, you think, 'Great, I've lost weight! Now I can have the foods I love and forget about the carb restrictions.' The Which Carbs 14-day meal plan will help you sail through the second phase without having to question what you're eating. I reintroduce carbohydrates in the form of high-fibre, low–simple sugar carbohydrates. Bran breakfast cereal helps start the day the low-carb way. Add to this dishes like Cheddar Scramble or a scrumptious Raspberry Smoothie. Tex-Mex Layered Salad or Roast Turkey and Tzatziki Sandwich are two tasty lunches. How does Chicken Provençal, Neapolitan Steak or Seared Sesame Tuna sound for dinner?

3 right carbs: permanent level with great food for a healthy lifestyle

So, what should you eat to maintain your weight loss? Right Carbs has the answers. Vietnamese Pancakes, Prawn Caesar Wrap and Chicken with Parmesan and Tomato Sauce are a breakfast, lunch and dinner that are quick to make, fit the guidelines and, most important of all, taste fabulous!

Does it mean you can't have desserts? No. Some of the meals include a dessert. In addition, I have created a guilt-free Dessert chapter to satisfy your sweet tooth. When you want to take the time to make a special dessert try Strawberry Pecan Whip or Mocha Fudge Cake.

So how does my husband handle holidays and blow-out weekends? No need to worry here. Remember, balance is the key. We have found that you can splurge on special occasions without negative effects when you return to eating the Right Carbs. In other words, the low-carbohydrate approach is forgiving. Following the programme, even with some deviations, will produce a good result. My husband found that returning to the Right Carbs is easy because it takes so little effort and the menus are so appealing. Any time you want to restart weight loss, you can go back to Quick Start for a week or two and work yourself back up to Right Carbs.

The 14-day meal plans in each of the three sections are organised to provide a day-to-day guide to low-carb eating. The breakfasts, lunches and dinners are presented as entire meals. While you can mix and match if you prefer a different side dish, the meals have been created to achieve the nutritional priorities of that phase. By all means, if you don't like or can't eat a particular food, simply replace that meal with a meal from the same section. Regardless of the section, feel free to substitute fish or chicken for each other.

Low-Carb Meals in Minutes is for all of you who want to eat healthily and be able to fit a low-carbohydrate weight-loss programme into your time-starved lives. The low-carb lifestyle has certainly changed our lives. My husband and I no longer think about what is and isn't low-carb – we just consider it good food that fits into our busy schedule.

Before starting a programme of this type, it is always best to check with your doctor first. This is especially true if you are taking any medication under a doctor's care – particularly if being treated for diabetes. It might be interesting to look at your cholesterol and related blood tests before and after to compare your results.

My goal in sharing these recipes with you is to help you enjoy good food for good health. My husband and I love good food. Now, with these recipes, we can live to eat and eat to live.

Bon Appétit.

smart shopping the low-carb way

When I was the Executive Director of a gourmet grocery chain, I used to hear people say, 'I hate shopping. I'd cook more if I had the ingredients at home.' Here are some tips that will help get you in and out of the shops quickly.

some advice

The adage of 'don't go shopping on an empty stomach' is true. If I go to the shops when I'm tired and hungry, I just get to a starving point and eat anything offered to me. Go after a meal, or have a snack before you go. This will help you concentrate on what you should be buying instead of what you shouldn't buy.

Try to go to the supermarket when it isn't crowded or directly after a long day's work. Carry a cool box in your car so you can stop on the way to work, during lunch or at other times. Alternatively, if you have use of an office refrigerator, use it to store groceries. Here's a hint: there have been many times when I've accidentally left my shopping at work or at a friend's house. The best solution is to put your car keys in one of the bags. You won't be able to go anywhere without them.

Keep the foods from the staples list on hand. (See pages 13–15.) You will only need to pick up a few fresh items to complete your meal.

supermarket savvy
let the markets help you

Supermarkets are in a 'meals solution' revolution. They are constantly updating their selection to help us get our meals on the table fast. Use them to your advantage.

dairy

Reduced-fat cheese has come a long way. Gone is the rubbery cheese that won't melt. Many producers have used new techniques to develop lower fat cheeses that melt well.

deli

Ask for roast chicken breast only. Look for new leaner cuts of cooked meats – gammon, roast beef and ham have been made leaner without the use of high carbs.

fruit and veg

Bags of washed, ready-to-eat salads are one of the best conveniences I've seen. Read the labels. If they don't say ready-to-eat or washed, then you will need to wash the ingredients prior to using.

Many supermarkets have ready-to-eat cubes of melon and pineapple.

meat

Look for lower fat or lean meats – many supermarkets now have separate sections for lean meats or mark them with special labels. There are many marinated or precooked meats available, but check their sugar, salt and fat content.

salad bar

Great for picking up a quick salad or lunch and buying cut vegetables and fruits for cooking at home.

supermarket aisles

There are many items that make our lives easier, with more coming out each day. Low-fat, no-sugar-added salad dressings and tomato-based pasta sauces are a few of the products. In fact, there are so many available, it's best to try a few and, when you find one you like, buy several bottles to keep on hand. Again, the most important advice is to read the nutritional labels and ingredients lists.

how to read the labels

It's worth spending a few minutes reading food labels, as many prepared foods have added salt and sugar. However, the terms used can be confusing:

The Food Safety Act of 1990 makes it an offence to falsely describe a food's contents. Other provisions cover specific terms.

- 'Low-fat' means 3g or less per 100g/ml.
- 'Low-sodium' means 40mg or less per 100g/ml.
- 'Sugar Free' means 0.2g or less per 100g/ml.
- 'No added sugar' means no sugar, or foods composed mainly of sugar are added to the food or its ingredients.
- 'Light' or 'lite' is not covered by law. This term can be used to describe the texture of a food, or to suggest it is low in fat.

staples

Keep these staples on hand and you'll only need to pick up a few fresh items to make quick meals.

bottled or tinned goods

Dijon mustard

Fat-free, low-sodium chicken stock

Haricot, cannellini and black beans and chickpeas

Mayonnaise made with olive or soya bean oil

Low-sodium, no-sugar-added chopped tomatoes

and tomato sauce

Low-sodium tomato juice

No-sugar-added oil and vinegar dressing

No-sugar-added tomato salsa

Palm hearts

Tuna packed in water

Water chestnuts

condiments

Hot pepper sauce

Low-sodium soy sauce

Worcestershire sauce

dairy

Eggs

Egg substitute (basically liquid egg whites)

Light yoghurt

Parmesan cheese

Reduced-fat Swiss, Cheddar and mozzarella cheese

Reduced-fat cottage cheese

Skimmed milk

deli

Chicken breast

Lean ham (not honey-smoked or sugar-glazed)

Lean gammon

Lean roast beef

Turkey breast

dry goods

Artificial sweetener, preferably granulated

High-fibre, no-sugar-added, bran breakfast cereal

Oatmeal

Salt

Wholemeal flour

Wholemeal pasta

freezer goods

Frozen, diced green sweet pepper

Frozen, diced onion

grains and breads

Barley

Brown rice

Ebly

Lentils

Multi-grain bread

100% wholemeal bread

Rye bread

Wholemeal pitta bread

Wholemeal tortillas

Wild rice

oils and vinegars

Balsamic vinegar

Distilled white vinegar

Olive oil

Olive oil spray

Rapeseed oil

Red wine vinegar

Rice vinegar

produce department

Celery

Cucumbers

Garlic

Lemon

Peppers

Red onions

Yellow onions

Tomatoes

spices and herbs

Black peppercorns

Cayenne pepper

Chilli powder

Ground cinnamon

Ground cumin

Dried chives

Dried dill

Dried oregano

Dried rosemary

Dried tarragon

equipment

You really don't need a lot of special equipment to make these meals. However, the following items will speed your preparation time and make your life easier.

food processor

A food processor or hand-held blender will quickly slice, chop and blend foods together.

garlic press

Some of the newer ones allow you to crush garlic without peeling the cloves. I also use it to crush fresh ginger.

knives

Sharp knives are important for fast and accurate cutting. A dull knife can be dangerous. It can slip or slide when you are trying to slice. Three different types are all you really need for most cutting tasks: a 33cm (13in), 20.5cm (8in) and a serrated knife for fruits or tomatoes.

meat thermometer

I love the new style probe that uses a cord. The cord is connected to a dial that sits on the counter. With the cord, it works well for items on the stove, in the oven or under the grill.

microwave oven

Use this fast-cooking tool. And remember, any dish that's microwave safe is dishwasher safe, too.

pots and pans

You can make most of the meals in this book using a medium 23–25.5cm (9–10in) non-stick frying pan, a large 3–4 litre (5–7 pint) saucepan and a wok. Nonstick frying pans are essential, as these recipes are designed for cooking with small amounts of oil. If you follow the instructions, your food will not stick.

scale

A small kitchen scale is very handy and inexpensive.

vegetable peeler

For easy peeling, make sure yours is sharp. These are actually little knives and should be replaced as they start to dull.

quick cooking tips and helpful hints

Each recipe has a helpful hints section. Knowing what to substitute, how best to prepare ingredients or some other shortcut can make a big difference to the time it takes you to get your meal on the table.

chopping fresh herbs

To quickly chop herbs, dry and snip the leaves right off the stem with scissors.

crisp stir-fry

For crisp, not steamed, stir-fried vegetables, start with a very hot wok or frying pan. Let the vegetables sit a minute before tossing to allow the wok to regain its heat.

dried spices and herbs

If using dried spices, make sure they are less than 6 months old. To bring out the flavour of dried herbs, chop them with fresh parsley. The juice from the parsley will help release the flavour of the herbs.

electric cooking

To get a quick high/low response from electric rings, heat two rings, one on medium-high and the other on low. Move the pan back and forth between them.

fluffy rice

I like to cook my rice like pasta, using a pot of boiling water that's large enough for the rice to roll freely. Use this method or follow the directions on the packet of rice.

food processor

To use the food processor for a recipe without having to stop to wash the bowl, first chop the dry ingredients (such as nuts), and then the wet ones (such as onion). You won't have to stop in the middle of preparing the ingredients.

fresh ginger

To chop fresh ginger quickly, cut it into small cubes and press through a garlic press with large holes. If using a press with small holes, just capture the juice that is squeezed out; it will give enough flavour for the recipe.

parmesan cheese

Buy good quality Parmesan cheese and grate it by hand or in a food processor. Freeze extra for quick use later – simply spoon out what you need and leave the rest frozen.

peeling prawns

Buying peeled prawns saves time otherwise spent shelling them yourself.

slices and weight

To determine the weight of sliced cheese or meat, divide the packet weight by the number of slices.

timely stir-fry

To keep from looking back at a recipe as you stir-fry the ingredients, line them up on a cutting board or plate in the order of use. You will know which ingredient comes next.

washing herbs

The quickest way to wash watercress, rocket, parsley or basil is to place the bunch, head first, into a bowl of water. Leave for a minute, then lift out and shake dry. The dirt and sand will be left behind. Repeat if necessary.

washing mushrooms

To clean whole mushrooms, wipe them with a damp paper towel.

low-carb food guidelines

After you've cooked several recipes in this book, you will begin to understand the types of ingredients and proportions that are part of a low-carb lifestyle. Use these foods to help you create your own menus.

Vegetables are an important part of a healthy eating lifestyle. You may find it hard to believe that vegetables have carbohydrates. Some have more than others. Here's a list of vegetables that are low in carbohydrates versus those with high carbs that should be eaten in smaller quantities.

eat as many of these vegetables as you like:

Alfalfa sprouts

Artichokes

Asparagus

Aubergine

Bok choy

Broccoli

Brussels sprouts

Cabbage

Cauliflower

Celery

Courgettes

Cucumber

Green beans

Herbs, all types

Kale

Leeks

Lettuce, all types: curly-leaved endive, escarole, chicory, romaine, iceberg or round

Mange tout

Mixed salad leaves

Mushrooms, all types

Onions

Okra

Peppers: green, red, yellow sweet peppers and all hot peppers

Radishes

Spinach

Spring onions

Swedes

Swiss chard

Tomatoes

Turnips

Yellow courgettes

eat these vegetables in measured amounts (about 75g/3oz per serving):

Beetroot

Carrots

Hard squash, such as acorn or butternut

Potatoes

Sweetcorn

fruits

Fruits are often high in carbohydrates, and they should be avoided during the Quick Start phase. They are reintroduced in the Which Carb and Right Carb stages. The amounts given below are guidelines for how much should be eaten at a serving:

Apple (1 small)

Apricots (4)

Apricots, dried (7 halves)

Banana (½)

Berries: strawberries, raspberries and blueberries (110g/4oz)

Cantaloupe (¼ whole cantaloupe)

Cherries (12 cherries)

Grapes (about 12)

Grapefruit (½)

Honeydew (¼ whole honeydew)

Kiwi (1)

Lemon juice (50ml/2fl oz)

Lime juice (50ml/2fl oz)

Nectarine (1)

Orange (1)

Tangerine (1)

Mango (½)

Peach (1)

Pear (1)

Pineapple (2 rings or 60g/2½oz)

Plums (2)

Watermelon (175g/6oz)

meats, poultry and seafood

From steak to prawns and all of the meats in between, here's a list of the leaner cuts:

beef

Fillet

Minced sirloin

Silverside

Sirloin

Topside

poultry (skinless)

Chicken breast

Chicken legs

Low-fat turkey sausage (keep in freezer for a quick dinner, lunch or breakfast)

Poussins

Spring chicken

Turkey breast

seafood

All types of shellfish. Tuna, salmon, sardines, mackerel, halibut and trout are high in omega-3 fatty acids. Try to eat one of these on a regular basis.

pork

Fillet

Lean gammon

Lean ham (no honey-baked or sugar-glazed)

veal

Escalope

Leg fillet

Loin chop

lamb

Leg (preferred)

Chops with visible fat removed

easy ways to turn meals into 'special events'

Presentation is as important as preparation. The appeal of a beautiful plate of food adds to our eating experience. Some meals are special with friends or when celebrating events and holidays, but all meals can have a special dimension if you follow these tips and utilise your own creativity.

Use attractive dinnerware (colourful plates with matching napkins) to create a warm and fun atmosphere. If possible, set your table with the theme of the meal in mind:

● Serve Asian dishes on Chinese-style plates and place chopsticks alongside the knives and forks.

● Mediterranean meals look great served in Italian pottery or presented on place mats and tablecloths using the blues, reds and saffron yellows of Provence.

● Serve Tex-Mex dishes on earthenware plates that reflect the hot, earthy colours of the South-western United States and Mexico.

● Set the table for Caribbean meals using tropical-coloured place mats or arrange some hibiscus or tropical plants for a centrepiece.

For larger parties, dress up a buffet table by placing the platters of food on different levels. Simply use large mixing bowls turned upside down or small boxes. Place them on a table and cover with an attractive tablecloth. You can also create a sparking atmosphere by placing votive candles around the centrepiece or at varying intervals on the table.

Day-to-day eating can be made special with minimal effort. For recipes that use the grill or oven, use oven-to-table ware and bring the sizzling serving dish to the table. The sound and smell are part of the enjoyment. You can also serve omelettes and frittatas from a cast-iron pan.

Sprinkle soups with fresh green herbs, choosing a herb to complement the flavour of the dish: fresh basil or oregano for Italian meals, coriander for a Latin American or Caribbean touch and chives or rocket for extra bite. When serving meat, fish or poultry, make an attractive fan by slicing to one narrow point, then spreading the slices into a fan.

Add coloured lettuce leaves as a garnish or base for

different dishes. For example, Grilled Cheddar and Chicken Salad can be served on a bed of red-leaf lettuce. Similarly, make salads with different coloured leaves. Romaine, radicchio, rocket or basil leaves add varied colour and flavour. Or you can mix pale chicory with spicy, deep green watercress.

Dress up salads with nasturtiums or other edible flowers. Arrange them attractively on the plate or cut the petals into strips and sprinkle them over the salad. Alternatively, you can create attractive salads by stacking the ingredients. Form them into a pyramid shape or create layers, with the salad greens as a base and the other ingredients in alternating colours. A layer of sliced red peppers, for instance, can be followed by a layer of sliced cucumbers, then topped with sliced or cherry tomatoes.

When serving wraps, cut them in half crosswise on the diagonal and lay one half on its side and lean the other half against it. This will make an attractive display on the plate and show the colourful layers inside the wrap.

When entertaining, serve Chicory Filled with Ham and Cottage Cheese, arranged in a pretty star shape on a round serving platter, or Roast Beef and Watercress Wraps cut into small circles. Both can be prepared in advance.

The desserts in this book can be served with flavoured decaffeinated coffee or herbal teas. My favorite dessert for a crowd is the Raspberry Parfait. It's very pretty and takes only a few minutes to make. Best of all, it can be prepared ahead and refrigerated until needed.

The recipes in this book include tips on presentation, and have been planned with colour and texture in mind. When creating your own meals, consider their appearance as well as their taste.

tips for eating out

One of the biggest challenges to eating a healthy diet is that many of our meals are prepared outside the home. We eat out, order in and eat on the run. Use the recipes in this book as a guide to eating out, and you will be able to order from the menu with confidence. Here are some additional hints and tips to eat well in spite of your schedule.

● Avoid all deep-fried foods.

● Avoid sugary drinks. Opt for water, unsweetened iced tea or diet soft drinks.

● Plain, soft tacos or tortilla-filled wraps are fine as long as they aren't filled with rice and beans.

● Roasted or grilled meats are best. Make sure you include vegetables with your meal and avoid sugar-based sauces, especially barbecue sauce and most glazes.

● Many meals are loaded with carbs. If possible, order two vegetables instead of a starch.

● Ask for your salad dressing on the side. You'll be surprised at how far 1 tablespoon of dressing will go, or just dip your salad into the dressing.

● If you order dessert, share it with the table or make sure you don't have a starch during dinner. Better still, order a fresh fruit salad or berries.

● Have a low-carb snack (vegetables, a few nuts, a slice of low-fat cheese) before you go out to eat. This will help you avoid the basket of bread while you're waiting for your meal.

● Don't go out for drinks on an empty stomach. One drink will make you hungry, and you'll eat the first thing you can find. Have a healthy snack before you go out. If you think it will be a long night, start with sparkling water with a piece of lemon or lime or a diet soft drink first.

● Fast food can be fine. Order grilled chicken or fish and discard the bread. Or, eat it as an open sandwich using half a roll. Stay away from baked potatoes, chips and crisps.

● Chinese food can be loaded with sugar. Order stir-fried meats and vegetables or skewered meats, and avoid soups with fried wontons, egg rolls, ribs in thick sauce and noodles. Some restaurants now offer brown rice as an alternative to white.

● Italian food doesn't have to mean a plate of pasta. Order an antipasto platter or any of the meats, salads or vegetables.

● French food can be very healthy. Order clear soups, salads, vegetables, meats or seafood, but avoid heavy sauces and bread.

● Japanese sushi is based on rice – very often with sugar added to it. Try miso soup or any of the cooked meats and vegetables instead.

● Mexican food can be high in saturated fat and carbohydrates. Fajitas (1 tortilla) with garnishes, grilled meats and salads are fine. Avoid rice, refried beans and nachos.

Watch portion size when eating out. Here's a guide to help you size up what you should be eating.

75g (3oz) cooked meat, poultry, or fish	a deck of cards
35g (1½oz) cheese	6 dice
1 tortilla	a 18cm- (7in-) plate
1 muffin	a large egg
1 teaspoon butter	a thumb tip
2 tablespoons peanut butter	a golf ball

sizing it up*

Snacks are important little meals that will help you through the day, especially during the Quick Start phase. They can prevent that sinking feeling at 4 or 5 p.m. when your energy is low, or the mid-morning, is-it-time-for-lunch clock watching.

*Food Insight News published by IFIC (International Food Information Council)

Knowing what to snack on and how to have it handy can help prevent raids on the vending machine to satiate sweet cravings.

here are some ideas

● If you've had an extra large salad for lunch, take some back to the office or home and use the remainder as an afternoon snack.

● 25g (1oz) low-fat cheese

● 50ml (2fl oz) low-fat cottage cheese

● 25g (1oz) nuts, such as almonds, pecans and walnuts. Keep portion-sized packets of nuts in your drawer at work, handbag or brief case.

● 50g (2oz) deli meats, such as lean ham, turkey, chicken or roast beef

● 1 hard-boiled egg. Keep a few hard-boiled eggs on hand for snacks. They need to be refrigerated.

● 25g (1oz) sunflower seeds

● 6 olives

● Any vegetables such as cucumber slices, celery sticks, broccoli or cauliflower florets and sliced pepper

quick start

introduction

This two-week meal plan is designed to start you off on cutting carbs from your meals. When I give cooking classes and show these meals, the response always surprises me: 'You mean I can eat all of that?' Knowing the quantities of each type of food you can eat will help you build your own recipes to fit your lifestyle.

There is a range of recipes in this section. Some of them involve only the assembly of ready-prepared foods from the supermarket. Another category involves cooking a few ingredients to create the finished product. Still others involve cooking an entire meal in just minutes. This gives you a wide variety to choose from. Some you'll want to make on the weekend when you have more time, while others will be grab-and-go for midweek.

I have organised the menus into a meal-at-a-glance chart with some easy and quick meals mid-week and those that take a little more time for the weekends. They are arranged to give variety throughout the day and over the course of the week. The meals appear in the same sequence within the chapter. Just follow the meals in the order given for a complete two-week plan.

breakfasts

There's plenty of variety in these breakfasts to fit all tastes, from Swiss Scramble to Sausage and Vegetable Stir Fry. Pick the ones you like and use them for this two-week period.

mid-morning snack

When you first start reducing carbs, you will need to eat a mid-morning snack. I have included a section with some suggestions (see page 23).

lunch

There's a lunch for any occasion here – quick lunches that can be eaten at home or taken with you – and more elaborate lunches for when you have more time or friends stop by.

Enjoy a Herby Chicken Caesar Salad, Greek Salad or Prawn Salad. These meals can be made at home and taken to work. They are commonly found on lunch menus. If you are eating out, use these recipes as a guide for the portions you should eat and remember to ask for your dressing on the side. (See pages 22–23 for more tips on eating out.)

Make vinaigrette dressing according to the instructions provided in the recipes and keep it refrigerated, or speed up preparation by buying a low-carbohydrate dressing to keep on hand. Read the labels carefully. There should be no more than 1 gram of carbohydrate per 2 tablespoon serving.

mid-afternoon snack

When you first start reducing carbs, you will need to eat a mid-afternoon snack (see page 23).

dinner

Do you feel like Chinese, French, Tex-Mex or American food tonight? There's something from each ethnic group – Pacific Rim Pork, Pecan-Crusted Fish with Vegetable Creole, Tex-Mex Meat Loaf and Sirloin Burger with Fresh Slaw are some of the tempting meals.

Salsa-baked Snapper is a 15-minute meal. Steak au Poivre and Rosemary-Roasted Pork take longer, about 30 minutes.

I've served these meals at dinner parties without telling anyone they were low-carb. No one knew and the only question asked was could they have the recipe.

How low is low-carb? It's important to reduce carbohydrate intake low enough for a period of time so that you eliminate the peaks of insulin secretion. Following the Quick Start 14-day plan, you will consume an average of 30 to 40 grams of carbohydrates per day. Carbohydrates percentage is based on carbohydrates less fibre consumed, which is the normal way of calculating carbohydrate consumption. The balance of these meals is 10 per cent of calories from carbohydrates, 36 per cent of calories from lean protein, 40 per cent of calories from mono-unsaturated fat, and 11 per cent of calories from saturated fat.

To achieve the correct balance, the recipes have been designed as complete meals. Whatever meal you pick, it's best to stay with the entire menu given.

quick start 14-day menu plan

week 1	breakfast	lunch	dinner
sunday	Smoked Salmon Pinwheels 29	Mozzarella Tomato Tower 44	Spicy Prawns with Roasted Asparagus 59–60
monday	Salsa and Sliced Eggs 30	Turkey Bundles 45	Asian Ginger Salmon 61–62
tuesday	Pesto Scramble 31	Tuna Salad Wraps 46	Glazed Balsamic Chicken with 63–64
wednesday	Cheesy Fried Eggs 32	Smoked Trout Salad 47	Tex-Mex Meat Loaf . . .65
thursday	Sautéed Ham and Tomatoes 33	Roast Beef and Watercress Wraps 48	Marsala Chicken . .66–67
friday	Florentine Eggs and Ham 34	Crunchy Chicken Salad 49	Sirloin Burger with Fresh Slaw 68
saturday	Sausage and Vegetable Stir Fry 35	Curried Chicken–stuffed Tomatoes 50	Pacific Rim Pork . . .69–70

week 2	breakfast	lunch	dinner
sunday	Pepper and Turkey Omelette 36	Salmon Balsamico 51	Veal Escalopes with Garlic Greens 71
monday	Smoked Chicken and Cheddar Grill 37	Ham and Cucumber Parcels 52	Pecan-crusted Fish with Vegetable Creole 72
tuesday	Devilish Eggs 38	Greek Salad 53	Sausage-pepper Sauté 73
wednesday	Swiss Scramble 39	Grilled Cheddar and Chicken Salad 54	Salsa-baked Snapper 74
thursday	Chicory filled with Ham and Cottage Cheese 40	Prawn Salad 55	Rosemary-roasted Pork 75–76
friday	Portobello and Gammon Omelette 41	Herby Chicken Caesar Salad 56	Herb-stuffed Chicken 77–78
saturday	Cheddar and Sausage Frittata 42	Portobellos Stuffed with Smoked Trout and Sun-dried Tomatoes 57	Steak au Poivre . . .79–80

quick start
breakfasts

smoked salmon pinwheels

Smoked salmon spread with cream cheese makes an elegant, quick breakfast for midweek or the weekend.

smoked salmon pinwheels

350g (12oz) smoked salmon
50g (2oz) low-fat cream cheese
1 tablespoon skimmed milk
1 medium cucumber, sliced
2 medium tomatoes, sliced
Salt and freshly ground black
    pepper to taste

Place salmon on a cutting board. Soften cream cheese with skimmed milk and mix until smooth. Spread on salmon. Roll up, slice crosswise into 1cm (½in) pinwheels, and place on 2 plates. Season the cucumber and tomato slices with salt and pepper and divide between the plates. *Makes 2 servings.*

One serving: 324 calories, 37g protein, 11g carbohydrate, 14g fat (6g saturated), 61mg cholesterol, 1468mg sodium, 1g fibre

countdown

- *Slice cucumber and tomatoes.*
- *Complete recipe.*

shopping list

TO BUY:
  1 small packet low-fat cream
    cheese (50g/2oz needed)
  350g (12oz) sliced smoked
    salmon
  1 medium cucumber
  2 medium tomatoes
STAPLES:
  Skimmed milk
  Salt
  Black peppercorns

salsa and sliced eggs

Salsa makes an appetising garnish for the eggs. Choose mild or hot, according to your taste. Keep hard-boiled eggs on hand, so this breakfast can be put together in minutes.

helpful hint

- *Use an egg slicer to quickly slice the eggs.*

countdown

- *Hard boil the eggs.*
- *Slice cucumbers.*
- *Assemble dish.*

shopping list

TO BUY:
   1 small jar no-sugar-added
      tomato salsa
   medium cucumber
STAPLES:
   Eggs

salsa and sliced eggs

4 eggs
1 medium cucumber, peeled
125ml (4fl oz) no-sugar-added
   tomato salsa

Place eggs in a small saucepan and cover with cold water. Bring to a boil. Reduce the heat and gently simmer for 12 minutes. Drain and rinse eggs under cold water. Peel and slice with an egg slicer or cut in half lengthwise.

Slice the cucumber in half crosswise; cut into 4 pieces lengthwise. Divide the egg slices between 2 plates and spoon with salsa. Arrange the cucumbers around the eggs and serve.
Makes 2 servings.

One serving: 201 calories, 15g protein, 12g carbohydrate, 11g fat (3g saturated), 426mg cholesterol, 511mg sodium, 3g fibre

pesto scramble

Fresh basil, parsley, pine nuts and Parmesan cheese are the ingredients of a good pesto.
● Using a jar of pesto bought in the supermarket, you can make these scrambled eggs in just minutes. They can even be made in the microwave. ● There are many good varieties of pesto available – look for one made with olive oil. ● The eggs are served on a bed of wilted lettuce. Most people don't think of cooking lettuce. It develops a tasty, nutty flavour.

pesto scramble

150g (5oz) washed, ready-to-eat, Italian-style salad leaves
225ml (8fl oz) egg substitute
2 teaspoons prepared pesto
2 teaspoons olive oil
2 tablespoons freshly grated Parmesan cheese

Place the lettuce in a microwave-safe bowl and microwave on high for 3 minutes. Place on 2 plates. Mix the egg substitute and pesto together. Heat the oil in a medium-sized non-stick frying pan over a high heat. Reduce the heat to low, or remove the pan from the heat, and add the egg mixture. Scramble for about 1 minute, or until set to desired consistency. Place over the lettuce and sprinkle with Parmesan cheese.
Makes 2 servings.

One serving: 279 calories, 18g protein, 10g carbohydrate, 18g fat (5g saturated), 236mg cholesterol, 147mg sodium, 1g fibre

helpful hints

● If you don't have a microwave oven, sauté the lettuce for about 1 minute in a frying pan, remove to a plate and scramble the egg in the same pan.
● Buy good quality Parmesan cheese and grate it yourself. Freeze extra for quick use later – simply spoon out what you need and leave the rest frozen.
● 2 whole eggs and 6 egg whites can be used instead of egg substitute.
● Any type of washed, ready-to-eat lettuce can be used.

countdown

● Microwave lettuce.
● Make scrambled eggs.

shopping list

TO BUY:
1 jar prepared pesto (50g/2oz needed)
1 bag washed, ready-to-eat, Italian-style salad leaves(150g/5oz needed)
STAPLES:
Olive oil
Egg substitute
Parmesan cheese

cheesy fried eggs

Eggs sunny side up are an American tradition. Here's a variation on the theme.

cheesy fried eggs

2 handfuls washed, ready-to-eat lettuce leaves

Half a cucumber, peeled and sliced

2 teaspoons olive oil

2 large eggs

Salt and freshly ground black pepper to taste

75g (3oz) sliced reduced-fat Swiss or Gruyère cheese (about 4 slices)

Place the lettuce on a plate and microwave on high for 1 minute. Divide the lettuce and cucumber between 2 plates, and heat the olive oil in a medium-sized non-stick frying pan over a medium-high heat. Break the eggs into the pan, and sprinkle with salt and pepper to taste. Cover and cook for 2 minutes. Remove the lid and place the cheese over the egg yolks. Cover and cook 1 minute. Serve the eggs on the cooked lettuce.

Makes 2 servings.

One serving: 265 calories, 23g protein, 8g carbohydrate, 17g fat (6g saturated), 236mg cholesterol, 147mg sodium, 1g fibre

smoked salmon pinwheels **p29**

florentine eggs and ham p34

sautéed ham and tomatoes

This is a quick, 5-minute breakfast that can be made in a frying pan, grill pan or microwave oven.

sautéed ham and tomatoes

225g (8oz) sliced lean ham
2 small tomatoes, sliced
2 teaspoons olive oil
Salt and freshly ground black
*   pepper to taste*

Sauté the ham in a medium-sized non-stick frying pan over a medium-high heat for 2 minutes, or until the ham begins to brown. Place the tomatoes on 2 plates and drizzle with olive oil. Sprinkle with salt and pepper to taste. Divide the ham between the plates and serve.
Makes 2 servings.

One serving: 305 calories, 30g protein, 12g carbohydrate, 16g fat (5g saturated), 136mg cholesterol, 797mg sodium, 3g fibre

helpful hint

● *Look for low-fat ham. Stay away from honey-baked ham.*

countdown

● *Preheat grill (if using).*
● *Cook ham.*
● *Assemble dish.*

shopping list

TO BUY:
225g (8oz) sliced lean ham
2 small tomatoes

staples:

Olive oil
Salt
Black peppercorns

florentine eggs and ham

Cooking the washed, ready-to-eat spinach in a microwave makes this a 15-minute breakfast.

helpful hints

- Buy good quality Parmesan cheese and grate it yourself. Freeze extra for quick use later – simply spoon out what you need and leave the rest frozen.
- If you prefer fried eggs add the olive oil to the same pan. Break the eggs into the pan and fry until set, about 1 minute. Using a spatula, gently turn the eggs over. Sprinkle with salt and pepper to taste.

countdown

- Make spinach.
- Make ham and eggs.

shopping list

TO BUY:

   225g (8oz) sliced lean ham

   1 bag washed, ready-to-eat fresh spinach (275g/10oz needed)

STAPLES:

   Eggs

   Parmesan cheese

   Olive oil

   Salt

   Black peppercorns

florentine eggs and ham

275g (10oz) washed, ready-to-eat fresh spinach

2 tablespoons freshly grated Parmesan cheese

Salt and freshly ground black pepper to taste

225g (8oz) sliced lean ham (about 8 slices), cut into strips

1 tablespoon distilled white vinegar

2 eggs

Place the spinach in a microwave-safe bowl and microwave on high for 5 minutes. Sprinkle with the Parmesan cheese and season with salt and pepper to taste. Chop the cooked spinach into bite-sized pieces and divide between 2 plates.

Set a medium-sized non-stick frying pan over a medium heat. Add the ham and sauté for 2 minutes, or until slightly browned. Divide evenly over the beds of spinach.

Next, add the vinegar to a pan of simmering water and create a whirlpool in its centre. Drop an egg into the whirlpool, turn off the heat and leave covered for 4 minutes, or until set. Repeat with the second egg. Serve the eggs over the ham and spinach.

Makes 2 servings.

One serving: 337 calories, 37g protein, 10g carbohydrate, 19g fat (5g saturated), 270mg cholesterol, 1501mg sodium, 7g fibre

sausage and vegetable stir fry

Here's a tasty breakfast made without eggs. If you can find them, keep frozen, diced onions and green pepper to use when really pressed for time. The flavour and texture are slightly different, but the results are good and save chopping time.

sausage and vegetable stir fry

275g (10oz) washed, ready-to-eat
    fresh spinach

Salt and freshly ground black
    pepper to taste

2 teaspoons olive oil

2 low-fat turkey sausages
    (175g/6oz), cut into 1cm
    (½in) slices

4 slices yellow onion

1 medium-sized green pepper,
    seeded and sliced

6 button mushrooms, sliced

Place the spinach in a microwave-safe bowl and microwave on high for 5 minutes. Add salt and pepper to taste. Divide the spinach between 2 plates. Heat the olive oil in a non-stick frying pan over a medium-high heat. Add sausages, onion, pepper and mushrooms. Sauté for 5 minutes or until sausages are cooked through. Season with salt and pepper to taste. Spoon over spinach. Makes 2 servings.

One serving: 271 calories, 22g protein,
18g carbohydrate, 13g fat (3g saturated),
45mg cholesterol, 715mg sodium, 7g fibre

helpful hints

● To determine the weight of each sausage, divide the packet weight by the number of sausages.

● To save time, buy sliced mushrooms.

● If using whole mushrooms, clean them with a damp paper towel.

countdown

● Microwave spinach.

● Sauté sausage and vegetables.

shopping list

TO BUY:

1 small packet low-fat turkey
    sausages (175g/6oz
    needed)

1 small bag washed, ready-
    to-eat fresh spinach

1 medium-sized green
    pepper

1 small packet button
    mushrooms

STAPLES:

Yellow onion

Olive oil

Salt

Black peppercorns

pepper and turkey omelette

Colourful peppers flavour this tasty omelette – and it takes only 20 minutes from start to finish. The recipe can easily be doubled, saving half for the next day. Simply rewarm in a microwave for about 2 minutes on high.

pepper and turkey omelette

225ml (8fl oz) egg substitute
25g (1oz) chopped fresh parsley
Salt and freshly ground black
    pepper to taste
2 teaspoons olive oil
1 medium-sized red pepper, sliced
1 medium-sized yellow pepper,
    sliced
175g (6oz) sliced smoked turkey
    breast, diced

Preheat the grill. Combine the egg substitute and parsley. Add salt and pepper to taste. Place a medium-sized non-stick frying pan over a medium-high heat and add the oil. Sauté the peppers for 5 minutes. Add the egg mixture and turkey and allow to set for 2 minutes. Place under the grill for 3 minutes. Remove from the grill, cut in half, slide out of the pan and serve hot. *Makes 2 servings.*

One serving: 289 calories, 39g protein,
13g carbohydrate, 8g fat (2g saturated),
60mg cholesterol, 295mg sodium, 0g fibre

smoked chicken and cheddar grill

This is an on-the-go breakfast that can be made in 5 minutes. Any type of lean or low-fat cooked meat can be used.

smoked chicken and cheddar grill

2 large cucumbers, peeled and sliced on the diagonal

2 tablespoons mayonnaise made with soya bean or olive oil

175g (6oz) sliced roasted chicken breast

Salt and freshly ground black pepper to taste

35g (1½oz) sliced reduced-fat Cheddar cheese (about 2 slices)

Preheat the grill. Place the cucumbers on a foil-lined baking tray and spread the slices with mayonnaise. Top with the chicken slices and season with salt and pepper to taste. Tear the cheese into pieces to cover the chicken. Place under the grill for 1 minute or until the cheese melts. Divide between 2 plates and serve.
Makes 2 servings.

One serving: 351 calories, 34g protein,
9g carbohydrate, 20g fat (5g saturated),
92mg cholesterol, 329mg sodium, 2g fibre

helpful hints

● *Slice the cucumber on the diagonal for a larger surface area and oval-shaped slice.*

● *To determine the weight of each slice of cheese, divide the packet weight by the number of slices.*

countdown

● *Preheat grill.*

● *Complete recipe.*

shopping list

TO BUY:

1 packet sliced reduced-fat Cheddar cheese (35g/ 1½oz) needed

175g (6oz) sliced roasted chicken breast

2 large cucumbers

STAPLES:

Mayonnaise made with soya bean or olive oil

Salt

Black peppercorns

devilish eggs

Devilled eggs are a classic comfort food. They can be made ahead, stored in the refrigerator and are easily carried with you for a breakfast or lunch on the run. In fact, it's a good idea to keep a few hard-boiled eggs on hand for quick meals or snacks.

devilish eggs

6 eggs (only 2 yolks used)

2 tablespoons mayonnaise made with soya bean or olive oil

2 teaspoons Dijon mustard

Large pinch of cayenne pepper

2 tablespoons snipped fresh chives

Salt and freshly ground black pepper to taste

8 celery stalks, cut into 10cm (4in) pieces

Place the eggs in a small saucepan and cover with cold water. Set over a medium-high heat and bring to a boil. Reduce the heat to low and gently simmer for 12 minutes. Drain, and then fill the pan with cold water. When the eggs are cool to the touch, peel and cut in half lengthwise. Remove and discard the yolks from 4 of the eggs. Set the egg whites on 2 plates. Place the remaining 2 whole eggs in the bowl of a food processor or mash with a fork in a mixing bowl. Add the mayonnaise, mustard, cayenne pepper and chives. Season with salt and pepper to taste. Process until smooth. Fill the egg whites with the mixture. Serve with celery.

Makes 2 servings.

One serving: 251 calories, 16g protein, 14g carbohydrate, 18g fat (3g saturated), 218mg cholesterol, 653mg sodium, 4g fibre

swiss scramble

This breakfast can be made in 15 minutes or less. Swiss cheese, sweet peppers and spring onions add flavour and colour to the light eggs.

swiss scramble

2 teaspoons olive oil

2 medium-sized green peppers, sliced

2 whole eggs

6 egg whites

150g (5oz) spring onions, sliced

75g (3oz) sliced reduced-fat Swiss or gruyère cheese (about 4 slices), torn into small pieces

Salt and freshly ground black pepper to taste

Heat the oil in a medium-sized non-stick frying pan. Add the peppers and sauté for 3 minutes. Combine the whole eggs, egg whites, spring onions and cheese in a medium-sized bowl and season with salt and pepper to taste. Add to the frying pan and scramble for 2 minutes, or until cooked to desired doneness. Spoon onto 2 plates and serve.

Makes 2 servings.

One serving: 346 calories, 35g protein, 15g carbohydrate, 17g fat (6g saturated), 236mg cholesterol, 311mg sodium, 0g fibre

helpful hints

● *225ml (8fl oz) egg substitute can be used instead of whole eggs.*

● *Any type of reduced-fat cheese can be used.*

● *To determine the weight of each slice of cheese, divide the packet weight by the number of slices.*

countdown

● *Prepare all ingredients.*

● *Make spinach.*

● *Make eggs.*

shopping list

TO BUY:

1 packet sliced reduced-fat Swiss or gruyère cheese (75g/3oz needed)

2 medium-sized green peppers

1 bunch spring onions

STAPLES:

Olive oil

Eggs

Salt

Black peppercorns

chicory filled with ham and cottage cheese

Walnuts, ham and cottage cheese make a crunchy, flavourful stuffing for chicory spears. It's also great as hors d'oeuvres or a quick snack. ● This is a good on-the-go breakfast. It takes just seconds to blend the stuffing to a creamy consistency.

chicory filled with ham and cottage cheese

275g (10oz) lean ham (about 10 slices)
24 walnuts (50g/2oz)
110g (4oz) low-fat cottage cheese
Salt and freshly ground black pepper to taste
2 medium heads chicory, leaves separated

Chop the ham, walnuts and cottage cheese in a food processor. Add salt and pepper to taste. Spread the mixture into wide base of each chicory leaf.
Makes 2 servings.

One serving: 432 calories, 39g protein, 11g carbohydrate, 27g fat (6g saturated), 72mg cholesterol, 1425mg sodium, 2g fibre

helpful hints

● *Buy large heads of chicory. The larger leaves are easier to fill.*
● *The best way to clean chicory is to wipe the outer leaves with damp kitchen paper. Try not to soak the leaves in water, as they tend to brown.*

countdown

● *Chop ham, walnuts and cheese.*
● *Fill chicory.*

shopping list

TO BUY:
1 tub low-fat cottage cheese (225g/8oz needed)
275g (10oz) sliced lean ham
1 small packet walnut pieces (50g/2oz needed)
2 medium heads chicory
STAPLES:
Salt
Black peppercorns

portobello and gammon omelette

Gammon, mushrooms and spring onions flavour this egg white omelette. ● Look for lean or low-fat gammon. There are several brands available in the supermarket, and they are all packaged to keep for several weeks in the refrigerator. I always buy extra to have on hand for snacks or lunch.

portobello and gammon omelette

8 egg whites
60g (2½oz) spring onions, sliced
Salt and freshly ground black
   pepper to taste
2 teaspoons olive oil
225g (8oz) portobello mushrooms,
   sliced
225g (8oz) sliced lean gammon,
   diced

Preheat the grill. Combine the egg whites and spring onions in a small mixing bowl and season with salt and pepper to taste. Heat the oil in a medium-sized non-stick frying pan over a medium-high heat. Add the mushrooms and gammon and sauté for 3 minutes. Add the egg mixture and allow to set for 2 minutes. Place under the grill for 3 minutes, or until just cooked. Cut the omelette in half, slide out of the pan and serve.
Makes 2 servings.

One serving: 297 calories, 37g protein,
10g carbohydrate, 8g fat (1g saturated),
260mg cholesterol, 282mg sodium, 0g fibre

helpful hints

- *Any type of mushrooms can be used for this recipe.*
- *If you prefer, cover the omelette with a lid instead of finishing it under the grill.*
- *To save time, use presliced portobello mushrooms. If the slices are too large, cut them in half.*
- *Use a pan with an ovenproof handle to go under the grill.*

countdown

- *Preheat grill.*
- *Make omelette.*

shopping list

TO BUY:
   225g (8oz) sliced lean gammon
   1 bunch spring onions (8 needed)
   225g (8oz) sliced portobello mushrooms
STAPLES:
   Eggs
   Olive oil
   Salt
   Black peppercorns

cheddar and sausage frittata

A frittata is a little like a crustless quiche and takes about 10 minutes to cook. It's great for breakfast, and when cooled and cut into squares, it makes great canapés or snacks.

cheddar and sausage frittata

2 teaspoons olive oil
225g (8oz) red onion, sliced
1 medium-sized red pepper, sliced
2 celery stalks, sliced
2 low-fat turkey sausages, cut into 1cm (½in) slices
175g (6oz) tinned water chestnuts, drained and sliced
225ml (8fl oz) egg substitute
50g (2oz) rocket, washed and sliced
50g (2oz) grated, reduced-fat Cheddar cheese
Salt and freshly ground black pepper to taste

Preheat the oven to 200°C/400°F/gas mark 6. Heat the olive oil in a medium-sized non-stick frying pan over a medium-high heat. Sauté the onion, pepper, celery, sausages and water chestnuts over a high heat for 3 minutes. Combine the egg substitute, rocket and cheese in a medium-sized bowl and season with salt and pepper to taste. Reduce the heat to medium and pour the egg mixture into the pan. Swirl in the pan to cover the vegetables. Allow to set for 3 minutes. Transfer to the oven for 7 minutes, or until the eggs set to the desired consistency. Cut the frittata in half, slide out of the pan onto 2 plates and serve.

Makes 2 servings.

One serving: 396 calories, 36g protein, 20g carbohydrate, 19g fat (7g saturated), 65mg cholesterol, 1088mg sodium, 3g fibre

quick start
lunches

mozzarella tomato tower

This tower is made by alternating tomato slices, mozzarella and fresh basil until the tomato is re-formed. It's a modern version of a tomato-mozzarella plate that's fun to serve and delicious, too.

mozzarella tomato tower

4 teaspoons olive oil
2 medium tomatoes, cut into 1cm (½in) slices
Salt and freshly ground black pepper to taste
225g (8oz) reduced-fat mozzarella cheese, sliced
150g (5oz) washed, ready-to-eat mixed salad leaves
2 tablespoons pine nuts
20 leaves fresh basil
2 tablespoons no-sugar-added oil and vinegar dressing

Drizzle 2 teaspoons of the olive oil over the tomato slices, and season with salt and pepper to taste. Drizzle the remaining 2 teaspoons of olive oil over the cheese, tossing to coat well. Divide the salad leaves between 2 plates. Sprinkle with the pine nuts. Place the stem slices of the tomatoes in the centre of the salad, skin side down. Sprinkle a little mozzarella on top of each. Place a few basil leaves on the mozzarella. Continue layering the tomato slices, mozzarella and basil leaves until the tomatoes are rebuilt, ending with a sprinkling of mozzarella on top. Gently press the slices together with the palm of your hand. Drizzle the tomatoes and salad leaves with the dressing and serve.
Makes 2 servings.

One serving: 427 calories, 35g protein, 12g carbohydrate, 24g fat (6g saturated), 16mg cholesterol, 971mg sodium, 4g fibre

turkey bundles

For the times when you don't have time to make a lunch, here is a dish you can make and eat in minutes.

turkey bundles

350g (12oz) sliced turkey breast
18 to 20 leaves romaine or other lettuce
100g (3¹/₂oz) coleslaw
2 small tomatoes, sliced

Place a slice of turkey on a lettuce leaf. Add a spoonful of coleslaw and a slice of tomato. Fold the lettuce. Continue with additional lettuce leaves until all the turkey is used.
Makes 2 servings.

One serving: 398 calories, 52g protein, 16g carbohydrate, 12g fat (3g saturated), 125mg cholesterol, 269mg sodium, 2g fibre

helpful hints

● *Check the ingredients of shop-bought coleslaw, as some prepared versions have added sugar.*
● *Drain the coleslaw before use.*

shopping list

TO BUY:
350g (12oz) sliced turkey breast
100g (3¹/₂oz) coleslaw
1 head romaine or other lettuce
2 small tomatoes

tuna salad wraps

You can find almost any type of food in wraps these days, including a whole dinner. I've used large lettuce leaves for the wrap in this recipe. ● These wraps are really portable and will last at least a day in the refrigerator. I take them out when we go sailing. They are great for a day outside – easy to serve and very delicious.

tuna salad wraps

12 or 14 large romaine lettuce leaves, washed and dried

500g (18oz) tinned tuna packed in water, rinsed and drained

50ml (2fl oz) mayonnaise made from soya bean or olive oil

25g (1oz) snipped chives

110g (4oz) red onion, diced

Salt and freshly ground black pepper to taste

12 x 30.5 x 10cm (11 x 4 in) rectangles foil, parchment paper or greaseproof paper

110g (4oz) fresh basil leaves, washed and dried

350g (12oz) alfalfa sprouts, tops only

Crush the stems of the lettuce leaves so they lie flat. In a small mixing bowl, break the tuna up with a fork and stir in the mayonnaise, chives and onion. Add salt and pepper to taste. Spread the foil pieces on the work surface. Place a romaine leaf on each square. Spoon some of the tuna salad on each leaf and top with the basil. Spoon the remaining tuna salad on top and sprinkle with alfalfa sprouts. Roll up each leaf like a cigar, and wrap tightly in the foil. Seal the ends and slice in half crosswise. Use immediately or place in plastic bags and refrigerate until needed.

Makes 2 servings.

One serving: 421 calories, 37g protein, 12g carbohydrate, 25g fat (3g saturated), 66mg cholesterol, 738mg sodium, 1g fibre

smoked trout salad

It takes only a few minutes to put this tasty lunch together. A good quality smoked trout needs very little added to it to make a great meal.

smoked trout salad

*175g (6oz) washed, ready-to-eat
    mixed salad leaves*
350g (12oz) smoked trout
25g (1oz) walnut pieces
2 teaspoons olive oil
*Salt and freshly ground black
    pepper to taste*

Place the salad leaves on individual dishes. Flake trout into 1cm (½in) pieces and place on top of the salad leaves. Sprinkle with the walnuts and drizzle with the oil. Season with salt and pepper to taste and serve.
Makes 2 servings.

One serving: 342 calories, 31g protein, 5g carbohydrate, 22g fat (4g saturated), 77mg cholesterol, 60mg sodium, 2g fibre

helpful hints

● *Any type of smoked fish can be used.*
● *Any type of lettuce can be used.*

countdown

● *Prepare ingredients.*
● *Assemble salad.*

shopping list

TO BUY:
    350g (12oz) smoked trout
    *1 small packet walnut pieces
       (25g/1oz needed)*
    *1 bag washed, ready-to-eat
       mixed salad leaves*
STAPLES:
    Olive oil
    Salt
    Black peppercorns

roast beef and watercress wraps

Rocket and horseradish give these roast beef wraps a spicy bite. Watercress adds a little crunch. Wraps are great finger food. This recipe uses large lettuce leaves instead of tortillas to wrap around the filling.

roast beef and watercress wraps

12 large round lettuce leaves, washed and dried

12 x 30.5 x 10cm (11 x 4in) rectangles foil, parchment paper or greaseproof paper

2 tablespoons mayonnaise made with soya bean or olive oil

2 tablespoons horseradish

350g (12oz) sliced lean roast beef

110g (4oz) fresh rocket, washed and dried

12 small sprigs watercress, washed and dried

Crush the stems of the lettuce leaves so they lie flat. Place the foil pieces on the work surface. Place one lettuce leaf on each piece of foil. Combine the mayonnaise and horseradish in a small bowl and spread on the leaves. Place one layer of roast beef on each leaf. Top with some rocket and a sprig of watercress. Roll up each leaf like a cigar, then wrap tightly in the foil. Seal the ends and slice in half crosswise to serve. *Makes 2 servings.*

One serving: 466 calories, 52g protein, 7g carbohydrate, 24g fat (6g saturated), 144mg cholesterol, 235mg sodium, 1g fibre

mozzarella tomato tower   **p44**

salmon balsamico p51

crunchy chicken salad

Here's a popular lunch or light dinner dish that appears on many restaurant menus.
● *The secret to this salad is to cut all of the ingredients into small, even cubes. This way every bite contains different colour and flavour combinations.* ● *This is a great way to use left over chicken.*

crunchy chicken salad

2 celery stalks, chopped into 5mm (1/4in) pieces

1 medium-sized green pepper, chopped into 5mm (1/4in) pieces

10 large red-leaf lettuce leaves, sliced into 5mm (1/4in) pieces

6–8 broccoli florets, chopped into 5mm (1/4in) pieces

50ml (2fl oz) no-sugar-added oil and vinegar dressing

2 spring onions, sliced into 5mm (1/4in) pieces

225g (8oz) roasted chicken breast, skinned and cut into 5mm (1/4in) pieces

Place the celery, sweet pepper, lettuce and broccoli in a medium-sized bowl. Add the dressing and toss. Add the spring onions and chicken, then toss again. Divide between 2 plates and serve.
Makes 2 servings.

One serving: 401 calories, 40g protein, 14g carbohydrate, 23g fat (4g saturated), 96mg cholesterol, 329mg sodium, 2g fibre

helpful hints

● *Roasted, skinless chicken is available pre-cut into small pieces. You can use it for this recipe, but read the label carefully to make sure there are no hidden carbs. Buy the original flavour rather than the honey-baked or barbecued variety.*

● *Any type of lean roasted meat can be used in the salad.*

countdown

● *Prepare ingredients.*
● *Assemble salad.*

shopping list

TO BUY:

225g (8oz) roasted chicken breast

1 medium-sized green pepper

1 small head red-leaf lettuce

1 small packet broccoli florets (6–8 florets needed)

1 small bunch spring onions (2 needed)

STAPLES:

Celery

No-sugar-added oil and vinegar dressing

helpful hints

- *Toasting ground spices before they are used releases their natural oils and flavours. This step can be omitted if you're pressed for time.*
- *To help the tomato halves sit straight, cut a thin slice from the rounded ends.*

countdown

- *Toast spices.*
- *Make recipe.*

shopping list

TO BUY:

175g (6oz) cooked chicken breast
1 small packet flaked almonds (25g/1oz needed)
1 jar curry powder
2 small tomatoes
1 medium-sized red pepper
1 small head any type of lettuce (several leaves needed)

STAPLES:

Celery
Mayonnaise made with soya bean or olive oil
Ground cumin
Salt
Black peppercorns

curried chicken–stuffed tomatoes

The pungent flavour of curry blends well with roasted chicken to make a tasty salad with a hint of India. ● *Authentic curries are made with a blend of about 15 spices. For this quick salad, I use curry powder, which loses its flavour quickly and should be not used if more than three to four months old.* ● *This recipe works for any type of leftover meat.* ● *Quick suggestion: Use chicken salad from the deli counter and add the other ingredients to it. Ask for the nutritional analysis, as some commercial chicken salads are made with sugar.*

curried chicken–stuffed tomatoes

1 tablespoon curry powder
2 teaspoons ground cumin
2 small tomatoes
2 tablespoons mayonnaise made with soya bean or olive oil
Salt and freshly ground black pepper to taste
175g (6oz) cooked chicken breast, skinned and chopped
1 celery stalk, diced
Half a medium-sized red pepper, diced
2½ tablespoons flaked almonds (25g/1oz)
Several lettuce leaves, washed and torn into bite-sized pieces

Toast the curry powder and cumin in a small non-stick frying pan for 1 minute or microwave on high for 30 seconds. Stem the tomatoes and slice in half crosswise. Scoop the pulp, seeds and juice from the tomato halves into the bowl of a food processor and blend until smooth. Alternatively, scoop the pulp onto a chopping board and the juice into a bowl. Chop the pulp by hand and add to the bowl. Set the tomato halves aside.

Add the spices and the mayonnaise to the bowl. Add salt and pepper to taste. Combine until smooth. Stir in the chicken, celery, pepper and almonds. Taste for seasoning and add more if necessary. Divide the lettuce between 2 plates and place the tomato halves on the lettuce. Fill the tomatoes with the chicken salad and serve. *Makes 2 servings.*

One serving: 381 calories, 34g protein, 15g carbohydrate, 23g fat (3g saturated), 77mg cholesterol, 197mg sodium, 2g fibre

salmon balsamico

Rich, flavourful salmon is easy to cook and very filling. The smooth, rich texture goes well with cool, crunchy salad leaves and vegetables.

salmon balsamico

2 teaspoons olive oil
225g (8oz) salmon fillet
Salt and freshly ground black pepper to taste
225g (8oz) sweet potatoes, peeled and cut into 1cm (½in) cubes
125ml (4fl oz) balsamic vinegar
150g (5oz) washed, ready-to-eat mixed salad leaves
2 tablespoons no-sugar-added oil and vinegar dressing

Heat the oil in a small non-stick frying pan over a medium-high heat. Rinse salmon and pat dry with kitchen paper. Sauté the salmon for 3 minutes, then turn and brown for 3 more minutes, or longer if the salmon is more than 2.5cm (1in) thick. Sprinkle the cooked salmon with salt and pepper to taste and set aside.

Fill another pan with water and bring to the boil. Add the sweet potato and cook for 5 minutes, then drain. Add the vinegar and sweet potatoes to the salmon, return to the heat and reduce for about 1 minute, or until the liquid is syrupy. Divide the salad leaves between 2 plates and toss with the salad dressing. Place the salmon on top of the salad leaves. Spoon the glaze and sweet potato cubes on top and serve.
Makes 2 servings.

One serving: 365 calories, 30g protein, 16g carbohydrate, 20g fat (3g saturated), 80mg cholesterol, 158mg sodium, 6g fibre

helpful hint

● *Any type of fish fillet can be used.*

countdown

● *Sauté salmon.*
● *Assemble salad.*

shopping list

TO BUY:
225g (8oz) salmon fillet
225g (8oz) sweet potatoes
1 bag washed, ready-to-eat mixed salad leaves
STAPLES:
Olive oil
No-sugar-added oil and vinegar dressing
Balsamic vinegar
Salt
Black peppercorns

ham and cucumber parcels

helpful hints

- *These travel well. Make them ahead, store in a plastic bag and refrigerate until needed.*
- *Any type of lettuce can be used. Large leaves are needed.*

shopping list

TO BUY:

350g (12oz) sliced lean ham

1 head romaine or other lettuce

2 medium cucumbers

STAPLES:

Dijon mustard

For the days when you don't have time to make a lunch, here is a dish you can prepare and eat in minutes.

ham and cucumber parcels

350g (12oz) sliced lean ham
18–20 leaves romaine or other lettuce
50ml (2fl oz) Dijon mustard
2 medium cucumbers, sliced

Place 1 slice of ham on a lettuce leaf. Spread the ham with Dijon mustard. Add a few slices of cucumber. Fold the lettuce. Continue with additional lettuce leaves until all the ham is used. *Makes 2 servings.*

One serving: 318 calories, 38g protein, 16g carbohydrate, 11g fat (3g saturated), 80mg cholesterol, 2218mg sodium, 3g fibre

greek salad

With the help of the supermarket deli, you can make this salad in less than 5 minutes. A traditional Greek salad has olives, feta cheese, radishes and good olive oil. You can also add sweet peppers, capers and anchovies, all of which can be found on the supermarket shelves. Use this recipe as the base and build your own salad with other fresh vegetables.

greek salad

2 tablespoons no-sugar-added oil and vinegar dressing

2 teaspoons dried oregano or 2 tablespoons fresh

225g (8oz) washed, ready-to-eat lettuce leaves

1 medium cucumber, peeled and sliced

12 black olives, chopped (preferably kalamata)

8 radishes, sliced

8 spring onions, sliced

35g (1½oz) drained capers

225g (8oz) medium-sliced lean turkey breast

75g (3oz) reduced-fat feta cheese, crumbled

Freshly ground black pepper to taste

Combine the oil and vinegar dressing and oregano together in a salad bowl. Add the lettuce, cucumber, olives, radishes, spring onions and capers. Toss well. Slice the turkey breast into 1cm (½in) strips. Sprinkle on top of the salad with the crumbled feta cheese. Add pepper to taste. Divide between 2 plates and serve.

Makes 2 servings.

One serving: 455 calories, 41g protein, 15g carbohydrate, 25g fat (9g saturated), 118mg cholesterol, 1639mg sodium, 2g fibre

helpful hints

- *Dried oregano is called for in this recipe for speed. Fresh oregano (available in most supermarkets) will add a sweeter flavour to the salad. Use it if you have time.*
- *If using dried oregano, make sure it is less than six months old.*
- *Any type of washed, ready-to-eat lettuce can be used.*

countdown

- *Make salad dressing.*
- *Make salad.*

shopping list

TO BUY:

1 packet reduced-fat feta cheese (75g/3oz needed)

225g (8oz) medium-sliced lean turkey breast

1 jar capers

1 packet black olives (preferably kalamata)

1 bag washed, ready-to-eat lettuce leaves

1 medium cucumber

1 small bunch radishes

1 bunch spring onions (8 needed)

STAPLES:

No-sugar-added oil and vinegar dressing

Dried oregano

Black peppercorns

grilled cheddar and chicken salad

This lunch can be made in 5 minutes by using either leftover chicken or roasted skinless chicken from the supermarket, but read the labels carefully to make sure there are no hidden carbs. Buy the original flavour rather than the honey-baked or barbecued variety. ● The cheese melts, providing a warm covering for the cool salad.

grilled cheddar and chicken salad

2 tablespoons mayonnaise made with olive or soya bean oil

2 tablespoons warm water

2 tablespoons Dijon mustard

225g (8oz) roasted chicken breast, chopped

1 medium-sized green pepper, seeded and chopped

110g (4oz) yellow onion, diced

25g (1oz) chopped fresh parsley

Salt and freshly ground black pepper to taste

2 large tomatoes, sliced

2 slices reduced-fat, mature Cheddar cheese (35g/1½oz)

Preheat the grill. Combine the mayonnaise, water and mustard in a medium-sized bowl. Add the chicken, pepper, onion and parsley. Add salt and pepper to taste and toss well. Place the tomato slices on an ovenproof dish or on a foil-lined baking tray and season with a little salt and pepper. Spread with chicken salad and tear cheese slices into small pieces to fit over the chicken salad. Grill for 2 minutes, or until the cheese melts, and serve.

Makes 2 servings.

One serving: 434 calories, 46g protein, 14g carbohydrate, 22g fat (6g saturated), 116mg cholesterol, 723mg sodium, 0g fibre

prawn salad

Juicy prawns, well seasoned, and crunchy celery make a delicious, quick lunch.

prawn salad

*50ml (2fl oz) mayonnaise made
   from soya bean or olive oil*

1 tablespoon fish seasoning

*350g (12oz) cooked prawns, cut
   into 1cm (½in) pieces*

8 celery stalks, finely chopped

*Salt and freshly ground black
   pepper to taste*

*12–14 large romaine lettuce
   leaves, washed and dried*

Combine the mayonnaise and fish seasoning in a medium-sized mixing bowl. Add the prawns and celery and season with salt and pepper to taste. Mix well. Serve on a bed of lettuce leaves.
Makes 2 servings.

One serving: 443 calories, 38g protein, 17g carbohydrate, 26g fat (3.6g saturated), 708mg cholesterol, 5mg sodium, 2g fibre

helpful hints

● *Any type of lettuce can be used.*

● *Buy cooked prawns from the fish department in the supermarket or buy good quality frozen, cooked prawns.*

● *If fish seasoning is unavailable use a mild pickling mix, or make your own from 1 bay leaf, 10 peppercorns, ½ teaspoon of mustard seeds and ¼ teaspoon each of allspice, cloves and ginger.*

countdown

● *Prepare all ingredients.*

● *Assemble salad.*

shopping list

TO BUY:
   350g (12oz) cooked prawns
   1 small jar fish seasoning
   1 head romaine lettuce
STAPLES:
   Celery
   *Mayonnaise made from soya
      bean or olive oil*
   Salt
   Black peppercorns

herby chicken caesar salad

Caesar salads make a popular lunch. Crisp lettuce and smooth, tangy dressing provide an enjoyable, mouth-watering combination. This is a recipe that you can easily make at home.
● Here's a tip when ordering a Caesar salad at a restaurant: ask for the salad without the croutons or remove them when the salad is served. Many salads come swimming in dressing, so ask for the dressing on the side and use only 2 tablespoons on your salad.

herby chicken caesar salad

2 tablespoons walnuts (10g/½oz)
6 medium-sized garlic cloves, crushed
2 teaspoons dried oregano
¼ teaspoon freshly ground black pepper
Pinch of salt
Grated rind from 1 lemon (½ tablespoon)
2 tablespoons freshly squeezed lemon juice (1 lemon)
2 egg whites
225g (8oz) boneless, skinless chicken breast
Olive oil spray
4 anchovies, mashed
4 teaspoons Worcestershire sauce
4 teaspoons olive oil
1 small head romaine lettuce, washed and cut into pieces
4 slices red onion
2 tablespoons freshly grated Parmesan cheese

Preheat the grill. Line a baking tray with foil. Place the walnuts on tray and grill for 1 minute, or until toasted. (Watch carefully to keep them from burning.) Combine 2 garlic cloves, the oregano, pepper, salt, grated lemon rind and ½ tablespoon of the lemon juice in a small bowl. In a separate bowl, whisk the egg whites lightly until just frothy. Dip the chicken into the egg whites and then roll in the garlic-lemon mixture. Spray the foil-lined baking tray with olive oil. Place the coated chicken on the baking tray and grill about 12.5cm (5in) from the heat for 5 minutes. Turn and grill for another 5 minutes. Remove from grill.

To make the dressing, place the anchovies, remaining lemon juice, 4 crushed garlic cloves, Worcestershire sauce and olive oil in the bowl of a food processor and blend thoroughly, scraping down the sides several times. Alternatively, mix the ingredients together by hand, mashing the anchovies and garlic to blend well. Place the lettuce in a salad bowl and toss with half the dressing. Divide the salad between 2 plates, add the walnuts and top with onion slices. Sprinkle with Parmesan cheese. Cut the chicken into thin slices and place on top. Spoon the remaining dressing over the top and serve.
Makes 2 servings.

One serving: 442 calories, 48g protein, 11g carbohydrate, 24g fat (5g saturated), 101mg cholesterol, 708mg sodium, 1g fibre

helpful hints

● Use the recipe below or purchase a low-carbohydrate, Caesar-salad dressing.
● Toasting walnuts can be tricky, as they burn quickly. Watch them carefully.
● To save cleaning time, use the same baking tray to toast the walnuts and grill the chicken.
● Buy good quality Parmesan cheese and grate it yourself. Freeze extra for quick use later – simply spoon out what you need and leave the rest frozen.

countdown
● Preheat grill.
● Make chicken.
● Make dressing.
● Assemble dish.

shopping list
TO BUY:
225g (8oz) boneless, skinless chicken breast
1 small packet walnut pieces (10g/½oz needed)
1 tin anchovies
1 lemon
1 small head romaine lettuce
STAPLES:
Eggs
Parmesan cheese
Red onion
Olive oil
Olive oil spray
Garlic
Dried oregano
Worcestershire sauce
Salt
Black peppercorns

portobellos stuffed with smoked trout and sun-dried tomatoes

Large portobello mushroom caps have an earthy flavour and meaty texture. They can be roasted, grilled or sautéed. This dish can be eaten warm or at room temperature, and it only takes about 15 minutes to make. ● Curly endive has lacy, green-trimmed leaves, but any type of lettuce can be used for this recipe.

portobellos stuffed with smoked trout and sun-dried tomatoes

Olive oil spray

4 large portobello mushroom caps, washed (225g/8oz)

Salt and freshly ground black pepper to taste

2 tablespoons mayonnaise made with olive or soya bean oil

1 tablespoon freshly squeezed lemon juice (about ½ lemon)

50ml (2fl oz) horseradish

225g (8oz) smoked trout or other smoked fish

175g (6oz) sun-dried tomatoes, drained and diced

Several leaves curly endive

Preheat the oven to 230°C/450°F/gas mark 8. Line a baking tray with foil and spray with olive oil. Place the mushrooms on the tray and spray both sides with olive oil until lightly coated. Bake for 5 minutes; turn and bake for 5 more minutes. Remove from the oven, and add salt and pepper to taste.

Combine the mayonnaise, lemon juice and horseradish in a medium-sized mixing bowl. Flake the smoked trout into the mayonnaise mixture. Stir in the sun-dried tomatoes, blending well. Season with salt and pepper to taste. Spoon the mixture into the mushroom caps. Divide the lettuce between 2 plates, top with the stuffed mushroom caps and serve. Makes 2 servings.

One serving: 476 calories, 33g protein, 17g carbohydrate, 30g fat (5g saturated), 82mg cholesterol, 179mg sodium, 4g fibre

helpful hints

● *To clean whole mushrooms, wipe them gently with damp kitchen paper.*

● *The smoked fish filling can be mixed in a food processor.*

countdown

● *Preheat oven to 230°C/450°F/gas mark 8.*

● *Roast mushrooms.*

● *Assemble dish.*

shopping list

TO BUY:

225g (8oz) smoked trout or other smoked fish

1 jar horseradish

1 jar sun-dried tomatoes

4 large portobello mushrooms (225g/8oz)

1 lemon

1 head curly endive

STAPLES:

Olive oil spray

Mayonnaise made with olive or soya bean oil

Salt

Black peppercorns

quick start
dinners

spicy prawns with roasted asparagus

When I made this dish for my husband, he couldn't believe it took only 5 minutes to make the sauce. The secret is red vermouth. It adds spice and depth to fresh tomatoes and goes perfectly with the prawns. ● *Roasting intensifies the flavour of fresh vegetables. The roasted asparagus takes only 15 minutes and goes perfectly with the simple leafy salad over leaf.*

spicy prawns

2 teaspoons olive oil
6 medium-sized garlic cloves, crushed
125ml (4fl oz) red vermouth
275g (10oz) diced tomatoes
350g (12oz) large raw prawns, peeled and deveined
25g (1oz) chopped fresh parsley
Several drops hot pepper sauce
Salt and freshly ground black pepper to taste

Heat the olive oil in a medium-sized non-stick frying pan over a medium-high heat. Sauté the garlic for a few seconds, then add the red vermouth and tomatoes. Cook for 5 minutes. Add the prawns and parsley and cook for 2–3 minutes until the prawns are pink. Season with hot pepper sauce, salt and pepper to taste. Divide between 2 plates and serve.
Makes 2 servings.

One serving: 297 calories, 37g protein, 10g carbohydrate, 8g fat (1g saturated), 260mg cholesterol, 282mg sodium, 0g fibre

roasted asparagus

225g (8oz) fresh asparagus
2 teaspoons olive oil
Salt and freshly ground black pepper to taste

Preheat the oven to 200°C/400°F/gas mark 6. Cut or snap off any fibrous stem on the asparagus and discard. Slice the remaining asparagus into 5cm (2in) pieces. Line a baking tray with foil and spoon the oil onto the foil. Sprinkle the oil with salt and pepper to taste. Add the asparagus and roll in oil, making sure all the spears are coated with the oil and seasoning. Spread the asparagus into a single layer and roast in the oven for 5 minutes. Roll the asparagus in the oil to recoat and roast, 10 more minutes for thick spears and 5 more minutes for thin ones. Remove from the oven and serve with the prawns.
Makes 2 servings.

One serving: 55 calories, 2g protein, 3g carbohydrate, 5g fat (1g saturated), 0mg cholesterol, 3mg sodium, 2g fibre

helpful hints

● *To save roasting time, the asparagus can be cooked in a microwave oven on high: 3 minutes for thin asparagus and 5 minutes for thick spears.*

● *Buy peeled prawns – it is well worth the time otherwise spent peeling them yourself.*

countdown

● *Preheat oven 200°C/400°F/gas mark 6.*
● *Start asparagus.*
● *Make prawns.*
● *Make Italian greens.*

shopping list

TO BUY:
   350g (12oz) large raw prawns
   1 small bottle red vermouth
   1 small bunch fresh parsley
   1 medium tomato
   225g (8oz) asparagus
   1 bag washed, ready-to-eat, Italian-style salad leaves
STAPLES:
   Olive oil
   No-sugar-added oil and vinegar dressing
   Garlic
   Hot pepper sauce
   Salt
   Black peppercorns

spicy prawns with roasted asparagus continued

italian greens

150g (5oz) washed, ready-to-eat, Italian-style salad leaves

2 tablespoons no-sugar-added oil and vinegar dressing

Salt and freshly ground black pepper to taste

Place the salad in a small bowl and drizzle with the dressing. Season with salt and pepper to taste. Toss well and serve.

Makes 2 servings.

One serving: 84 calories, 1g protein, 2g carbohydrate, 8g fat (1g saturated), 0mg cholesterol, 81mg sodium, 0g fibre

asian ginger salmon

This is a very simple 15-minute dinner. It's a basic recipe that you can use as a blueprint to make other similar dinners. Boneless, skinless chicken breast can be used instead of salmon, cauliflower instead of broccoli and yellow beans instead of green.

asian ginger salmon

Olive oil spray
350g (12oz) salmon fillet
Salt and freshly ground black
    pepper to taste
2 tablespoons low-sodium soy
    sauce
2 tablespoons water
2 tablespoons chopped fresh
    ginger

Heat a non-stick frying pan over a medium-high heat and spray with olive oil. Add the salmon and brown for 2 minutes. Turn, season the cooked side, then brown the second side for 2 minutes. Lower the heat and sauté for 5 minutes. Combine the soy sauce, water and ginger in a small bowl. Remove the salmon from the pan, add the soy sauce mixture to the pan and cook for several seconds. Divide the salmon between 2 plates and spoon the sauce over the salmon.
Makes 2 servings.

One serving: 310 calories, 43g protein, 2g carbohydrate, 12g fat (3g saturated), 120mg cholesterol, 714mg sodium, 0g fibre

sesame broccoli

110g (4oz) broccoli florets
2 teaspoons olive oil
25g (1oz) sesame seeds
Salt and freshly ground black
    pepper to taste

Place the broccoli in a microwave-safe bowl and microwave on high for 5 minutes. Alternatively, bring a pot of water to the boil and add the broccoli. Boil for 2 minutes and then drain. Heat the oil in a non-stick frying pan over a medium-high heat. Sauté the broccoli and sesame seeds for 3 to 4 minutes, or until the sesame seeds are golden and the broccoli is bright green, but crisp. Season with salt and pepper to taste. Serve with the salmon.
Makes 2 servings.

One serving: 158 calories, 7g protein, 6g carbohydrate, 14g fat (2g saturated), 0mg cholesterol, 79mg sodium, 2g fibre

helpful hints

● *Broccoli and beans can be microwaved at the same time for 3 minutes on high.*
● *To save washing an extra pan, prepare the salmon and cover with foil to keep warm. Use same pan to sauté the broccoli.*
● *A washed, ready-to-eat salad can be substituted for one of the vegetables.*
● *To chop fresh ginger quickly, cut it into small cubes and press through a garlic press with large holes. If using a press with small holes, just capture the juice that is squeezed out; it will give enough flavour for the recipe.*

countdown

● *Make salmon.*
● *Make broccoli.*
● *Make beans.*

shopping list

TO BUY:
    350g (12oz) salmon fillet
    1 small packet sesame seeds
    225g (8oz) French beans
    110g (4oz) broccoli florets
    1 small piece fresh ginger

asian ginger salmon continued

STAPLES:
  Olive oil
  Olive oil spray
  No-sugar-added olive oil and
    vinegar dressing
  Low-sodium soy sauce
  Salt
  Black peppercorns

green bean salad

225g (8oz) French beans, trimmed
  and cut in half
2 tablespoons no-sugar-added
  olive oil and vinegar dressing
Salt and freshly ground black
  pepper to taste

Place the beans in a microwave-safe bowl and microwave on high for 3 minutes. Alternatively, bring a pot of water to the boil and add the beans. Boil for 2 minutes, and then drain. Toss the cooked beans with the salad dressing. Season with salt and pepper to taste and serve. *Makes 2 servings.*

One serving: 119 calories, 2g protein, 10g carbohydrate, 9g fat (1g saturated), 0mg cholesterol, 79mg sodium, 2g fibre

glazed balsamic chicken

Balsamic vinegar makes a zesty glaze for chicken – and adds very few calories in the process.
● *Roasting or grilling intensifies the flavour of vegetables. The courgettes are left to cook while you prepare the chicken and mange tout.*

glazed balsamic chicken

Olive oil spray
350g (12oz) boneless, skinless chicken breast
Salt and freshly ground black pepper to taste
125ml (4fl oz) good quality balsamic vinegar
25g (1oz) pine nuts
1 tablespoon Dijon mustard

Heat a medium-sized non-stick frying pan over a medium-high heat and spray with olive oil. Brown the chicken for 3 minutes, turn and cook for another 3 minutes. Remove from the heat, cover with a lid and let sit for 3 minutes. Remove the chicken to a plate, season with salt and pepper to taste and cover with a plate or foil to keep warm. In the same pan, add the vinegar and pine nuts. Cook over a medium-high heat to reduce, about 30 seconds, or until about half the amount of liquid remains. Add the mustard and mix well to make a smooth glaze. Return the chicken to the pan, turning to coat both sides with the glaze. Cook for another minute, then divide between 2 plates to serve and spoon any remaining glaze on top.
Makes 2 servings.

One serving: 378 calories, 54g protein, 4g carbohydrate, 11g fat (2g saturated), 144mg cholesterol, 306mg sodium, 0g fibre

helpful hint

● *To save cleaning time, sauté the chicken and remove to a plate. Cover with another plate or foil to keep warm. Use the same pan to sauté the mange tout.*
● *If yellow courgettes are unavailable, use green ones instead.*

countdown

● *Preheat grill.*
● *Start courgettes.*
● *Make chicken.*
● *Sauté mange tout.*

shopping list

TO BUY:
  350g (12oz) boneless, skinless chicken breast
  1 small packet pine nuts
  225g (8oz) mange tout
  225g (8oz) yellow courgettes
  1 medium-sized red pepper
STAPLES:
  Olive oil
  Olive oil spray
  Balsamic vinegar
  Dijon mustard
  Garlic
  Salt
  Black peppercorns

glazed balsamic chicken continued

grilled courgettes

Olive oil spray

2 teaspoons olive oil

2 medium-sized garlic cloves, crushed

1 tablespoon water

225g (8oz) yellow courgettes, cut into 2.5cm (1in) slices

1 medium-sized red pepper, cut into 2.5cm (1in) pieces

Salt and freshly ground black pepper to taste

Preheat the grill. Line a baking sheet with foil and spray with olive oil. Place the foil-lined sheet under the grill 12.5cm (5in) from the heat. Combine the olive oil with garlic and water in a small mixing bowl. Remove the baking sheet from the grill and place the vegetables on the sheet. Spoon half of the olive oil mixture over the vegetables and toss well. Spread the vegetables out to form a single layer. Grill for 10 minutes. Turn the vegetables over and spoon with the remaining olive oil mixture. Grill for another 10 minutes. The courgettes should be cooked through, but not black. Sprinkle with salt and pepper to taste. Serve with the chicken. *Makes 2 servings.*

One serving: 104 calories, 3g protein, 11g carbohydrate, 7g fat (1g saturated), 0mg cholesterol, 4mg sodium, 1g fibre

mange tout

2 teaspoons olive oil

225g (8oz) mange tout, trimmed

Salt and freshly ground black pepper to taste

Heat the olive oil in a non-stick frying pan over a medium-high heat. Add the mange tout and sauté for 2 minutes, tossing continuously. Season with salt and pepper to taste. Serve with the chicken. *Makes 2 servings.*

One serving: 66 calories, 2g protein, 5g carbohydrate, 5g fat (1g saturated), 0mg cholesterol, 3mg sodium, 2g fibre

tex-mex meat loaf

This moist, well-seasoned meat loaf smothered in spicy salsa makes a great, homely meal. By forming the meat into small loaves instead of one large loaf, it takes only 20 minutes to cook, rather than the usual 45–60 minutes.● The heat circulates more quickly around the loaves. I The cooked loaves will keep a day in the refrigerator. If you have time, double the recipe and form 4 loaves. Save the other two for another quick meal.

tex-mex meat loaf

Olive oil spray
50g (2oz) red onion, thinly sliced
110g (4oz) mushrooms, thinly sliced
275g (10oz) minced veal
2 egg whites
Salt and freshly ground black pepper to taste

1 large tomato, diced
25g (1oz) chopped fresh coriander
1 small jalapeño pepper, seeded and chopped
½ teaspoon ground cumin
1 tablespoon freshly squeezed lime juice

Preheat the oven to 200°C/400°F/gas mark 6. Line a baking tray with foil and spray with olive oil. Heat a non-stick frying pan over a medium-high heat and spray with olive oil. Add the onion and mushrooms and sauté for 5 minutes. Combine the vegetables with the minced veal and egg whites in a medium-sized mixing bowl. Add salt and pepper to taste. Place the meat directly on the foil-lined baking tray and shape into 2 loaves about 15 x 8cm (6 x 3in) each. Bake for 20 minutes.

While the loaves bake, combine the diced tomato, coriander, jalapeño, cumin and lime juice in a small bowl. Season with salt and pepper to taste. Spoon the salsa over the baked meat loaves and serve on 2 plates with the avocado.
Makes 2 servings.

One serving: 407 calories, 45g protein, 13g carbohydrate, 17g fat (10g saturated), 125mg cholesterol, 164mg sodium, 2g fibre

sliced avocado

½ small avocado, stoned, peeled, and sliced
1 tablespoon no-sugar-added oil and vinegar dressing
Salt and freshly ground black pepper to taste

Arrange the avocado slices next to the meat loaves and drizzle with dressing. Season with salt and pepper to taste. Serve with the meat loaf. Makes 2 servings.

One serving: 114 calories, 1g protein, 3g carbohydrate, 12g fat (2g saturated), 0mg cholesterol, 43mg sodium, 2g fibre

helpful hint

● *Use the salsa recipe given or purchase a no-sugar-added version.*

countdown

● *Preheat oven to 200°C/400°F/gas mark 6.*
● *Make meat loaf.*
● *Prepare avocado.*

shopping list

TO BUY:
275g (10oz) minced veal
1 small avocado
1 small packet sliced mushrooms (50g/2oz needed)
2 limes
1 large tomato
1 small bunch coriander
1 small jalapeño pepper
STAPLES:
Olive oil spray
Red onion
Eggs
No-sugar-added oil and vinegar dressing
Ground cumin
Salt
Black peppercorns

marsala chicken

The rich, smoky flavour of Sicily's Marsala wine makes a quick glaze for this chicken. To help cook the chicken faster, I flatten the chicken breast to about 1cm (½in) thick. This also enlarges the surface area available to absorb the glaze.

marsala chicken

275g (10oz) boneless, skinless chicken breasts

2 teaspoons olive oil

Salt and freshly ground black pepper to taste

125ml (4fl oz) medium-dry Marsala wine

1 tablespoon crème fraîche

Remove all visible fat from the chicken. Pound with the palm of your hand to flatten to about 1cm (½in) thick. Heat the oil in a non-stick frying pan over a medium-high heat. Brown the chicken, about 2 minutes on each side. Season each cooked side with salt and pepper to taste. Add the Marsala wine to the pan and continue to cook for 2–3 minutes. Remove the chicken to 2 plates. Continue to simmer the sauce for about 1 minute to reduce. Add the crème fraîche and season with salt and pepper to taste. Spoon the sauce over the chicken and cover with foil to keep warm before serving.

Makes 2 servings.

> One serving: 394 calories, 45g protein, 7g carbohydrate, 14g fat (4g saturated), 131mg cholesterol, 113mg sodium, 0g fibre

roman spinach

275g (10oz) fresh washed, ready-to-eat fresh spinach

2 teaspoons olive oil

4 medium-sized garlic cloves, crushed

Salt and freshly ground black pepper to taste

Place the spinach in a large saucepan (do not add water). Cover and cook for 5 minutes, tossing once or twice, then drain. Alternatively, place in a microwave-safe bowl and microwave on high for 5 minutes. Heat the olive oil in the same saucepan over a medium heat and add the garlic. Stir for about 30 seconds. Return the spinach to the pan. Season with salt and pepper to taste. Serve with the chicken.

Makes 2 servings.

> One serving: 97 calories, 7g protein, 10g carbohydrate, 5g fat (1g saturated), 0mg cholesterol, 172mg sodium, 7g fibre

radicchio salad

1 small head radicchio, torn into
  bite-sized pieces
12 radishes
1 tablespoon no-sugar-added oil
  and vinegar dressing
Salt and freshly ground black
  pepper to taste

Divide the radicchio leaves between 2 plates
and grate the radishes on top. Alternatively,
grate the radishes in a food processor fitted with
a grating blade. Spoon the dressing over the
salad and season with salt and pepper to taste
before serving.
Makes 2 servings.

One serving: 103 calories, 1g protein,
6g carbohydrate, 9g fat (1g saturated),
0mg cholesterol, 96mg sodium, 1g fibre

sirloin burger with fresh slaw

helpful hints

- If pressed for time, use a shop-bought coleslaw instead of the recipe given. Check the nutritional analysis of shop-bought coleslaw, as some prepared versions have added sugar.
- To determine the weight of each slice of cheese, divide the packet weight by the number of slices.

countdown

- Make coleslaw.
- Make burger.

shopping list

TO BUY:

1 packet sliced reduced-fat
    Cheddar cheese
    (35g/1½oz needed)
225g (8oz) minced lean sirloin
1 bag presliced cabbage and
    carrot mix (450g/1lb
    needed)
2 medium tomatoes

STAPLES:

Red onion
Olive oil spray
Mayonnaise made with soya
    bean or olive oil
Dijon mustard
Distilled white vinegar
Artificial sweetener
Salt
Black peppercorns

In the mood for a burger? Here's a quick one made with lean sirloin and accompanied by coleslaw. Sliced, ready-to-use cabbage and carrot can be found in the fruit and veg section of the supermarket, making homemade coleslaw a breeze.

sirloin burger

50g (2oz) red onion, chopped
225g (8oz) minced lean sirloin
Salt and freshly ground black
    pepper to taste
Olive oil spray
35g (1½oz) sliced reduced-fat
    Cheddar cheese (about 2 slices)
4 teaspoons Dijon mustard

Combine the onion and minced sirloin in a medium-sized bowl. Season with salt and pepper to taste. Form into 2 patties. Set a medium-sized non-stick frying pan over medium-high heat and spray with olive oil. Cook the sirloin burgers for 5 minutes. Turn and top each burger with a slice of cheese. Continue cooking for 3 more minutes. Top the cheese with mustard and serve.

Makes 2 servings.

One serving: 338 calories, 46g protein, 2g carbohydrate, 17g fat (8g saturated), 117mg cholesterol, 496mg sodium, 0g fibre

fresh slaw

2 tablespoons mayonnaise made
    with soya bean or olive oil
2 tablespoons distilled white
    vinegar
4 teaspoons Dijon mustard
4g (⅛oz) artificial sweetener
Salt and freshly ground black
    pepper to taste
4 slices red onion
450g (1lb) presliced cabbage and
    carrot mix
2 medium tomatoes, sliced

Combine the mayonnaise, vinegar, mustard and artificial sweetener in a medium-sized bowl. Season with salt and pepper to taste. Add the cabbage, carrot and onion and toss well. Add more salt and pepper, if needed. Divide between 2 plates, and arrange the tomato slices on the side.

Makes 2 servings.

One serving: 191 calories, 5g protein, 18g carbohydrate, 12g fat (2g saturated), 5mg cholesterol, 355mg sodium, 2g fibre

pacific rim pork

Spicy, Pacific Rim flavours add zest to this easy-to-prepare dinner. ● The pickled vegetable salad makes a great snack. Make extra and store in a plastic bag. Serve it on its own, or add it to chicken or tuna salads.

pacific rim pork

350g (12oz) pork tenderloin, visible fat removed

For marinade:
50ml (2fl oz) low-salt soy sauce
50ml (2fl oz) distilled white vinegar
4 medium-sized garlic cloves, crushed
4 teaspoons Dijon mustard
2 teaspoons ground ginger
Dash of freshly ground black pepper

Preheat the grill and place the rack on the top rung of the oven. Line a baking sheet with foil. Cut the pork almost in half lengthwise and open like a book. Do not cut all of the way through. Combine the marinade ingredients in a small bowl. Add the pork and allow to marinate for 20 minutes. Remove from the marinade and place the pork on the foil-lined baking sheet. Grill for 5 minutes, turn and grill for 3 more minutes. The pork is done when a meat thermometer inserted in the centre registers 70°C/160°F. Slice and serve with the salad and vegetables.
Makes 2 servings.

One serving: 293 calories, 50g protein, 2g carbohydrate, 8g fat (3g saturated), 159mg cholesterol, 478mg sodium, 0g fibre

pickled radish salad

225ml (8fl oz) water
150ml (5fl oz) distilled white vinegar
10g (½oz) artificial sweetener
1 teaspoon crushed red pepper
1 teaspoon salt
Half a cucumber, peeled and sliced
175g (6oz) radishes, peeled and sliced
2 tablespoons yellow onion, chopped

Mix the water, vinegar, sweetener, crushed red pepper and salt together in a medium-sized bowl. Add the cucumber, radish and onion and marinate for 15 minutes. Drain and serve.
Makes 2 servings.

One serving: 34 calories, 1g protein, 9g carbohydrate, 0g fat (0g saturated), 0mg cholesterol, 276mg sodium, 1g fibre

helpful hints

● If possible use white radish in the salad. Daikon radish is a white, Oriental radish with a sweet, fresh flavour. Otherwise, red radishes can be used.
● To keep from having to look back at the recipe as you stir-fry the ingredients, line them up on a chopping board or plate in the order of use so you know which ingredient comes next.
● For crisp, not steamed, stir-fried vegetables, start with a very hot wok or frying pan. Let the vegetables sit for a minute before tossing to allow the wok to regain its heat.

countdown

● Preheat grill.
● Marinate pork.
● Make salad.
● Prepare stir-fry vegetable ingredients.
● Grill pork.
● While pork cooks, make stir-fry vegetables.

shopping list

TO BUY:
350g (12oz) pork tenderloin
1 small jar ground ginger
1 bottle sesame oil
1 small head Chinese cabbage (Chinese leaf)
1 packet fresh bean sprouts
1 jar crushed red pepper
Half a cucumber
175g (6oz) radishes

pacific rim pork continued

ginger-garlic stir-fry vegetables

STAPLES:
STAPLES:
  Garlic
  Yellow onion
  Dijon mustard
  Low-sodium soy sauce
  Distilled white vinegar
  Artificial sweetener
  Salt
  Black peppercorns

2 teaspoons sesame oil

2 teaspoons ground ginger

225g (8oz) Chinese cabbage (Chinese leaf), washed and sliced

150g (5oz) fresh bean sprouts

4 medium-sized garlic cloves, crushed

Pour the oil into a wok or non-stick frying pan and place over a high heat. When the oil begins to smoke, add the ginger, lettuce, bean sprouts and garlic. Stir-fry for 6 minutes and then serve. Makes 2 servings.

One serving: 92 calories, 4g protein, 10g carbohydrate, 5g fat (1g saturated), 0mg cholesterol, 13mg sodium, 2g fibre

veal escalopes with garlic greens

In this dish, romaine and radicchio leaves are just wilted in a pan and flavoured with garlic to form a crunchy, colourful topping for the veal escalopes. ● *Veal escalopes take only a few minutes to cook. The secret to keeping them juicy is to brown them in a hot frying pan for 1 minute on each side, then remove them to a plate and cover to keep warm. Boneless, skinless chicken breasts can be substituted, though they will need to cook longer.* ● *Saffron is the stigmas from a saffron crocus. It is pricy because it is harvested by hand. Fortunately, a little goes a long way.*

veal escalopes with garlic greens

Olive oil spray
350g (12oz) veal escalopes pounded to 2–3mm (1/8–1/16in) thick
Salt and freshly ground black pepper to taste
4 medium-sized garlic cloves, crushed
150g (5oz) cos and radicchio leaves torn into bite-sized pieces

Set a medium-sized non-stick frying pan over a high heat and spray with olive oil. Brown the veal for 1 minute on each side. Season the cooked sides and remove to 2 plates. Add the garlic and salad leaves to the pan. Toss for 1 minute, or until the leaves just start to wilt. Season with salt and pepper to taste. Serve the salad leaves over the veal escalopes.
Makes 2 servings.

One serving: 398 calories, 46g protein, 3g carbohydrate, 20g fat (12g saturated), 150mg cholesterol, 114mg sodium, 0g fibre

saffron cauliflower

225g (8oz) cauliflower florets
4 teaspoons olive oil
1/4 teaspoon saffron strands
Salt and freshly ground black pepper to taste

Place the cauliflower in a vegetable steamer set over boiling water. Steam for 6–7 minutes, or until tender. Alternatively, place in a microwave-safe dish – do not add water – and microwave on high for 5 minutes. Spoon the olive oil into a large serving bowl and add the saffron. Microwave on high for 10 seconds. Add the cauliflower to the oil, season with salt and pepper to taste and toss well before serving.
Makes 2 servings.

One serving: 130 calories, 4g protein, 10g carbohydrate, 9g fat (1g saturated), 0mg cholesterol, 60mg sodium, 5g fibre

helpful hints

● *Turmeric or bijol can be used instead of the saffron.*
● *Buy cauliflower already cut into florets.*
● *Washed, ready-to-eat salad can be used. Make sure the leaves are firm. Baby gourmet salad leaves or lamb's lettuce will be too soft to work in this recipe.*

countdown

● *Make cauliflower, cover to keep warm.*
● *Prepare veal and garlic greens.*

shopping list

TO BUY:
350g (12oz) veal escalopes
1 small packet saffron strands
225g (8oz) cauliflower florets
1 small head romaine lettuce
1 small head radicchio lettuce
STAPLES:
Olive oil
Olive oil spray
Garlic
Salt
Black peppercorns

pecan-crusted fish with vegetable creole

helpful hints

- For an extra fiery bite, add another 1/8 teaspoon cayenne pepper to the fish recipe.
- Vegetable creole keeps well. Make extra and save for another dinner.
- To save cleaning time, make the fish and creole in the same pan.
- Any type of firm, non-oily white fish can be used, for example turbot, halibut or monkfish.

countdown

- Preheat oven to 200°C/400°F/gas mark 6.
- Make fish.
- Make vegetable creole.

shopping list

TO BUY:
  350g (12oz) fish fillet
  1 small packet pecan pieces (50g/2oz needed)
  1 tin no-sugar-added diced tomatoes (450g/1lb needed)
  1 medium-sized green pepper
  1 courgette
STAPLES:
  Eggs
  Yellow onion
  Garlic
  Worcestershire sauce
  Olive oil
  Olive oil spray
  Artificial sweetener
  Cayenne pepper
  Salt
  Black peppercorns

Pecan-flavoured fish and vegetable creole are updated versions of Southern American comfort foods. ● *To cook fish fast, preheat the baking tray in the oven. The hot tray will help to cook the fish on the underside without having to turn the fish.*

pecan-crusted fish

1/4 teaspoon salt
1/4 teaspoon freshly ground black pepper
1/4 teaspoon cayenne pepper
2 egg whites, lightly beaten
50g (2oz) pecans, finely chopped
350g (12oz) fish fillet
2 teaspoons olive oil
Olive oil spray

Preheat the oven to 200°C/400°F/gas mark 6. Line a baking tray with foil and place in the oven to heat. Combine the salt, black pepper and cayenne on a plate. Line up the spice mixture, the beaten egg whites and the pecans in a row on the work surface for easy coating of the fish. First, roll the fish in the spice mixture, coating both sides. Next, dip the fish into the egg whites and then roll in the pecans.

Heat the olive oil in a non-stick frying pan over a medium-high heat. When the oil is hot, brown the fish for 2 minutes. Turn and brown the other side for 1 minute. Remove the baking tray from the oven and spray with olive oil. Place the fish on the tray and return the tray to the oven for 5 minutes to finish cooking. Serve with the creole.
Makes 2 servings.

> One serving: 399 calories, 39g protein, 4g carbohydrate, 26g fat (3g saturated), 62mg cholesterol, 412mg sodium, 3g fibre

vegetable creole

2 teaspoons olive oil
110g (4oz) yellow onion, sliced
1 medium-sized green pepper, sliced
1 courgette, sliced
4 medium-sized garlic cloves, crushed
450g (1lb) tinned no-sugar-added, diced tomatoes
1 tablespoon Worcestershire sauce
2g (1/16oz) artificial sweetener

Heat the olive oil in a non-stick frying pan over a medium-high heat. Add the onion, pepper, courgette and garlic and sauté for 5 minutes. Lower the heat to medium. Add the tomatoes, Worcestershire sauce and artificial sweetener. Cover with a lid and cook for 5 minutes. Serve hot with the fish.
Makes 2 servings.

> One serving: 156 calories, 6g protein, 22g carbohydrate, 5g fat (1g saturated), 0mg cholesterol, 378mg sodium, 7g fibre

sausage-pepper sauté

This is a 15-minute meal. I keep low-fat turkey sausages in my freezer for emergency meals and use whatever is in my vegetable drawer to go with it – peppers, celery, mushrooms, broccoli or cauliflower. Use this recipe as a base and create your own sausage meal. ● A jar of marinated artichokes or palm hearts from the pantry can be made into an instant salad to complete a great, quick meal.

sausage-pepper sauté

Olive oil spray
4 low-fat turkey sausages
    (350g/12oz), cut into 2.5cm
    (1in) slices
1 medium-sized red pepper, sliced
2 medium-sized garlic cloves,
    crushed
Salt and freshly ground black
    pepper to taste
25g (1oz) fresh basil leaves, torn
    into small pieces

Set a medium-sized non-stick frying pan over a medium-high heat and spray with olive oil. Add the sausage, pepper and garlic and sauté for 10 minutes. Season with salt and pepper to taste. Sprinkle with the basil and serve.
Makes 2 servings.

One serving: 344 calories, 30g protein,
14g carbohydrate, 18g fat (5g saturated),
90mg cholesterol, 1084mg sodium, 0g fibre

marinated artichoke salad

350g (12oz) jars marinated
    artichoke hearts, drained
110g (4oz) washed, ready-to-eat,
    Italian-style salad leaves
2 tablespoons no-sugar-added oil
    and vinegar dressing
Salt and freshly ground black
    pepper to taste

Cut the artichoke hearts in half. Place the salad leaves in a small bowl and toss with the dressing. Season with salt and pepper to taste. Place the artichoke hearts on top and serve.
Makes 2 servings.

One serving: 229 calories, 3g protein,
13g carbohydrate, 17g fat (1g saturated),
0mg cholesterol, 618mg sodium, 3g fibre

helpful hints

● *Most supermarkets sell marinated artichoke hearts in a jar or tin.*
● *To determine the weight of each sausage, divide the packet weight by the number of sausages.*

countdown

● *Make sausage and peppers.*
● *Make artichoke salad.*

shopping list

TO BUY:
  1 packet low-fat turkey
    sausages (350g/12oz
    needed)
  2 jars marinated artichoke
    hearts (350g/12oz needed)
  1 medium-sized red pepper
  1 bag washed, ready-to-eat,
    Italian-style salad leaves
  1 small bunch basil
STAPLES:
  Olive oil spray
  No-sugar-added oil and
    vinegar dressing
  Garlic
  Salt
  Black peppercorns

salsa-baked snapper

helpful hints

- Any type of salsa can be used – just make sure it does not have sugar added.
- Any type of thin fish fillet, such as sole, flounder or bream can be used.
- Buy good quality Parmesan cheese and grate it yourself. Freeze extra for quick use later – simply spoon out what you need and leave the rest frozen.
- For optimum taste, make sure the dried oregano is less than 6 months old.

countdown

- Preheat oven to 200°C/400°F/gas mark 6.
- Make fish.
- While fish bakes, make courgettes.
- Make salad.

shopping list

TO BUY:
  350g (12oz) snapper fillet
  1 jar no-sugar-added tomato salsa
  1 bag washed, ready-to-eat, Italian-style salad leaves
  225g (8oz) courgettes
STAPLES:
  Olive oil
  Olive oil spray
  No-sugar-added oil and vinegar dressing
  Parmesan cheese
  Dried oregano
  Salt
  Black peppercorns

This is a great meal for those evenings you need to get a tasty dinner on the table in 15 minutes. Fresh fish is the original fast food. Simply cover the fish with salsa, grill and serve.

salsa-baked snapper

Olive oil spray
350g (12oz) snapper fillet
Salt and freshly ground black pepper to taste
225ml (8fl oz) no-sugar-added tomato salsa

Preheat the oven to 200°C/400°F/gas mark 6. Line a baking tray with foil and spray with olive oil. Place the fish on the baking sheet, spray with olive oil and season with salt and pepper to taste. Bake for 10 minutes. Spoon the salsa over the fish and bake for 5 more minutes before serving.
Makes 2 servings.

One serving: 244 calories, 39g protein, 10g carbohydrate, 4g fat (1g saturated), 62mg cholesterol, 872mg sodium, 4g fibre

courgette parmesan

225g (8oz) courgettes, sliced
4 teaspoons olive oil
Salt and freshly ground black pepper to taste
2 tablespoons freshly grated Parmesan cheese

Place the courgettes in a microwave-safe bowl and heat on high for 5 minutes. Alternatively, bring a medium saucepan of water to a boil and add the courgettes. Boil for 3 minutes and drain. Toss with the olive oil and season with salt and pepper to taste. Sprinkle with Parmesan cheese and serve.
Makes 2 servings.

One serving: 123 calories, 4g protein, 4g carbohydrate, 11g fat (2g saturated), 4mg cholesterol, 110mg sodium, 1g fibre

italian greens

2 tablespoons no-sugar-added oil and vinegar dressing
2 teaspoons dried oregano
150g (5oz) washed, ready-to-eat, Italian-style salad leaves

Spoon the dressing into a salad bowl and stir in the oregano. Add the salad, toss well and serve.
Makes 2 servings.

One serving: 88 calories, 1g protein, 3g carbohydrate, 9g fat (1g saturated), 0mg cholesterol, 81mg sodium, 1g fibre

rosemary-roasted pork

Northern Italy inspired this roasted pork dinner served with fennel gratin and Brussels sprouts. The secret to roasting the pork in only 15 minutes is to butterfly it by cutting it in half lengthwise. ● *Pecorino cheese is an alternative to using Parmesan cheese, but with a sharper flavour. It's made from sheep's milk and the most popular kinds are hard and perfect for grating.* ● *Fennel has a pale green bulb and stalk with feathery leaves. It has a slight anise or liquorice flavour when raw that becomes even milder when cooked.*

rosemary-roasted pork

Olive oil spray
350g (12oz) pork tenderloin
2 teaspoons olive oil
2 tablespoons chopped fresh rosemary or 2 teaspoons dried
Salt and freshly ground black pepper to taste

Preheat the oven to 200°C/400°F/gas mark 6. Line a baking tray with foil, spray with olive oil and place in the oven to heat. Remove all visible fat from the pork and cut the loin nearly in half lengthwise. Open the pork and lay flat like a book. Pound it flat with the palm of your hand or with the bottom of a pan. Rub the pork with olive oil and sprinkle with rosemary on both sides. Place the pork on the hot baking tray. Roast for 15 minutes. Remove from the oven, cover with foil and let the meat rest for 5 minutes. Season with salt and pepper to taste. Slice and serve.
Makes 2 servings.

One serving: 345 calories, 49g protein, 0g carbohydrate, 15g fat (4g saturated), 159mg cholesterol, 115mg sodium, 0g fibre

helpful hints

● *Parmesan cheese can be used instead of pecorino cheese.*
● *A quick way to chop fresh rosemary is to snip it right from the stem with scissors.*
● *Celery can be substituted for the fennel in the recipe.*

countdown

● *Preheat oven to 400°F/200°C/gas mark 6.*
● *Start pork.*
● *Make fennel.*
● *Steam Brussels sprouts.*

shopping list

TO BUY:
  1 small piece pecorino cheese
  350g (12oz) pork tenderloin
  1 small bunch fresh rosemary or 1 jar dried
  1 medium bulb fennel
  110g (4oz) Brussels sprouts
STAPLES:
  Olive oil spray
  Olive oil
  Salt
  Black peppercorns

rosemary-roasted pork continued

fennel gratin

4 teaspoons olive oil

half medium bulb fennel, stalks
and leaves removed, thinly
sliced

Salt and freshly ground black
pepper to taste

2 tablespoons grated pecorino
cheese

Heat the olive oil in a non-stick frying pan over a medium-high heat. Add the fennel and toss in the oil. Cover with a lid and cook for 2 minutes. Alternatively, place in a microwave-safe bowl, add the oil, and toss to coat. Cover and microwave on high for 8 minutes. Season the cooked fennel with salt and pepper to taste and toss well. Sprinkle with the cheese and place in the oven with the pork for 5 minutes, or until the cheese starts to melt. Use the same baking tray as the pork to save clean-up time. Serve with the pork. *Makes 2 servings.*

One serving: 135 calories, 2g protein, 0g carbohydrate, 11g fat (2g saturated), 4mg cholesterol, 106mg sodium, 0g fibre

brussels sprouts

110g (4oz) Brussels sprouts,
damaged outer leaves removed
and sprouts halved

2 teaspoons olive oil

Salt and freshly ground black
pepper to taste

Place the Brussels sprouts in the basket of a vegetable steamer. Place over boiling water and steam for 6–7 minutes. Alternatively, microwave on high for 5 minutes. Transfer the cooked Brussels sprouts to a serving bowl. Add the olive oil and season with salt and pepper to taste. Toss well before serving. *Makes 2 servings.*

One serving: 60 calories, 1g protein, 4g carbohydrate, 5g fat (1g saturated), 0mg cholesterol, 12mg sodium, 1g fibre

herb-stuffed chicken

This fresh herb stuffing gives a fragrant flavour to the chicken and keeps it moist during cooking. The stuffing, a combination of chopped fresh tarragon, spring onions and mushrooms, is so simple, it really only takes minutes to make. The herbs and mushrooms can be chopped in a food processor to save even more time. ● Small, baby turnips are sweet and need only a little sautéing to bring out their flavour and keep their crunchy texture.

herb-stuffed chicken

2 x 175g (6oz) boneless, skinless chicken breasts

2 tablespoons fresh tarragon or 2 teaspoons dried

2 spring onions, sliced

2 medium-sized button mushrooms

2 tablespoons fat-free plain yoghurt

Salt and freshly ground black pepper to taste

Olive oil spray

Holding the chicken breast flat with the palm of your hand, make a horizontal slit in each breast. It should be deep enough to form a pocket the length of the chicken breast. In a food processor or by hand, chop the tarragon, spring onions and mushrooms together. Add the yoghurt and blend well. Season with salt and pepper to taste. Season the inside slits of the chicken. Spoon the herb stuffing into the slit. Gently press the chicken breast together to close the slits. Set a medium-sized non-stick frying pan over a medium-high heat, and spray with olive oil. Brown the chicken breasts for 2 minutes on each side, seasoning each cooked side with salt and pepper. Lower the heat to medium, cover with a lid and cook for 6 more minutes. Serve hot. *Makes 2 servings.*

One serving: 309 calories, 55g protein, 2g carbohydrate, 10g fat (2g saturated), 144mg cholesterol, 138mg sodium, 0g fibre

helpful hint

● *Dried tarragon can be substituted for fresh. Make sure the dried leaves are green. If they have started to turn brown, it's time to buy a new jar.*

countdown

● *Prepare all ingredients.*
● *Start chicken.*
● *While chicken cooks, make asparagus and turnips.*

shopping list

TO BUY:

1 small pot fat-free plain yoghurt

2 x 175 (6oz) boneless, skinless chicken breasts

225g (8oz) fresh asparagus

225g (8oz) baby turnips

1 small bunch fresh tarragon or 1 jar dried

1 small packet button mushrooms

1 small bunch spring onions (2 needed)

STAPLES:

Olive oil

Olive oil spray

Garlic

Salt

Black peppercorns

herb-stuffed chicken continued

pan-roasted asparagus and baby turnips

225g (8oz) fresh asparagus
4 teaspoons olive oil
225g (8oz) baby turnips, peeled and cut into 2.5cm (1in) cubes
1 medium-sized garlic clove, crushed
Salt and freshly ground black pepper to taste

Cut or snap off the 2.5cm (1in) fibrous stem on the asparagus and discard. Slice the remaining asparagus into 5cm (2in) pieces. Heat the olive oil in a medium-sized non-stick frying pan over a medium-high heat and add the turnips. Sauté for 5 minutes, turning to make sure all sides are browned. Add the asparagus and garlic and continue to sauté, 5 minutes for thin asparagus and 10 minutes for thick. Season with salt and pepper to taste. Serve with the chicken.
Makes 2 servings.

One serving: 134 calories, 3g protein, 12g carbohydrate, 9g fat (1g saturated), 0mg cholesterol, 90mg sodium, 5g fibre

steak au poivre

Here's a meal that's perfect for those evenings when you want something a little special.
● *Steak au Poivre, or black pepper steak, is a very simple, very French dish. This recipe calls for cracked or coarsely broken black peppercorns, which are available in the spice section of the supermarket.* ● *Crème fraîche adds a tangy flavour and creamy texture to the sauce.*
● *Brandy is the generic name for cognac or Armagnac. You can buy brandy in miniature bottles at many supermarkets and most off-licences.* ● *Palm hearts are the tender heart of the Sabal palm tree.*

steak au poivre

2 x 150g (5oz) fillets of beef
1 tablespoon cracked black
    pepper
4 teaspoons rapeseed oil
Salt to taste
2 tablespoons cognac
    or brandy
1 tablespoon crème fraîche

Cover the steaks with the cracked pepper, pressing it into the meat with the palm of your hand. Heat the oil in a non-stick frying pan over a medium-high heat. Brown the steaks for 4 minutes. If the steaks are browning too quickly, reduce the heat to medium. Turn and salt the cooked sides to taste. Brown the second side for 2 minutes, or until a meat thermometer registers 60°C/140°F. Remove the steaks to 2 plates.

Add the cognac to the hot pan, scraping up the brown bits as it cooks. Add the crème fraîche and mix well. Taste for salt and adjust the seasoning if necessary. Spoon the sauce on top of the steaks and serve.
Makes 2 servings.

One serving: 376 calories, 30g protein,
2g carbohydrate, 24g fat (8g saturated),
98mg cholesterol, 81mg sodium, 0g fibre

helpful hints

● *If pressed for time, use a bottled, no-sugar-added oil and vinegar dressing instead of the recipe provided here.*
● *Sirloin steaks can be used instead of beef fillets.*
● *Any type of lettuce leaves can be used instead of red lettuce.*
● *Artichoke hearts can be used instead of palm hearts.*
● *Ordinary green beans can be used instead of French green beans and cut in half.*
● *To save cleaning an extra pan, prepare the steaks and green beans in the same pan.*

countdown

● *Make the palm hearts salad.*
● *Blanch the green beans.*
● *Make the steak.*
● *Sauté the green beans.*

shopping list

TO BUY:

1 small pot crème fraîche

2 x 150g (5oz) beef fillets

1 jar cracked black pepper

1 small bottle brandy, preferably cognac

1 jar or tin palm hearts (275g/10oz needed)

225g (8oz) French green beans (haricots verts)

1 small head red lettuce

STAPLES:

Garlic

Rapeseed oil

Red wine vinegar

Dijon mustard

Salt

Black peppercorns

steak au poivre continued

french green beans

225g (8oz) French green beans (haricots verts), trimmed

4 teaspoons rapeseed oil

2 medium-sized garlic cloves, crushed

Salt and freshly ground black pepper to taste

Bring a medium saucepan full of water to a boil. Add the beans. As soon as the water comes back to a boil, drain the beans. Return the beans to the pan and fill the pan with iced water to stop the cooking. Drain the beans. In the same saucepan, heat the oil over a high heat. Add the beans and garlic, and sauté for 2–3 minutes until the beans are crisp. Season with salt and pepper to taste and serve with the steak.

Makes 2 servings.

One serving: 88 calories, 3g protein, 11g carbohydrate, 5g fat (1g saturated), 0mg cholesterol, 4mg sodium, 2g fibre

palm hearts salad

1 tablespoon red wine vinegar

4 teaspoons Dijon mustard

Salt and freshly ground black pepper to taste

2 teaspoons rapeseed oil

275g (10oz) palm hearts, drained and cut into 1cm (½in) slices

Several red lettuce leaves

In a salad bowl, whisk the vinegar and mustard together until smooth. Season with salt and pepper to taste. Whisk in the oil and adjust for seasoning as necessary. Add the palm hearts to the dressing. Toss well. Place the lettuce on 2 small plates, spoon the palm hearts on top and serve.

Makes 2 servings.

One serving: 100 calories, 5g protein, 9g carbohydrate, 6g fat (1g saturated), 0mg cholesterol, 868mg sodium, 4g fibre

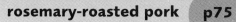
rosemary-roasted pork   **p75**

chicory filled with cheese and roasted peppers   **p96**

which carbs

introduction

When I teach classes, I find that this is the most important phase. My students are afraid to start reintroducing carbs for fear they will negate all of the benefits they've achieved. This section shows you how to start bringing carbs back into your life without gaining weight. I have carefully chosen these recipes to reincorporate high-fibre, low simple-sugar carbohydrates. Organised into a meal-at-a-glance chart, these recipes include some easy and quick meals for busy mid-week schedules and some more elaborate recipes suited to a relaxed weekend pace. They are arranged to give variety throughout the day and over the course of the week. For an overview see the 14-day meal plan. Otherwise, the meals appear in the same sequence within the chapter, so just follow the meals in the order given.

breakfast

You can choose from a variety of breakfasts. Quick ideas like Cheddar Scramble and Dijon Ham and Cheddar Grill can be made in less than 5 minutes. You can also enjoy Pecan Ham Roll-Ups or Prawn, Pepper and Tomato Frittata.

lunch

Chicken Salad Amandine and Salad Niçoise from the French Riviera are two tempting choices.

dinner

Neapolitan Steak, Spicy Chicken Legs and Whisky Pork Chops are some of the meals that have been carefully planned to slowly reintroduce carbohydrates.

During the Which Carb 14-day meal plan, you will consume an average of 75–85g (3–3$^{1}/_{2}$oz) of carbohydrate per day. This percentage is based on carbohydrates less fibre consumed – the normal way of calculating carbohydrate consumption. The balance of these meals is 23 per cent of calories from carbohydrates, 38 per cent of calories from lean protein, 27 per cent of calories from mono-unsaturated fat and 8 per cent of calories from saturated fat.

quick carbs 14-day menu plan

week 1	breakfast	lunch	dinner
sunday	Sausage and Mushroom Egg Pizzetta 85	Tex-Mex Layered Salad 100	Thai Peanut-Rub Pork 115
monday	Rocket and Ham Scramble 86	Smoked Haddock Salad 101	Pesto Chicken . .116–117
tuesday	Turkey and Cottage Cheese 87	Salad Niçoise 102	Grilled Scallops Parmigiana 118–119
wednesday	Dijon Ham and Cheddar Grill 88	Chicken Salad Amandine 103	Breaded Veal Escalopes 120
thursday	Quick Herb Omelette 89	Roast Turkey and Tzatziki Sandwich . . .104	Garlic Prawn Stir Fry 121–122
friday	Smoked Turkey Roll-ups 90	California Chef's Salad 105	Sole Amandine 123
saturday	Prawn, Pepper and Tomato Frittata 91	Turkey, Salsa and Citrus Salad 106	Smothered Steak with Caramelised Onions 124–125

week 2	breakfast	lunch	dinner
sunday	Asian Omelette 92	Jerk Chicken with Palm Hearts 107	Whisky Pork Chops 126–127
monday	Tuna-stuffed Peppers 93	Deli Salad 108	Seared Sesame Tuna 128–129
tuesday	Pecan Ham Roll-ups 94	Gammon and Egg Salad 109	Chicken Provençal 130–131
wednesday	Cheddar Scramble 95	Balsamic and Dill Salmon Salad 110	Mussels Marinière . . .132
thursday	Chicory Filled with Cheese and Roasted Pepper . . .96	Hollywood Cobb Salad 111	Spicy Crab and Vegetable Stir Fry 133–134
friday	Spanish Omelette 97	Black Bean and Salsa Wraps 112	Neapolitan Steak 135–136
saturday	Raspberry Smoothie with Toasted Walnut Oatmeal 98	Grilled Chilli Chicken 113	Spicy Chicken Legs 137–138

which carbs
breakfasts

sausage and mushroom egg pizzetta

Sausage, mushrooms, onion and tomato sauce form the topping for an egg pizza base. This is a fun breakfast that takes about 15 minutes to make. It's great for a weekday or weekend treat, breakfast, lunch or dinner.

sausage and mushroom egg pizzetta

225ml (8fl oz) egg substitute

Freshly ground black pepper

Olive oil spray

125ml (4fl oz) low-fat, no-sugar-added tomato sauce for pasta

2 small low-fat turkey sausages, cut into 2.5cm (1in) slices

6 button mushrooms, sliced

1 tablespoon diced red onion

4 slices reduced-fat mozzarella cheese (75g/3oz)

Preheat the grill. Season the egg substitute with pepper to taste. Set a small (20.5cm/8in) frying pan over a medium-high heat. Spray with olive oil and pour in half the egg substitute. Swirl in the pan to make a thin layer. Allow to cook for 2 minutes, turn over for 1 minute and remove from the heat. Spread the tomato sauce on top. Add the sausage, mushrooms, onion and mozzarella cheese. Place under the grill about 25.5cm (10in) from the heat. Grill for 10 minutes. Carefully slide onto a plate and serve. Repeat for the second serving.
Makes 2 servings.

bran cereal

50g (2oz) high-fibre, no-sugar-added bran cereal

225ml (8fl oz) skimmed milk

Divide between 2 cereal bowls.
Makes 2 servings.

Total breakfast one serving: 387 calories, 38g protein, 39g carbohydrate, 13g fat (5g saturated), 55mg cholesterol, 1189mg sodium, 15g fibre

helpful hints

● Sliced mushrooms can be found in the fruit and veg section of the supermarket.

● 2 whole eggs can be used instead of egg substitute.

● To determine the weight of each sausage or slice of cheese, divide the packet weight by the number of sausages or slices.

countdown

● Preheat grill.

● Make egg pizza base.

● Complete pizza.

shopping list

TO BUY:

1 ball reduced-fat mozzarella cheese (75g/3oz needed)

1 packet low-fat turkey sausages (175g/6oz needed)

1 jar low-fat, no-sugar-added tomato sauce for pasta (110g/4oz needed)

1 packet button mushrooms (6 mushrooms needed)

STAPLES:

Red onion

Olive oil spray

Egg substitute

High-fibre, no-sugar-added bran cereal

Skimmed milk

Black peppercorns

rocket and ham scramble

helpful hints

- To quickly wash rocket, place it in a bowl of cold water, and then lift it out of the bowl. The sand will be left behind.
- To quickly chop or slice the rocket for this dish, place the leaves on top of each other and slice them all at the same time.
- 2 whole eggs and 6 egg whites can be used instead of egg substitute.
- Use spinach if rocket is unavailable.

countdown

- Prepare all ingredients.
- Make eggs.
- Make oatmeal.

shopping list

TO BUY:

225g (8oz) sliced lean ham
1 small bunch rocket

STAPLES:

Egg substitute
Olive oil
Oatmeal
Skimmed milk
Artificial sweetener
Black peppercorns

Ham blends well with savoury rocket in this simple-to-make scrambled egg dish.

rocket and ham scramble

225ml (8fl oz) egg substitute
110g (4oz) rocket, coarsely chopped or sliced
Freshly ground black pepper to taste
2 teaspoons olive oil
225g (8oz) sliced lean ham, cubed (about 8 slices)

Combine the egg substitute and rocket, seasoning with pepper to taste. Heat the oil in a medium-sized non-stick frying pan over a medium-high heat. Add the ham and sauté for 2 minutes. Add the rocket and egg mixture. Scramble for 1 minute, or until the egg is set to desired consistency. Serve.
Makes 2 servings.

oatmeal

110g (3½oz) oatmeal
450ml (16fl oz) water
225ml (8fl oz) skimmed milk
2g (1/16oz) artificial sweetener (optional)

To prepare in the microwave, combine the oatmeal and water in a microwave-safe bowl. Microwave on high for 4 minutes. Stir in the milk and sweetener, divide between 2 bowls and serve warm.

Alternatively, to prepare on the hob, combine the oatmeal and water in a small saucepan over a medium-high heat, and bring to a boil. Reduce the heat to medium and cook for about 5 more minutes, stirring occasionally. Stir in the milk and sweetener, divide between 2 bowls and serve warm.
Makes 2 servings.

Total breakfast one serving: 427 calories,
41g protein, 42g carbohydrate, 11g fat (2g saturated),
54mg cholesterol, 1274mg sodium, 4g fibre

turkey and cottage cheese

This breakfast is ideal when you're on the go, as it takes only a few minutes to make. ● *The addition of a few pecans to the oatmeal gives it a crunchy texture and nutty flavour.*

turkey and cottage cheese

225g (8oz) low-fat cottage cheese
2 tablespoons dried chives
225g (8oz) sliced roast turkey
  breast

Combine the cottage cheese and chives in a small bowl. Place the turkey slices on 2 plates and spoon the cottage cheese mixture on the slices. Fold the turkey slices in half and serve. *Makes 2 servings.*

pecan oatmeal

75g (3oz) oatmeal
450ml (16fl oz) water
25g (1oz) pecan pieces
225ml (8fl oz) skimmed milk
2g (¹/₁₆oz) artificial sweetener
  (optional)

To prepare in the microwave, combine the oatmeal and water in a microwave-safe bowl. Microwave on high for 4 minutes.

Alternatively, to prepare on the hob, combine the oatmeal and water in a small saucepan over a medium-high heat and bring to a boil. Reduce the heat to medium and cook about 5 more minutes, stirring occasionally.

Place the pecans on a foil-lined tray and toast under the grill for 1 minute, or until golden. Stir the milk, sweetener and toasted pecans into the oatmeal. Divide between 2 bowls and serve. *Makes 2 servings.*

Total breakfast one serving: 473 calories,
40g protein, 40g carbohydrate, 17g fat (4g saturated),
52mg cholesterol, 439mg sodium, 5g fibre

helpful hints

● *Other types of fresh herbs such as dill, parsley or basil can be used in place of chives.*
● *Toasting pecans can be tricky, as they burn quickly. Watch them carefully.*

countdown

● *Make turkey.*
● *Make oatmeal.*

shopping list

TO BUY:
  1 small pot low-fat cottage
    cheese (225g/8oz needed)
  225g (8oz) sliced roast turkey
    breast
  1 packet pecan pieces
    (25g/1oz needed)
  1 jar dried chives
STAPLES:
  Oatmeal
  Skimmed milk
  Artificial sweetener

dijon ham and cheddar grill

For those mornings when you don't feel like eggs, try this quick cheese and ham melt.
If you like spicy food, adjust the amount of cayenne accordingly.

dijon ham and cheddar grill

225g (8oz) sliced lean smoked
    ham (about 8 slices)
75g (3oz) sliced reduced-fat,
    mature Cheddar cheese
2 tablespoons Dijon mustard
Pinch cayenne pepper
1 medium tomato, cut into 1cm
    (½in) slices

Line a baking tray with foil. Place the ham on foil and cheese on top. Spread the cheese with mustard and sprinkle with cayenne. Place under the grill for 4 minutes, or until the cheese melts. Place the tomato slices on 2 plates with the ham and cheese to serve.
Makes 2 servings.

cinnamon oatmeal

75g (3oz) oatmeal
450ml (16fl oz) water
225ml (8fl oz) skimmed milk
½ teaspoon ground cinnamon
2g (¹⁄₁₆oz) artificial sweetener
    (optional)

To prepare in the microwave, combine the oatmeal and water in a microwave-safe bowl. Microwave on high for 4 minutes. Stir in the milk, cinnamon and sweetener, divide between 2 bowls and serve warm.

Alternatively, to prepare on the hob, combine the oatmeal and water in a small saucepan over a medium-high heat and bring to a boil. Reduce the heat to medium and cook for about 5 more minutes, stirring occasionally. Stir in the milk, cinnamon and sweetener, divide between 2 bowls and serve warm.
Makes 2 servings.

Total breakfast one serving: 484 calories,
40g protein, 43g carbohydrate, 16g fat (8g saturated),
84mg cholesterol, 1773mg sodium, 4g fibre

helpful hints

- To determine the weight of each slice of cheese or ham, divide the packet weight by the number of slices.
- No-sugar-added instant oatmeal can be used.

countdown

- Preheat grill.
- Make cheese and ham melt.
- Make oatmeal.

shopping list

TO BUY:
1 packet sliced reduced-fat, mature Cheddar cheese (75g/3oz needed)
225g (8oz) sliced lean smoked ham
1 medium tomato
STAPLES:
Oatmeal
Skimmed milk
Ground cinnamon
Dijon mustard
Cayenne pepper
Artificial sweetener

quick herb omelette

Omelette aux Fines Herbes is on almost every French bistro menu. This is a quick version of this very French dish. ● *The secret here is to chop the dried herbs with the fresh parsley. The moisture from the parsley helps to release the juices from the dried herbs.*

quick herb omelette

1 tablespoon dried chives
½ tablespoon dried tarragon
50g (2oz) fresh parsley leaves
2 eggs
6 egg whites
Salt and freshly ground black pepper to taste
2 teaspoons olive oil
35g (1½oz) sliced reduced-fat Swiss cheese (about 2 slices)

Chop the chives, tarragon and parsley together. Whisk the eggs and egg whites together in a medium-sized bowl. Stir in the herbs and add salt and pepper to taste. Heat the oil in a medium-sized non-stick frying pan over a medium-high heat. Pour in the egg mixture and allow to set for 1 minute. Cover with a lid and cook 2–3 minutes more, or until the egg is almost set. Turn the omelette over, place the cheese slices on top and cover. Cook for 1 more minute. Slide a knife under the omelette and fold in half. Cut the folded omelette in half and serve on 2 plates.
Makes 2 servings.

bran cereal

225ml (8fl oz) skimmed milk
75g (3oz) high-fibre, no-sugar-added bran cereal

Divide the milk and cereal between 2 bowls.
Makes 2 servings.

Total breakfast one serving: 343 calories, 33g protein, 36g carbohydrate, 15g fat (4g saturated), 226mg cholesterol, 488mg sodium, 13g fibre

helpful hints

● *To determine the weight of each slice of cheese, divide the packet weight by the number of slices.*
● *Make sure the dried chives and tarragon are less than 6 months old.*
● *Parsley, chives and tarragon can be chopped together in a food processor or with a hand held blender.*

countdown

● *Prepare all ingredients.*
● *Make omelette.*
● *Assemble bran cereal.*

shopping list

TO BUY:
  1 small packet sliced reduced-fat Swiss cheese (35g/1½oz needed)
  1 jar dried chives
  1 large bunch fresh parsley
STAPLES:
  Eggs
  Skimmed milk
  High-fibre, no-sugar-added bran cereal
  Olive oil
  Dried tarragon
  Salt
  Black peppercorns

smoked turkey roll-ups

Turkey slices filled with nutty-flavoured rocket and alfalfa sprouts provide a quick-grab breakfast. The roll-ups can be made the night before and eaten on the run..

smoked turkey roll-ups

225g (8oz) sliced lean smoked turkey breast

2 tablespoons mayonnaise made with olive or soya bean oil

Several rocket leaves

110g (4oz) alfalfa sprouts

Place the turkey slices on a work surface or plate. Spread the turkey with mayonnaise. Top with rocket leaves and sprouts. Roll up, divide between 2 plates and serve.
Makes 2 servings.

spiced oatmeal

75g (3oz) oatmeal

450ml (16fl oz) water

2g (¹/₁₆oz) artificial sweetener (optional)

½ teaspoon ground nutmeg

225ml (8fl oz) skimmed milk

To prepare in the microwave, combine the oatmeal and water in a microwave-safe bowl. Microwave on high for 4 minutes. Stir in the sweetener and nutmeg. Stir in the milk, divide between 2 bowls and serve warm.

Alternatively, to prepare on the hob, combine the oatmeal and water in a small saucepan over a medium-high heat and bring to a boil. Reduce the heat to medium and cook for about 5 more minutes, stirring occasionally. Stir in the sweetener and nutmeg. Stir in the milk, divide between 2 bowls and serve warm.
Makes 2 servings.

Total breakfast one serving: 484 calories, 43g protein, 36g carbohydrate, 18g fat (3g saturated), 87mg cholesterol, 218mg sodium, 5g fibre

prawn, pepper and tomato frittata

This is an unusual frittata topped with sliced tomatoes and melted cheese.

prawn, pepper and tomato frittata

2 whole eggs

6 egg whites

Salt and freshly ground black pepper to taste

2 teaspoons olive oil

1 medium-sized red pepper, sliced

225g (8oz) cooked prawns, cut in half crosswise

1 medium-sized tomato, sliced

25g (1oz) grated, reduced-fat Cheddar cheese

Preheat the oven to 200°C/400°F/gas mark 6. Lightly beat the whole eggs and egg whites together in a medium-sized bowl and season with salt and pepper to taste.

Pour the oil into a medium-sized non-stick frying pan and place over a medium heat. Add the pepper and sauté for 3 minutes. Add the prawns and pour the egg mixture into the pan, swirling in the pan to cover the pepper. Allow to set for 1 minute. Place the tomato slices on top and sprinkle with the cheese.

Place in the oven for 5 minutes, or until the eggs are set to the desired consistency. Divide the frittata between 2 plates and serve.

Makes 2 servings.

yoghurt bran cup

225ml (8fl oz) low-fat flavoured yoghurt

75g (3oz) high-fibre, no-sugar-added bran cereal

Divide the yoghurt between 2 bowls and sprinkle with the bran.

Makes 2 servings.

Total breakfast one serving: 467 calories, 53g protein, 41g carbohydrate, 17g fat (5g saturated), 399mg cholesterol, 716mg sodium, 13g fibre

helpful hints

- *Use a pan with an ovenproof handle, and be careful of the hot handle when removing the pan from the oven.*
- *Buy cooked prawns in the seafood section of the supermarket, or look for good quality, large, frozen cooked prawns.*
- *To determine the weight of each slice of cheese, divide the packet weight by the number of slices.*

countdown

- *Preheat oven to 200°C/400°F/gas mark 6.*
- *Make frittata.*
- *Assemble bran cup.*

shopping list

TO BUY:

1 packet grated, reduced-fat Cheddar cheese (25g/1oz needed)

1 pot low-fat flavoured yoghurt

225g (8oz) cooked prawns

1 medium-sized red pepper

1 medium-sized tomato

STAPLES:

Eggs

Olive oil

High-fibre, no-sugar-added bran cereal

Salt

Black peppercorns

asian omelette

helpful hint

- *To save time, buy sliced water chestnuts.*
- *4 whole eggs and 8 egg whites can be used instead of egg substitute.*

countdown

- *Make omelette.*
- *Assemble cereal.*

shopping list

TO BUY:

   110g (4oz) sliced lean ham
   1 small tin water chestnuts
   1 small packet fresh bean sprouts

STAPLES:

   Egg substitute
   Olive oil
   Skimmed milk
   High-fibre, no-sugar-added bran cereal
   Black peppercorns

Crisp water chestnuts and bean sprouts give an Oriental flavour to this omelette. It's adapted from the popular Chinese dish, Egg Foo Yong.

asian omelette

2 teaspoons olive oil
25g (1oz) fresh bean sprouts
75g (3oz) water chestnuts, drained and sliced
Freshly ground black pepper to taste
450ml (16fl oz) egg substitute
110g (4oz) sliced lean ham, chopped (about 4 slices)

Heat the oil in a non-stick frying pan over a medium-high heat. Add the bean sprouts and water chestnuts and sauté for 1 minute. Season the egg substitute with pepper to taste and pour into the pan, swirling to cover the vegetables. Allow to set for 1 minute. Sprinkle the ham on top, cover and cook 2–3 minutes longer, or until the egg sets to desired consistency. Cut the omelette in half, slide out of the pan and serve. *Makes 2 servings*.

bran cereal

225ml (8fl oz) skimmed milk
75g (3oz) high-fibre, no-sugar-added bran cereal

Divide the milk and cereal between 2 bowls. *Makes 2 servings*.

Total breakfast one serving: 369 calories, 42g protein, 44g carbohydrate, 8g fat (1g saturated), 28mg cholesterol, 1146mg sodium, 15g fibre

tuna-stuffed peppers

This popular combination of tuna salad and melted cheese works well for breakfast.

tuna–stuffed peppers

175g (6oz) tinned tuna packed in water, drained and rinsed

2 tablespoons mayonnaise made from soya bean or olive oil

6 to 8 fresh basil leaves, torn into bite-sized pieces (about 4 tablespoons)

Salt and freshly ground black pepper to taste

2 small red peppers, seeded and halved

75g (3oz) sliced reduced-fat Cheddar cheese (about 4 slices)

Preheat the grill. Line a baking tray with foil. In a small bowl, flake the tuna with a fork. Stir in the mayonnaise and basil and season with salt and pepper to taste. Spoon the tuna salad into the pepper halves and top with the cheese. Grill for 2 minutes, or until the cheese has melted. Divide between 2 plates and serve.

Makes 2 servings.

bran cereal

225ml (8fl oz) skimmed milk

75g (3oz) high-fibre, no-sugar-added bran cereal

Divide the milk and cereal between 2 bowls.

Makes 2 servings.

Total breakfast one serving: 455 calories, 43g protein, 39g carbohydrate, 21g fat (6g saturated), 60mg cholesterol, 957mg sodium, 13g fibre

helpful hint

● *Any reduced-fat strong cheese can be substituted for the Cheddar cheese.*

countdown

● *Preheat grill.*
● *Make tuna melt.*
● *Assemble cereal.*

shopping list

TO BUY:

1 packet sliced reduced-fat Cheddar cheese (75g/3oz needed)

175g (6oz) tinned tuna packed in water

1 small bunch fresh basil

2 small red peppers

STAPLES:

Mayonnaise made from soya bean or olive oil

High-fibre, no-sugar-added bran cereal

Skimmed milk

Salt

Black peppercorns

pecan ham roll-ups

Cream cheese and pecans make a quick filling for sliced ham. These can be made a day ahead and used for a quick-take breakfast.

helpful hints

● *To determine the weight of each slice of ham, divide the packet weight by the number of slices.*

● *Warm water can be used instead of skimmed milk to soften the cream cheese.*

countdown

● *Make ham roll-ups.*
● *Make oatmeal.*

shopping list

TO BUY:

50g (2oz) reduced-fat cream cheese

225g (8oz) sliced lean ham

1 small packet pecan pieces (10g/¹⁄₂oz needed)

STAPLES:

Oatmeal

Skimmed milk

Ground cinnamon

Artificial sweetener

pecan ham roll-ups

50g (2oz) reduced-fat cream cheese
2 tablespoons skimmed milk
6 pecans, chopped (2 tablespoons)
225g (8oz) sliced lean ham (about 8 slices)

Blend the cream cheese, milk and pecans in a food processor. Or, chop the pecans by hand and combine with the cream cheese and milk. Lay the ham slices on the work surface or plate and spread with the cream cheese mixture. Roll up, divide between 2 plates and serve.
Makes 2 servings.

cinnamon oatmeal

75g (3oz) oatmeal
450ml (16fl oz) water
225ml (8fl oz) skimmed milk
¹⁄₂ teaspoon ground cinnamon
2g (¹⁄₁₆oz) artificial sweetener (optional)

To prepare in the microwave, combine the oatmeal and water in a microwave-safe bowl. Microwave on high for 4 minutes. Stir in the milk, cinnamon and sweetener, divide between 2 bowls and serve warm.

Alternatively, to prepare on the hob, combine the oatmeal and water in a small saucepan over a medium-high heat and bring to a boil. Reduce the heat to medium and cook about 5 more minutes, stirring occasionally. Stir in the milk, cinnamon and sweetener. Divide between 2 bowls and serve warm.
Makes 2 servings.

Total breakfast one serving: 449 calories, 32g protein, 42g carbohydrate, 18g fat (6g saturated), 76mg cholesterol, 1169mg sodium, 5g fibre

cheddar scramble

This is a breakfast you can make on the run. The eggs take 1¹/₂ minutes to cook and, best of all, there's no pan to wash.

cheddar scramble

450ml (16fl oz) egg substitute

75g (3oz) sliced reduced-fat Cheddar cheese, (about 4 slices)

Freshly ground black pepper to taste

Combine half of the egg substitute with 2 slices of the cheese in a microwave-safe bowl. Season with pepper to taste. Microwave on high for 1½ minutes. Stir and then heat for another 30 seconds. Repeat for the second serving. Serve hot.
Makes 2 servings.

bran cereal

225ml (8fl oz) skimmed milk

75g (3oz) high-fibre, no-sugar-added bran cereal

Divide the milk and cereal between 2 bowls.
Makes 2 servings.

Total breakfast one serving: 358 calories, 41g protein, 35g carbohydrate, 10g fat (6g saturated), 32mg cholesterol, 998mg sodium, 13g fibre

helpful hint

- *2 whole eggs and 6 egg whites can be used instead of egg substitute.*
- *To determine the weight of each slice of cheese, divide the packet weight by the number of slices.*

countdown

- *Make eggs.*
- *Assemble cereal.*

shopping list

TO BUY:

1 small packet sliced reduced-fat Cheddar cheese (75g/3oz needed)

STAPLES:

Egg substitute

Skimmed milk

High-fibre, no-sugar-added bran cereal

Black peppercorns

chicory filled with cheese and roasted peppers

This is a quick breakfast that you can put together in minutes. In fact, it's also a good snack. Keep the mixture in the refrigerator and use it as a dip or spread with other vegetables.

chicory filled with cheese and roasted peppers

450g (1lb) low-fat cottage cheese
50g (2oz) low-fat cream cheese
350g (12oz) roasted red peppers, drained and diced
50g (2oz) purple basil, chopped
Salt and freshly ground black pepper to taste
2 large heads chicory

Combine the cottage cheese, cream cheese, roasted red pepper and purple basil by hand in a medium-sized bowl or in a food processor. Season with salt and pepper to taste. Remove any damaged outer leaves from the chicory, break off leaves and divide between 2 plates. Spoon the filling onto the wide end of each leaf and serve.

Makes 2 servings.

bran cereal

225ml (8fl oz) skimmed milk
75g (3oz) high-fibre, no-sugar-added bran cereal

Divide the milk and cereal between 2 bowls.

Makes 2 servings.

Total breakfast one serving: 394 calories, 36g protein, 47g carbohydrate, 11g fat (8g saturated), 44mg cholesterol, 1005mg sodium, 13g fibre

turkey and tzatsiki sandwich | **p104**

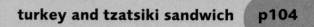

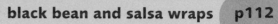

black bean and salsa wraps   p112

spanish omelette

This zesty breakfast classic is updated here to make a quick meal. You can add chillies, garlic and peppers for variety and additional spice. Just use this recipe as a guideline.

spanish omelette

2 whole eggs
4 egg whites
225g (8oz) sliced turkey breast, chopped
8 spring onions, sliced
Salt and freshly ground black pepper to taste
2 teaspoons olive oil
1 medium tomato, cubed

Preheat the grill. Whisk the whole eggs and egg whites together in a medium-sized mixing bowl. Stir in the turkey and spring onions and season with salt and pepper to taste. Heat the oil in a medium-sized non-stick frying pan over a medium-high heat. Add the tomato and sauté for 3 minutes. Add the egg mixture, swirling to cover the tomato. Allow to set for 1 minute and then place under the grill for 5 minutes. Divide the omelette in half, slide out of the pan and serve on 2 plates.
Makes 2 servings.

bran cereal

225ml (8fl oz) skimmed milk
75g (3oz) high-fibre, no-sugar-added bran cereal

Divide the milk and cereal between 2 bowls.
Makes 2 servings.

> Total breakfast one serving: 465 calories, 54g protein, 39g carbohydrate, 16g fat (4g saturated), 295mg cholesterol, 455mg sodium, 13g fibre

helpful hint

● *Use a pan with an ovenproof handle, but be careful with the hot handle when removing the pan from the oven.*

countdown

● *Preheat grill.*
● *Make omelette.*
● *Assemble cereal.*

shopping list

TO BUY:
  110g (4oz) sliced turkey breast
  1 small bunch spring onions (8 needed)
  1 medium tomato
STAPLES:
  Eggs
  Skimmed milk
  Olive oil
  High-fibre, no-sugar-added bran cereal
  Salt
  Black peppercorns

raspberry smoothie with toasted walnut oatmeal

helpful hints

- If using frozen raspberries, make sure they are not packed in syrup.
- Any type of lettuce can be used.
- No-sugar-added, instant oatmeal can be used.
- Toasting walnuts can be tricky, as they burn quickly. Watch them carefully.

countdown

- Make smoothie.
- Make oatmeal.
- Assemble turkey.

shopping list

TO BUY:
- 1 pot low-fat raspberry-flavoured yoghurt
- 175g (6oz) sliced smoked turkey breast
- 1 small packet walnuts (25g/1oz needed)
- 1 small punnet fresh or 1 small bag frozen raspberries
- 1 small head lettuce

STAPLES:
- Vanilla extract
- Oatmeal
- Skimmed milk
- Artificial sweetener

When I did some research into smoothies, I was astounded at their high carbohydrate content. But the cool, smooth, frozen drinks are so good that I decided to create one that was quick, easy, delicious – and good for us too. My family proclaimed this one a winner. ● Use a microwave to make the oatmeal, and this breakfast will take only 10 minutes to make.

raspberry-red smoothie

110g (4oz) fresh or frozen raspberries
125ml (4fl oz) light raspberry-flavoured yoghurt
2 teaspoons vanilla essence
2g (1/16oz) artificial sweetener
1 1/2 pint glasses full of ice cubes

Place the raspberries, yoghurt, vanilla essence and sweetener in a blender. Blend until smooth. Add the ice cubes and blend until thick. Pour into 2 glasses and serve cold.
Makes 2 servings.

toasted walnut oatmeal

75g (3oz) oatmeal
450ml (16fl oz) water
25g (1oz) walnuts
225ml (8fl oz) skimmed milk
2g (1/16oz) artificial sweetener (optional)

To prepare in the microwave, combine the oatmeal and water in a microwave-safe bowl. Microwave on high for 4 minutes.

Alternatively, to prepare on the hob, combine the oatmeal and water in a small saucepan over a medium-high heat and bring to a boil. Reduce the heat to medium and cook about 5 more minutes, stirring occasionally.

Place the walnuts on a foil-lined tray and toast under the grill for 1 minute, or until lightly toasted. Stir the milk, sweetener and toasted walnuts into the oatmeal. Divide between 2 bowls and serve warm.
Makes 2 servings.

smoked turkey breast

175g (6oz) sliced smoked turkey breast, cubed
Several lettuce leaves

Place lettuce on 2 plates with the turkey cubes on top, and serve.
Makes 2 servings.

Total breakfast one serving: 492 calories, 38g protein, 49g carbohydrate, 16g fat (2g saturated), 63mg cholesterol, 149mg sodium, 8g fibre

which carbs

lunches

helpful hint

- Buy ready-to-eat, shredded lettuce.

countdown

- Prepare ingredients.
- Make salad.

shopping list

TO BUY:

225g (8oz) sliced smoked lean turkey breast

1 small tin black beans

1 medium tomato

1 jalapeño pepper

1 head iceberg lettuce

1 medium-sized green pepper

STAPLES:

Red onion

No-sugar-added oil and vinegar dressing

Ground cumin

Salt

Black peppercorns

tex-mex layered salad

This is a very pretty salad that will impress guests. Arrange the salad in a large glass bowl so that the layers of colours show through. The salad can be made several hours in advance. Keep covered and refrigerated, and add the dressing just before serving.

tex-mex layered salad

1 medium tomato

110g (4oz) red onion, chopped

1 jalapeño pepper, seeded and chopped

1/2 teaspoon ground cumin

Salt and freshly ground black pepper to taste

175g (6oz) tinned black beans, rinsed and drained

350g (12oz) iceberg lettuce, washed and shredded

1 medium-sized green pepper, chopped

225g (8oz) sliced smoked lean turkey breast, cut into 1cm (1/2in) strips

50ml (2fl oz) no-sugar-added oil and vinegar dressing

Chop half of the tomato and slice the remaining half. Combine the chopped tomato with the onion and jalapeño in a medium-sized bowl. Stir in the ground cumin. (These steps can be done in a food processor or by hand.) Season with salt and pepper to taste. Gently stir in the black beans. Layer the lettuce, pepper, half the black bean mixture and turkey in a medium glass bowl. Arrange the tomato slices on the turkey and spoon the remaining black beans over the tomatoes. Pour the dressing over the salad and serve.

Makes 2 servings.

One serving: 467 calories, 41g protein, 27g carbohydrate, 21g fat (4g saturated), 80mg cholesterol, 238mg sodium, 3g fibre

smoked haddock salad

Haddock has a firm texture and, if properly smoked, a subtle colouring and smoky aroma.

smoked haddock salad

*2 tablespoons mayonnaise made
with olive or soya bean oil*

*2 tablespoons low-fat, plain
yoghurt*

*10g (¹/₂oz) snipped fresh dill or
1 teaspoon dried*

*225g (8oz) smoked haddock,
flaked*

4 spring onions, sliced

2 celery stalks, sliced

*Salt and freshly ground black
pepper to taste*

Several round lettuce leaves

2 medium tomatoes, sliced

2 slices rye bread

Combine the mayonnaise, yoghurt and dill in a
medium-sized bowl. Add the haddock, spring
onions and celery. Season with salt and pepper
to taste. Toss well. Serve on 2 plates over the
lettuce with sliced tomatoes and bread.
Makes 2 servings.

**One serving: 327 calories, 34g protein,
22g carbohydrate, 14g fat (2g saturated),
43mg cholesterol, 1447mg sodium, 4g fibre**

helpful hints

● *If using fresh dill, simply
snip the leaves with scissors.*

● *Make sure dried dill is less
than 6 months old. It should
be green, not brown or grey.*

countdown

● *Prepare ingredients.*

● *Make salad.*

shopping list

TO BUY:

1 pot low-fat, plain yoghurt

225g (8oz) smoked haddock

*1 bunch fresh dill or 1 jar
dried*

*1 small bunch spring onions
(4 needed)*

1 small head round lettuce

2 medium tomatoes

STAPLES:

Celery

*Mayonnaise made with olive
or soya bean oil*

Rye bread

Salt

Black peppercorns

salad niçoise

helpful hint

- Use the dressing recipe provided here or buy a no-sugar-added oil and vinegar dressing and add diced red onion.

countdown

- Make dressing.
- Blanch asparagus.
- Assemble salad.

shopping list

TO BUY:

350g (12oz) tinned low-sodium, solid white tuna, packed in water

1 jar or tin pitted black olives

225g (8oz) fresh asparagus

1 bag washed, ready-to-eat lamb's lettuce or French-style salad leaves

2 medium tomatoes

2 medium oranges

STAPLES:

Red onion

Dijon mustard

Red wine vinegar

Olive oil

Salt

Black peppercorns

This quick salad from the French Riviera is filled with olives, tomatoes, asparagus and tuna. These ingredients were chosen to give a variety of textures, colours and flavours: crisp, pale green lettuce; ripe red tomatoes; soft, pink tuna; and dark green asparagus. Use this recipe as a base and create your own version of this classic, using other ingredients or leftovers.

salad niçoise

50ml (2fl oz) red wine vinegar

2 tablespoons Dijon mustard

50g (2oz) red onion, diced

2 tablespoons water

2 tablespoons olive oil

Salt and freshly ground black pepper to taste

350g (12oz) low-sodium, solid white tuna, drained and rinsed

225g (8oz) fresh asparagus

150g (5oz) washed, ready-to-eat lamb's lettuce or French-style salad leaves

2 medium tomatoes, cut into wedges

8 pitted black olives, quartered

To prepare the vinaigrette dressing, whisk the vinegar and mustard together in a large bowl with the onion and water. Whisk in the oil to a smooth consistency. Season with salt and pepper to taste. Flake the tuna into the vinaigrette.

Cut or snap off the 2.5cm (1in) fibrous stem on the asparagus and discard. Slice the remaining asparagus into 5cm (2in) pieces. Bring a medium-sized saucepan of water to a boil. Add the asparagus. As soon as the water comes back to a boil, drain the asparagus and refresh in cold water. (If using thick asparagus boil for 5 minutes.) To microwave the asparagus instead, place asparagus in a microwave-safe bowl and microwave on high for 4 minutes. Add the asparagus to the tuna mixture and toss gently. Divide the lettuce between 2 plates. Spoon the tuna-asparagus mixture over the lettuce. Arrange the tomato wedges around the plate, sprinkle the olives over the top and serve. *Makes 2 servings.*

One serving: 424 calories, 51g protein, 14g carbohydrate, 20g fat (2g saturated), 75mg cholesterol, 1283mg sodium, 3g fibre

citrus

2 medium oranges

Divide the oranges between 2 plates and serve. *Makes 2 servings.*

One serving: 62 calories, 1g protein, 15g carbohydrate, 0g fat (0g saturated), 0mg cholesterol, 0mg sodium, 3g fibre

chicken salad amandine

*Almonds and apples add a crunchy texture and varied flavours to this chicken salad. Use
leftover roasted chicken or shop-bought roasted chicken for a fast meal.*

chicken salad amandine

2 tablespoons flaked almonds

*2 tablespoons mayonnaise made
    with olive or soya bean oil*

50ml (2fl oz) non-fat, plain yoghurt

4 teaspoons dried tarragon

*Salt and freshly ground black
    pepper to taste*

*225g (8oz) roast chicken breast,
    skin removed and cut into
    2.5cm (1in) pieces*

2 celery stalks, sliced

*1 Golden Delicious apple, cored
    and cut into 1cm (½in) cubes*

1 small head radicchio

Place almonds on a foil-lined tray and toast
under the grill for 1 minute. Alternatively, toast
in a non-stick frying pan over a medium heat for
1 minute, or until golden. Combine the
mayonnaise, yoghurt and tarragon in a medium-
size bowl. Season with salt and pepper to taste.
Add the chicken, celery, toasted almonds and
apple. Toss well and adjust seasonings if
necessary. Carefully remove the leaves from the
radicchio, making them into small cups. Spoon
the chicken salad into the radicchio leaves.
Serve on 2 plates.
Makes 2 servings.

One serving: 457 calories, 43g protein,
24g carbohydrate, 23g fat (3g saturated),
101mg cholesterol, 282mg sodium, 5g fibre

helpful hints

● *Make sure the bottle of
dried tarragon is less than 6
months old. It should be a
green colour, not brown or
grey. This freshness will
make a marked difference to
the flavour of the salad.*

● *Any type of lettuce can be
used.*

● *Toasting almonds
intensifies their flavour, but
can be tricky. Watch them
carefully, as they burn easily.
This step can be omitted.*

countdown

● *Toast almonds.*

● *Make salad.*

shopping list

TO BUY:

   1 pot non-fat, plain yoghurt

   *225g (8oz) roast chicken
      breast*

   *1 small packet flaked
      almonds (25g/1oz needed)*

   1 Golden Delicious apple

   1 small head radicchio

STAPLES:

   Celery

   *Mayonnaise made with olive
      or soya bean oil*

   Dried tarragon

   Salt

   Black peppercorns

helpful hint

- *Buy ready-to-eat shredded lettuce.*

countdown

- *Make tzatziki.*
- *Make sandwich.*

shopping list

TO BUY:

1 pot low-fat plain yoghurt

225g (8oz) sliced roast turkey breast

1 small packet pistachio nuts (35g/1½oz needed)

Half a cucumber

1 bunch fresh mint

1 bag washed, ready-to-eat, shredded lettuce

STAPLES:

Garlic

Red onion

Wholemeal bread

Salt

Black peppercorns

turkey and tzatziki sandwich

The refreshing flavour of mint and cucumber mingle with roasted turkey in this grilled Middle Eastern sandwich. Tzatziki is a yoghurt sauce that can also be used as a vegetable dip. It takes only seconds to make in a food processor.

turkey and tzatziki sandwich

Half a cucumber, peeled and seeded

125ml (4fl oz) low-fat, plain yoghurt

2 medium-sized garlic cloves, crushed

2 tablespoons chopped fresh mint

50g (2oz) red onion, chopped

Salt and freshly ground black pepper to taste

2 slices wholemeal bread, toasted

225g (8oz) sliced roast turkey breast, skinned and cut into 2.5cm (1in) pieces

75g (3oz) washed, ready-to-eat, shredded lettuce

Chop the cucumber in the bowl of a food processor and drain. Stir the yoghurt, garlic, mint and onion into the food processor bowl with the drained cucumber. Season with salt and pepper to taste.

Place a slice of toasted bread on each plate. Top with roast turkey and shredded lettuce. Spoon a little tzatziki over the lettuce. Serve any extra lettuce and sauce on the side.

Makes 2 servings.

One serving: 302 calories, 40g protein, 23g carbohydrate, 6g fat (1g saturated), 81mg cholesterol, 241mg sodium, 6g fibre

pistachios

35g (1½oz) shelled pistachio nuts

Divide the pistachios between 2 plates and serve.

Makes 2 servings.

One serving: 131 calories, 5g protein, 6g carbohydrate, 11g fat (1g saturated), 0mg cholesterol, 2mg sodium, 0g fibre

california chef's salad

Julienned slices of ham, turkey, roast beef and cheese alongside an array of fresh vegetables are the basis for this American favourite. The addition of alfalfa sprouts gives this dish a modern 'California' touch. • Traditionally, the ingredients in a Chef's Salad are cut in julienne strips (large match sticks). However, if you are pressed for time, you can slice them in a food processor fitted with a thick slicing blade. • You can use whatever lean cold meats and vegetables you have on hand, referring to the proportions given in the recipe as a guideline.

california chef's salad

50ml (2fl oz) balsamic vinegar

1 tablespoon Dijon mustard

2 tablespoons water

2 tablespoons rapeseed oil

Salt and freshly ground black pepper to taste

8 large cos lettuce leaves, washed, dried and sliced

Half a cucumber, peeled and julienned

1 medium-sized red pepper, julienned

35g (1$^1/_2$oz) reduced-fat Swiss or Gruyère cheese, julienned

50g (2oz) sliced smoked deli chicken breast, julienned

50g (2oz) sliced lean deli roast beef, julienned

50g (2oz) sliced lean deli ham, julienned

1 large handful alfalfa sprouts

Mix the vinegar and mustard together in a small bowl until smooth. Add the water and oil, blending well. Season with salt and pepper to taste. Divide the lettuce leaves between 2 plates. Place the remaining ingredients on the leaves in pie-shaped segments, like the spokes of a wheel. Spoon the dressing over the top and serve.

Makes 2 servings.

One serving: 400 calories, 34g protein, 19g carbohydrate, 22g fat (5g saturated), 71mg cholesterol, 519mg sodium, 2g fibre

helpful hints

● *Ask the deli to cut the meat in 1cm (½in) slices. You can then easily cut the slices into 1cm (½in) julienne strips.*

● *If reduced-fat Swiss or Gruyère cheese is not available, use another reduced-fat cheese. Alternatively, use regular Swiss or Gruyère, although the fat content and total calories will be increased.*

● *Use any type of sprouts.*

● *If making salad in advance, add dressing just before serving.*

● *Any type of no-sugar-added dressing can be used instead of the dressing recipe given.*

countdown

● *Make dressing.*

● *Prepare ingredients.*

● *Assemble salad.*

shopping list

TO BUY:

35g (1½oz) reduced-fat Swiss or Gruyère cheese

50g (2oz) sliced smoked deli chicken breast

50g (2oz) sliced lean roast beef

50g (2oz) sliced lean deli ham

1 head cos lettuce

Half a cucumber

1 medium-sized red pepper

1 container alfalfa sprouts

STAPLES:

Rapeseed oil

Dijon mustard

Balsamic vinegar

Salt

Black pepper

turkey, salsa and citrus salad

The nutty flavour and creamy texture of ripe avocado blends well with sweet orange and smoky turkey in this quick salad – only 5 minutes from start to finish. • Ask the greengrocer for a ripe avocado if you don't find one displayed. Sometimes they don't display ones that will ripen within a day. A quick way to help avocados ripen is to remove the stem, place the avocado in a paper bag and leave in a warm spot. • Curly endive has a loose head with lacy, green-rimmed leaves that curl at the pointed tips.

turkey, salsa and citrus salad

225g (8oz) sliced lean smoked turkey breast, cut into 2.5cm (1in) cubes

1 ripe small avocado, pitted and cut into 2.5cm (1in) cubes

225g (8oz) no-sugar-added tomato salsa

2 small oranges, peeled and cut into 2.5cm (1in) cubes

1 large handful alfalfa sprouts

Salt and freshly ground black pepper to taste

Several curly endive leaves

Combine the turkey, avocado and salsa in a medium-sized bowl, tossing well. Gently stir in the orange cubes and sprouts. Season with salt and pepper to taste. Place the curly endive on 2 plates, spoon the turkey-avocado mixture on top and serve.

Makes 2 servings.

One serving: 464 calories, 40g protein, 33g carbohydrate, 19g fat (3g saturated), 80mg cholesterol, 850mg sodium, 12g fibre

plum plate

2 medium plums, halved and stoned

Slice the plums. Divide between 2 plates and serve.

Makes 2 servings.

One serving: 36 calories, 1g protein, 9g carbohydrate, 0g fat (0g saturated), 0mg cholesterol, 0mg sodium, 0.5g fibre

jerk chicken with palm hearts

'Jerking' is an old Jamaican method for preserving and cooking meat. It's a long process that involves marinating the meat and then slowly cooking it over a pimento (allspice) wood fire. For this recipe, I adapted the flavours and inspiration of jerk cooking to create an exotic, quick meal.

jerk chicken with palm hearts

1 tablespoon chopped yellow onion

2 teaspoons dried thyme

Pinch of salt

½ teaspoon ground nutmeg

2g (16oz) artificial sweetener

1 teaspoon freshly ground black pepper

350g (12oz) boneless, skinless chicken breast

Olive oil spray

Half a small head cos lettuce, torn into bite-sized pieces

350g (12oz) sliced palm hearts

2 tablespoons no-sugar-added oil and vinegar dressing

In a food processor or by hand, combine the onion, thyme, salt, nutmeg, sweetener and black pepper. The juice from the onion will bind the ingredients together. Remove any visible fat from the chicken breast and poke several holes in the meat with a knife or fork. Spoon the jerk seasoning over both sides of the chicken and let marinate for 15 minutes before cooking.

Set a non-stick frying pan over a medium heat and spray with olive oil. Sauté the chicken for 5 minutes, then turn and sauté for 5 more minutes, or until a meat thermometer registers 70°C (160°F).

Divide the lettuce between 2 plates. Scatter the palm heart slices over the lettuce. Drizzle the dressing over the lettuce. Slice the chicken into strips and arrange on the lettuce to serve. *Makes 2 servings.*

> One serving: 437 calories, 60g protein, 15g carbohydrate, 18g fat (3g saturated), 144mg cholesterol, 981mg sodium, 5g fibre

clementine

2 medium clementines

Divide the clementines between 2 plates. *Makes 2 servings.*

> One serving: 37 calories, 1g protein, 9g carbohydrate, 0g fat (0g saturated), 0mg cholesterol, 1mg sodium, 0g fibre

helpful hints

- *Use the jerk recipe provided or purchase a jerk seasoning or marinade. Make sure it does not have added sugar.*
- *Artichoke hearts can be used instead of palm hearts.*
- *Make sure the dried thyme is less than 6 months old.*
- *This jerk chicken will keep 1 to 2 days in the refrigerator. Double the recipe and save half for another lunch.*

countdown

- *Prepare ingredients.*
- *Make chicken.*
- *While chicken cooks, arrange palm hearts and lettuce on plate.*

shopping list

TO BUY:

350g (12oz) boneless, skinless chicken breast

1 jar or tin palm hearts

1 small head cos lettuce

2 medium clementines or satsumas

STAPLES:

Yellow onion

Dried thyme

Ground nutmeg

Olive oil spray

No-sugar-added oil and vinegar dressing

Artificial sweetener

Salt

Black peppercorns

deli salad

You can put this salad together in minutes with whatever you have in the refrigerator. Use the proportions in this recipe as a guideline for ordering similar dishes in restaurants or eating at salad bars.

<table>
<tr><td>

helpful hints

- *Any type of lean deli meats can be used.*
- *Any type of vegetables can be used.*
- *Fresh cantaloupe cubes can be found in the fruit and veg section of most supermarkets.*
- *Ask for the nutritional analysis of shop-bought coleslaw, as some prepared versions have added sugar.*

countdown

- *Prepare the ingredients.*
- *Assemble plate.*

shopping list

TO BUY:

110g (4oz) sliced smoked turkey breast

110g (4oz) sliced lean roast beef

1 container no-sugar-added deli coleslaw (100g/3¹/₂oz needed)

1 jar horseradish

Half a cucumber

1 cantaloupe or cut cantaloupe cubes

STAPLES:

Mayonnaise made with olive or soya bean oil

</td>
<td>

deli salad

110g (4oz) sliced smoked turkey breast

110g (4oz) sliced lean roast beef

50g (2oz) no-sugar-added deli coleslaw

half a cucumber, peeled and sliced

2 tablespoons mayonnaise made with olive or soya bean oil

2 tablespoons horseradish

cantaloupe

¹/₂ cantaloupe, cubed

</td>
<td>

Arrange the meat slices with the coleslaw and cucumber on 2 plates. Mix the mayonnaise and horseradish together and spoon over the meat to serve.

Makes 2 servings.

> One serving: 406 calories, 34g protein, 13g carbohydrate, 23g fat (5g saturated), 96mg cholesterol, 305mg sodium, 2g fibre

Divide the cantaloupe between 2 dessert bowls and serve.

Makes 2 servings.

> One serving: 39 calories, 1g protein, 9g carbohydrate, 0g fat (0g saturated), 0mg cholesterol, 10mg sodium, 1g fibre

</td>
</tr>
</table>

gammon and egg salad

Egg salad is available on lunch menus, or it can be made from scratch at home. Wherever you eat it, use this recipe as a portion guideline. It is made with 2 whole eggs and 6 egg whites to produce a light, tasty result.

gammon and egg salad

8 eggs (only 2 yolks are used)

225g (8oz) sliced lean gammon

2 tablespoons mayonnaise made
    with olive or soya bean oil

2 tablespoons Dijon mustard

2 tablespoons warm water

2 tablespoons diced red onion

10g (½oz) fresh flat leaf parsley,
    chopped

2 celery stalks, diced

Salt and freshly ground black
    pepper to taste

Several cos leaves, torn into bite-
    sized pieces

2 medium tomatoes, quartered

Preheat the grill. Place the eggs in a medium saucepan and cover with cold water. Set over a medium-high heat and bring to a boil. Reduce the heat to low and gently simmer for 12 minutes. Drain the hot water and fill the pan with cold water. When the eggs are cool to the touch, peel, cut in half and discard 6 of the yolks. Mash the remaining 2 whole eggs and 6 egg whites with a fork.

Meanwhile, place the gammon in one layer on a foil-lined tray and toast under the grill until brown. Combine the mayonnaise, mustard, water, onion and parsley in a bowl. Stir in the eggs and celery, mixing well. Season with salt and pepper to taste. Place the lettuce and tomatoes on 2 plates. Spoon the egg salad on top of the lettuce. Cut the browned gammon into bite-sized pieces and sprinkle over the egg salad. Serve.

Makes 2 servings.

One serving: 411 calories, 41g protein,
17g carbohydrate, 21g fat (4g saturated),
270mg cholesterol, 1743mg sodium, 1g fibre

fresh berries

4 good handfuls fresh
    strawberries

Divide the strawberries between 2 dessert bowls and serve.

Makes 2 servings.

One serving: 45 calories, 1g protein,
11g carbohydrate, 1g fat (0g saturated),
0mg cholesterol, 2mg sodium, 3g fibre

helpful hints

● You can make the egg salad in a food processor or with a hand-held blender. Be careful to pulse the blades and watch that it does not become too finely chopped or mushy.

countdown

● Preheat grill.
● Make hard-boiled eggs.
● Make egg salad.

shopping list

TO BUY:

225g (8oz) sliced lean
    gammon

1 bunch flat leaf parsley

1 head cos lettuce

2 medium tomatoes

1 punnet fresh strawberries

STAPLES:

Celery

Eggs

Mayonnaise made with olive
    or soya bean oil

Dijon mustard

Red onion

Salt

Black peppercorns

helpful hints

● This can be made with any type of fresh or leftover fish.

● Make sure the bottle of dried dill is less than 6 months old. For optimum flavour, the dill should be a green colour, not brown or grey.

countdown

● Sauté salmon.
● Make salad.

shopping list

TO BUY:

225g (8oz) salmon fillet

Half a cucumber

1 small bunch fresh dill or 1 jar dried

2 medium-sized green peppers

1 punnet fresh raspberries

STAPLES:

Olive oil spray

Mayonnaise made with olive or soya bean oil

Balsamic vinegar

Salt

Black peppercorns

balsamic and dill salmon salad

Fresh salmon mixed with cucumber and dill makes a richly-flavoured, yet light, salmon salad. If you have time, double the recipe and save half for another lunch.

balsamic and dill salmon salad

2 tablespoons mayonnaise made with olive or soya bean oil

4 teaspoons balsamic vinegar

10g (½oz) fresh dill or 2 teaspoons dried

Half a cucumber, deseeded and diced

Olive oil spray

225g (8oz) salmon fillet

Salt and freshly ground black pepper to taste

2 medium-sized green peppers, halved and deseeded

Combine the mayonnaise, balsamic vinegar, dill and cucumber in a small bowl. Set a non-stick frying pan over a medium-high heat and spray with olive oil. Add the salmon and sauté for 3 minutes. Turn and sauté for 2 more minutes. Flake the salmon into the mayonnaise mixture with a fork. Season with salt and pepper to taste and mix gently. Spoon the mixture into the pepper halves and serve.

Makes 2 servings.

One serving: 364 calories, 31g protein, 13g carbohydrate, 20g fat (4g saturated), 85mg cholesterol, 159mg sodium, 1g fibre

raspberries

350g (12oz) fresh raspberries

Divide the raspberries between 2 dessert bowls and serve.

Makes 2 servings.

One serving: 61 calories, 1g protein, 14g carbohydrate, 1g fat (0g saturated), 0mg cholesterol, 0mg sodium, 6g fibre

hollywood cobb salad

Roasted chicken breast, avocado and lettuce were key ingredients in Robert Cobb's first Cobb salad, which he served at the Brown Derby restaurant at Hollywood and Vine in the 1930s. It was so popular among the Hollywood moguls that it has become a favourite on restaurant menus throughout the States.

hollywood cobb salad

175g (6oz) finely sliced iceberg lettuce

75g (3oz) finely sliced chicory or curly endive

2 medium tomatoes, cut into large dice

225g (8oz) sliced skinless deli chicken breast, cut into 2.5cm (1in) cubes

half a small ripe avocado, stoned, peeled and cubed

2 tablespoons dried chives

2 tablespoons no-sugar-added oil and vinegar dressing

Arrange the iceberg and curly endive lettuce in 2 shallow bowls or on 2 plates. Arrange the tomatoes, chicken and avocado in rows over the lettuce. Sprinkle with the chives, drizzle with dressing and serve.

Makes 2 servings

> One serving: 378 calories, 40g protein, 11g carbohydrate, 21g fat (4g saturated), 96mg cholesterol, 183mg sodium, 3g fibre

peaches

2 medium peaches

Divide the peaches between 2 plates and serve.
Makes 2 servings.

> One serving: 37 calories, 1g protein, 10g carbohydrate, 0g fat (0g saturated), 0mg cholesterol, 0mg sodium, 1g fibre

helpful hints

- *Ask the deli to cut the chicken breast into 2.5cm (1in) thick slices to make it easier to cut into cubes.*
- *A hard-boiled egg can be substituted for the avocado.*
- *To speed the ripening of an avocado, remove the stem and store it in a paper bag in a warm spot.*

countdown

- *Make dressing.*
- *Prepare ingredients.*
- *Assemble salad.*

shopping list

TO BUY:

225g (8oz) sliced skinless deli chicken breast

1 jar dried chives

1 head iceberg lettuce

1 small head chicory or curly endive

2 medium tomatoes

1 small avocado

2 medium peaches

STAPLES:

No-sugar-added oil and vinegar dressing

black bean and salsa wraps

helpful hints

- Look for cos lettuce with large leaves.
- Black bean pâté is usually located with the dips and nachos in the snack section of the supermarket.
- If black bean pâté is unavailable use reduced-fat refried beans instead.

countdown

- Prepare ingredients.
- Assemble wraps.

shopping list

TO BUY:

1 pot light fruit-flavoured yoghurt

1 packet grated, reduced-fat Cheddar cheese (50g/2oz needed)

225g (8oz) sliced turkey breast

1 jar no-sugar-added black bean pâté

1 jar no-sugar-added tomato salsa (110g/4oz needed)

1 head cos lettuce

With the help of prepared black bean pâté and deli turkey breast, you can assemble this lunch in 5 minutes. It can be made the night before and stored in the refrigerator until needed for lunch. You can use these wraps as hors d'oeuvres or eat them on a picnic.

black bean and salsa wraps

12 large cos leaves, washed and patted dry

12 x 30.5 x 10cm (11 x 4in) rectangles foil, parchment paper or greaseproof paper

50g (2oz) prepared no-sugar-added black bean pâté

50g (2oz) grated reduced-fat Cheddar cheese

225g (8oz) sliced turkey breast

225g (8oz) no-sugar-added tomato salsa

Remove 1 inch of the thick stem from each lettuce leaf and crush the remaining stem so that the leaf lies flat. Place the rectangles of foil on the work surface. Place one leaf on each square. Spread the pâté on each leaf and sprinkle with cheese. Top with a layer of turkey. Roll the lettuce up lengthwise like a cigar. Wrap the foil tightly around the lettuce to hold it in place. Cut in half crosswise and serve on 2 plates with the salsa on the side.

Makes 2 servings.

One serving: 349 calories, 15g protein, 17g carbohydrate, 5g fat (3g saturated), 10mg cholesterol, 1070mg sodium, 5g fibre

yoghurt

225g (8oz) light fruit-flavoured yoghurt

Divide the yoghurt between 2 dessert bowls and serve.

Makes 2 servings.

One serving: 50 calories, 32g protein, 0g carbohydrate, 4g fat (1g saturated), 80mg cholesterol, 72mg sodium, 0g fibre

grilled chilli chicken

This chicken dish is full of hot, spicy Southwestern flavours, and it tastes delicious served over a cool bed of lettuce with the Green Onion Dressing.

grilled chilli chicken

110g (4oz) red onion, chopped

2 medium-sized garlic cloves, crushed

1 tablespoon chilli powder

1 teaspoon ground cumin

Pinch salt

Pinch freshly ground black pepper

225g (8oz) boneless, skinless chicken breasts

50ml (2fl oz) freshly squeezed lemon juice (2 medium lemons)

2 tablespoons Dijon mustard

4 teaspoons olive oil

1 tablespoon water

4 spring onions, sliced

Half a small head cos lettuce, torn into bite-sized pieces

2 medium tomatoes, cut into wedges

Preheat the grill. Combine the onion, garlic, chilli powder, cumin, salt and pepper in a small bowl. Remove any visible fat from the chicken and poke several holes in the meat with a knife or fork. Place in a bowl and spread the marinade evenly over the chicken. Let it marinate for 15 minutes, turning once. Cover a baking tray with foil. Place the chicken on the tray and grill it 10–12.5cm (4–5in) from the heat for 5 minutes. Turn and grill for another 5 minutes. Remove from the grill and let cool. When cool, slice into strips. Whisk the lemon juice and mustard together in a small bowl. Whisk in the oil and then the water. Stir in the spring onions. Place the lettuce on 2 plates. Top with the tomatoes and chicken strips. Drizzle the dressing over the salad or serve on the side.
Makes 2 servings.

One serving: 367 calories, 41g protein, 18g carbohydrate, 16g fat (3g saturated), 96mg cholesterol, 603mg sodium, 1g fibre

helpful hints

- *Chop onion, garlic and spices together in a food processor to make a quick marinade.*
- *If pressed for time, use a bottled, no-sugar-added dressing and add spring onions to it.*

countdown

- *Preheat grill.*
- *While chicken marinates, prepare greens and make dressing.*

shopping list

TO BUY:

225g (8oz) boneless, skinless chicken breast

1 small head cos lettuce

2 medium tomatoes

2 lemons

1 small bunch spring onions (4 needed)

STAPLES:

Red onion

Garlic

Olive oil

Ground cumin

Chilli powder

Dijon mustard

Salt

Black peppercorns

which carbs
dinners

thai peanut-rub pork

This blend of spices and peanuts rubbed into the pork forms a well-seasoned crust. Rubs are a quick way to add flavour to meats and a great alternative to marinades, since you don't have to wait for the meat to absorb the marinade flavours. These Thai spices are fun, easy to use, and provide a different way to spice up pork tenderloin.

thai peanut-rub pork

Olive oil spray

20 dry-roasted, unsalted peanuts
  (2 tablespoons when ground)

10g (½oz) fresh coriander leaves

1½ teaspoons garlic powder

1 tablespoon ground coriander

2g (¹⁄₁₆oz) artificial sweetener

Pinch of cayenne pepper

275g (10oz) pork tenderloin

Preheat the grill. Line a baking tray with foil, and spray with olive oil. Chop the peanuts and coriander leaves in a food processor. Add the garlic powder, ground coriander, artificial sweetener and cayenne, pulsing to incorporate. Alternatively, chop and mix by hand. Remove any visible fat from the pork. Rub the mixture on both sides of the pork, pressing the mixture onto the meat and making sure all the sides are coated. Place on baking tray and grill 20.5cm (8in) from the heat for 7 minutes, then turn and grill for another 8 minutes. The pork is done when a meat thermometer registers 70°C (160°F). Remove the pork to a plate and cover with foil to keep warm. Slice before serving.

Makes 2 servings.

One serving: 333 calories, 45g protein, 6g carbohydrate, 15g fat (4g saturated), 133mg cholesterol, 137mg sodium, 1g fibre

stir-fry broccoli noodles

50g (2oz) wholemeal noodles

110g (4oz) broccoli florets

2 tablespoons oyster sauce

2 tablespoons rice vinegar

Olive oil spray

4 medium-sized garlic cloves,
  crushed

10g (½oz) chopped fresh
  coriander leaves

Bring a large saucepan of water to the boil, add the noodles and boil for 8 minutes. Add the broccoli and boil for 2 minutes. Drain and set aside. Combine the oyster sauce and vinegar, then set aside. Spray a wok or frying pan with olive oil and place over a high heat. Add the noodles, broccoli and garlic. Stir-fry for 2 minutes, then push the ingredients to the sides of the pan. Add the oyster sauce mixture and toss well. Serve sprinkled with chopped coriander leaves.

Makes 2 servings.

One serving: 208 calories, 10g protein, 37g carbohydrate, 3g fat (1g saturated), 0mg cholesterol, 491mg sodium, 6g fibre

helpful hints

- *If rice vinegar is unavailable, substitute 1 tablespoon water mixed with distilled white vinegar.*
- *Chop the coriander leaves for both recipes at one time and divide accordingly.*
- *To keep from looking back at the recipe as you stir-fry the ingredients, line them up on a chopping board or plate in the order of use.*
- *For crisp, not steamed, stir-fried vegetables, start with a very hot wok. Let the vegetables sit for a minute before tossing to allow the wok to regain its heat.*

countdown

- *Preheat grill.*
- *Make pork dish.*
- *While pork cooks, make broccoli noodles.*

shopping list

TO BUY:

  275g (10oz) pork tenderloin

  1 small packet dry roasted, unsalted peanuts (25g/1oz needed)

  1 small packet wholemeal tagliatelle (50g/2oz needed)

  1 small bottle oyster sauce

  1 small bottle rice vinegar

  1 small bunch fresh coriander

  1 packet broccoli florets (110g/4oz needed)

STAPLES:

  Garlic

  Olive oil spray

  Garlic powder

  Ground coriander

  Artificial sweetener

  Cayenne pepper

pesto chicken

helpful hints

- Pesto can be found in jars on the supermarket shelves.
- Artichokes are not available all year round. Asparagus or broccoli can be steamed or microwaved and served with this dressing instead.
- Fresh figs are not available all year round. Plums, apricots or pears can be substituted.

countdown

- Start artichokes.
- Make pasta.
- Make chicken.

shopping list

TO BUY:

   350g (12oz) boneless, skinless chicken breast

   1 small jar pesto

   1 packet wholemeal tagliatelle (50g/2oz needed)

   2 medium artichokes

   4 medium figs

STAPLES:

   No-sugar-added oil and vinegar dressing

   Salt

   Black peppercorns

Pesto is a flavourful Italian sauce filled with garlic, basil, pine nuts, parsley and olive oil. It's most widely used as a luscious dressing for pasta. Typically, pesto is not cooked. In this recipe, the sauce is added to the cooked chicken for a minute just before serving. The sauce is warmed by the chicken, while still preserving the fresh basil and parsley flavours.

● Steaming or boiling artichokes takes about 45 minutes. To cut the time in half, cut the artichokes in half and cook them in about 5cm (2in) of water for 20 minutes. The artichokes can also be cooked in a microwave, as described in this recipe. ● Artichokes may be served hot or cold. To eat, pull off the outer petals one at a time. Dip the base of each petal into the sauce; pull the petal through your teeth to remove the soft, pulpy portion of petal, then discard. For this recipe, the fuzzy section near the base, called the choke, will be removed. The bottom, or heart, of the artichoke is entirely edible. Many think it's the best part. Cut it into small pieces and dip in the sauce.

pesto chicken

50g (2oz) wholemeal tagliatelle

Salt and freshly ground black pepper to taste

350g (12oz) boneless, skinless chicken breast

50g (2oz) shop-bought pesto

Bring a large saucepan of water to a boil. Add the pasta and boil for 8 minutes, or according to the packet's instructions. Do not overcook. Drain, leaving about 3 tablespoons of pasta water on the pasta. Divide between 2 dinner plates and season with salt and pepper to taste.

Remove all visible fat from the chicken and pound the breast flat with the palm of your hand or a heavy pan to about 1cm (½in) thick. Set a non-stick frying pan over a medium-high heat and add the chicken. Brown for 2 minutes on each side, seasoning the cooked sides with salt and pepper. Lower the heat to medium and sauté for another minute. Spoon the pesto over the chicken. Remove the pan from the heat. Cover and let sit for 1 minute. Divide the chicken and spoon over the pasta to serve. *Makes 2 servings.*

One serving: 427 calories, 57g protein, 6g carbohydrate, 20g fat (5g saturated), 154mg cholesterol, 416mg sodium, 2g fibre

steamed artichokes

2 medium artichokes
2 tablespoons no-sugar-added oil and vinegar dressing

Cut the stem off the artichokes as close to the base as possible. Cut off the top quarter and prickly points of visible leaves. Slice the artichokes in half from top to stem. Scrape out the fuzzy chokes with a spoon. Remove the small inner leaves (they're usually purple) and discard. Fill a large non-stick frying pan with 2.5cm (1in) of water, place the artichokes cut-side down and bring to the boil. Cover and boil for 20 minutes. Check after the first 10 minutes and add more water if needed.

Alternatively, to cook artichokes in the microwave, set the artichokes in a deep, microwave-safe bowl. Add 125ml (4fl oz) water, cover the bowl with cling film and microwave for 7–8 minutes on high, giving the bowl a quarter turn halfway through the cooking time. Allow to stand for 5 minutes.

The artichokes are done when a petal pulls off easily. Remove the cooked artichokes from the pan and place on 2 plates. Place the dressing in 2 small bowls on the side and use as dipping sauce for the artichoke leaves and hearts.
Makes 2 servings.

One serving: 181 calories, 6g protein, 25g carbohydrate, 9g fat (1g saturated), 0mg cholesterol, 233mg sodium, 0g fibre

fresh figs

4 medium figs

Divide the figs between 2 plates and serve.
Makes 2 servings.

One serving: 74 calories, 1g protein, 19g carbohydrate, 0.5g fat (0g saturated), 0mg cholesterol, 0mg sodium, 3g fibre

grilled scallops parmigiana

Sweet, juicy scallops are easy to cook. The secret to this meal is buying fresh, good quality scallops. ● *These baked Parmesan scallops take only 15 minutes to make, and the courgettes can be cooked while the scallops bake, so the entire meal can be prepared in 15 to 20 minutes.* ● *Scallops are readily available. You can use any type for this recipe. If you buy small scallops, then bake them for only 10 minutes.*

grilled scallops parmigiana

350g (12oz) large scallops, rinsed
50ml (2fl oz) white wine
2 teaspoons olive oil
2 large handfuls washed, ready-to-eat fresh spinach
10g (½oz) freshly grated Parmesan cheese
Salt and freshly ground black pepper to taste

Preheat the oven to 180°C/350°F/gas mark 4. Place the scallops in a small baking dish just large enough to hold the scallops in one layer. Add the wine, tossing to coat the scallops. Bake for 15 minutes. While the scallops are baking, heat the oil in a medium-sized non-stick frying pan over a medium-high heat. Add the spinach, and sauté 2–3 minutes, or until wilted. Spoon onto 2 dinner plates. Remove the scallops from the oven and turn on the grill. When the grill is hot, sprinkle Parmesan cheese over the scallops and place under the grill for 1 minute, or until golden. Watch them carefully, as they will brown very quickly. Season with salt and pepper to taste. Spoon over the spinach and serve.
Makes 2 servings.

One serving: 286 calories, 37g protein, 9g carbohydrate, 10g fat (3g saturated), 63mg cholesterol, 573mg sodium, 4g fibre

lemon-pepper courgettes

2 teaspoons olive oil
225g (8oz) courgettes, sliced
2 tablespoons freshly squeezed lemon juice (1 lemon)
¼ teaspoon freshly ground black pepper
Salt to taste

In the frying pan used for the spinach, heat the oil over a medium-high heat. Add the courgettes and sauté for 5 minutes. Toss with the lemon juice and pepper. Season with salt to taste. Serve with the scallops.
Makes 2 servings.

One serving: 62 calories, 2g protein, 5g carbohydrate, 5g fat (1g saturated), 0mg cholesterol, 4mg sodium, 1g fibre

kiwi-berry jumble

2 kiwis, peeled and cubed
175g (6oz) fresh raspberries

Combine the kiwi cubes and the raspberries.
Spoon into 2 dessert bowls and serve.
Makes 2 servings.

One serving: 77 calories, 1g protein,
18g carbohydrate, 1g fat (0g saturated),
0mg cholesterol, 4mg sodium, 3g fibre

shopping list

TO BUY:
    350g (12oz) large scallops
    1 small bottle dry white wine
    1 bag washed, ready-to-eat
       fresh spinach
    225g (8oz) courgettes
    2 lemons
    2 kiwis
    1 punnet fresh raspberries
STAPLES:
    Olive oil
    Parmesan cheese
    Salt
    Black peppercorns

breaded veal escalopes

This meal takes only 15 minutes to make. ● *The breading adds flavour and keeps the veal moist.*

helpful hints

● *Buy good quality Parmesan cheese and grate it yourself. Freeze extra for quick use later – simply spoon out what you need and leave the rest frozen.*

● *Any type of wholemeal pasta can be used.*

countdown

● *Prepare all ingredients.*
● *Make pasta.*
● *Make veal.*
● *Make spinach.*

shopping list

TO BUY:

225g (8oz) veal escalopes
1 small packet plain bread crumbs, wholemeal if possible
1 packet thin wholemeal spaghetti (50g/2oz needed)
1 jar no-sugar-added pasta sauce (225g/8oz needed)
1 small bunch fresh oregano or 1 jar dried
1 bag washed, ready-to-eat fresh spinach

STAPLES:

Olive oil
Eggs
Parmesan cheese
Salt
Black peppercorns

breaded veal escalopes

225g (8oz) veal escalopes
Salt and freshly ground black pepper to taste
1 tablespoon fresh oregano or 2 teaspoons dried
25g (1oz) plain bread crumbs, wholemeal if possible
2 egg whites, lightly beaten
2 teaspoons olive oil

Sprinkle both sides of the veal escalopes with a little salt and pepper. Combine the oregano with the bread crumbs on a plate. Roll the veal in the bread crumb mixture, coating well. Dip the veal into the egg whites. Roll the veal in the bread crumbs again. Heat the oil in a non-stick frying pan over a medium-high heat. Sauté the veal for 1 minute, turn and sauté for 2 more minutes. Season with salt and pepper and serve with the spaghetti and spinach.

Makes 2 servings.

One serving: 314 calories, 34g protein, 3g carbohydrate, 17g fat (8g saturated), 100mg cholesterol, 155mg sodium, 0g fibre

spaghetti

50g (2oz) thin wholemeal spaghetti
125ml (4fl oz) no-sugar-added pasta sauce

Bring a large saucepan filled with water to a boil. Add the spaghetti and boil for 5 minutes, or according to the packet's instructions. Do not overcook. Drain, leaving about 3 tablespoons of water in the pan. Return the spaghetti to the pan, add the sauce and toss well.

Makes 2 servings.

One serving: 163 calories, 8g protein, 29g carbohydrate, 1g fat (1g saturated), 0mg cholesterol, 208mg sodium, 5g fibre

parmesan spinach

4 large handfuls washed, ready-to-eat fresh spinach
2 tablespoons freshly grated Parmesan cheese
Salt and freshly ground black pepper to taste

Place the spinach in a microwave-safe bowl and microwave on high for 6 minutes. Or, place the spinach in a saucepan over a medium heat. Do not add water: the spinach will release enough of its own liquid. Cover and cook until the spinach is wilted, about 5 minutes, making sure it does not burn. Add the Parmesan cheese and season with salt and pepper.

Makes 2 servings.

One serving: 74 calories, 9g protein, 8g carbohydrate, 3g fat (1g saturated), 4mg cholesterol, 278mg sodium, 7g fibre

garlic prawn stir-fry

Garlic, cashew nuts and sesame oil flavour this quick prawn dinner. ● The cooking time for this dinner is about 8 minutes. ● Use the helpful hint suggestions for quick preparation of the ingredients to make this a complete 15-minute meal.

garlic prawn stir-fry

2 tablespoons low-sodium soy sauce

2 tablespoons rice vinegar

2 tablespoons chopped fresh ginger

6 medium-sized garlic cloves, crushed

Several drops hot pepper sauce

4 teaspoons sesame oil

2 slices yellow onion

½ medium-sized red pepper, sliced

350g (12oz) medium prawns, peeled and deveined

225g (8oz) mange tout, trimmed

2 tablespoons cashews

Combine the soy sauce, rice vinegar, ginger, garlic and hot sauce in a small bowl. Make sure all ingredients are prepared and ready for cooking.

Heat the sesame oil in a wok or frying pan over a high heat. When the oil is smoking, add the onion and red pepper. Stir-fry for 3 minutes. Add the prawns and mange tout and stir-fry for 2 minutes. Add the cashews and sauce and continue to stir-fry, tossing continuously for 2 minutes. Add salt to taste. Divide between 2 plates and serve.

Makes 2 servings.

One serving: 411 calories, 41g protein, 21g carbohydrate, 18g fat (3g saturated), 260mg cholesterol, 944mg sodium, 2g fibre

helpful hints

● *Buy peeled prawns – it is well worth the time otherwise spent shelling them yourself.*

● *Washed and sliced cabbage can be used instead of the Chinese cabbage, but should be microwaved for 1 minute first.*

● *To chop fresh ginger quickly, cut it into small cubes and press through a garlic press with large holes. If using a press with small holes, just capture the juice that is squeezed out; it will give enough flavour for the recipe.*

● *If rice vinegar is unavailable, substitute 1 tablespoon water mixed with 1 tablespoon distilled white wine vinegar.*

● *To keep from having to look back at the recipe as you stir-fry the ingredients, line them up on a chopping board or plate in the order of use so you know which ingredient comes next.*

● *For crisp, not steamed, stir-fried vegetables, start with a very hot wok or frying pan. Let the vegetables sit a minute before tossing to allow the wok to regain its heat.*

countdown

- *Prepare ingredients.*
- *Make cabbage and bean sprouts.*
- *Make prawn stir-fry.*

shopping list

TO BUY:

350g (12oz) medium prawns

1 small packet cashew nuts (25g/1oz needed)

1 small bottle sesame oil

1 small bottle low-carbohydrate miso dressing

1 small bottle rice vinegar

1 medium-sized red pepper

1 small piece fresh ginger

225g (8oz) mange tout

1 small head Chinese cabbage (Chinese leaves)

1 small packet fresh bean sprouts

STAPLES:

Yellow onion

Garlic

Hot pepper sauce

Low-sodium soy sauce

garlic prawn stir-fry continued

chinese cabbage and bean sprouts

50g (2oz) thinly sliced Chinese cabbage (Chinese leaves)

60g (2½oz) fresh bean sprouts

2 tablespoons low-carbohydrate miso dressing

Place the cabbage and bean sprouts in a small bowl and toss with dressing. Serve with the stir-fry.

Makes 2 servings.

One serving: 73 calories, 5g protein, 8g carbohydrate, 3g fat (0.5g saturated), 0mg cholesterol, 321mg sodium, 1g fibre

sole amandine

Sole Amandine, a French classic, appears on menus at French restaurants, from the most elegant to simple brasseries. Dressed up or down, lemon juice and almonds are all the fillet of sole needs to give it a wonderful flavour. ● This quick dinner takes only 10 minutes to make. It's a perfect mid-week meal when you're on the run.

sole amandine

350g (12oz) sole fillet

4 teaspoons olive oil

Salt and freshly ground black pepper to taste

2 tablespoons flaked almonds

2 tablespoons freshly squeezed lemon juice (1 lemon)

2 tablespoons freshly chopped parsley (optional)

Rinse the sole and pat dry with kitchen paper. Heat the oil in a medium-sized non-stick frying pan over a medium-high heat. Sauté the fish for 2 minutes on each side. Remove to 2 plates, season with salt and pepper to taste and cover with foil to keep warm. Add the almonds to the same frying pan and sauté until slightly golden, about 1 minute. Sprinkle the fish with lemon juice, almonds and parsley and serve.
Makes 2 servings.

One serving: 264 calories, 28g protein, 4g carbohydrate, 17g fat (2g saturated), 60mg cholesterol, 98mg sodium, 1g fibre

butter beans

450g (1lb) butter beans

2 teaspoons olive oil

Salt and freshly ground black pepper to taste

Heat the beans in a small pan, then drain. Add the oil to the same frying pan used for the fish and heat on high. Sauté the beans for 1 minute. Add salt and pepper to taste.
Makes 2 servings.

One serving: 154 calories, 7g protein, 21g carbohydrate, 5g fat (1g saturated), 0mg cholesterol, 3mg sodium, 4g fibre

grilled tomatoes

2 medium tomatoes, halved

Salt and freshly ground black pepper to taste

Preheat the grill. Season the tomato halves with salt and pepper to taste. Grill for 4 minutes and serve with the fish and butter beans.
Makes 2 servings.

One serving: 25 calories, 2g protein, 5g carbohydrate, 0g fat (0g saturated), 0mg cholesterol, 10mg sodium, 0g fibre

helpful hints

● *Any type of non-oily fish fillet can be used.*

● *To save washing another pan, use the same pan for the fish and butter beans.*

countdown

● *Preheat grill.*

● *Make fish.*

● *Make butter beans.*

● *Make salad.*

shopping list

TO BUY:

350g (12oz) sole fillet

1 small packet flaked almonds (25g/1oz needed)

450g (1lb) tinned butter beans

1 lemon

1 small bunch parsley (optional)

2 medium tomatoes

STAPLES:

Olive oil

Salt

Black peppercorns

smothered steak with caramelised onions

helpful hints

- Beef fillet, sirloin, rump, skirt or flank steak can also be used.
- Fresh pineapple cubes are available in the fruit and veg sections of some supermarkets.
- Any type of lettuce can be used.
- If pressed for time, omit the Pineapple Kebabs and serve 110g (4oz) of pineapple cubes per person.

countdown

- Preheat grill.
- Make steak.
- Make salad.
- Assemble pineapple.

Caramelised onions, mushrooms and garlic are perfect toppings for steak. There's no reason to shy away from enjoying a steak if you pick a lean cut. ● Here it is served with succulent artichoke hearts and followed by a simple pineapple dessert.

smothered steak with caramelised onions

275g (10oz) top loin steak, visible fat removed

Olive oil spray

225g (8oz) red onion, sliced

125ml (4fl oz) fat-free, low-salt chicken stock

4 medium-sized garlic cloves, crushed

225g (8oz) portobello mushrooms, sliced

Salt and freshly ground black pepper to taste

Line a baking tray with foil and place under the grill. Spray the steak with oil on both sides and set aside. Heat a small non-stick frying pan over a medium-high heat and add the onion. Sauté for 1 minute. Add the chicken stock, cover with a lid and cook over a high heat for 3 minutes. Uncover and cook for another minute, or until all of the liquid has evaporated. Add the garlic and mushrooms and sauté for 2 minutes. Season with salt and pepper to taste. Remove the hot baking tray from the grill and place the steak on tray. Grill for 4 minutes for a 2.5cm (1in) thick steak, another 4 minutes for thicker steak and 2 minutes for a thinner one. Turn the steak and season the cooked side. Transfer the steak to 2 plates, smother with the onion and mushrooms and serve.

Makes 2 servings.

One serving: 365 calories, 53g protein, 10g carbohydrate, 14g fat (6g saturated), 127mg cholesterol, 237mg sodium, 0g fibre

salad of artichoke hearts

Several red lettuce leaves, washed and torn into bite-sized pieces

75g (3oz) artichoke hearts, drained and sliced thinly

2 tablespoons no-sugar-added oil and vinegar dressing

Place lettuce on 2 plates and top with the artichoke hearts. Drizzle with salad dressing and serve.

Makes 2 servings.

One serving: 90 calories, 1g protein, 3g carbohydrate, 9g fat (1g saturated), 0mg cholesterol, 234mg sodium, 1g fibre

pineapple kebabs

1 tablespoon ground cinnamon

2g (¹/₁₆ oz) artificial sweetener

275g (10oz) pineapple cubes

2 skewers

Line a baking tray with foil. Mix the cinnamon and sweetener together in a medium-sized bowl. Toss the pineapple cubes in the mixture, making sure all sides are coated. Thread the cubes onto 2 skewers and place on the baking tray. Grill 6 to 7 inches from the heat for 5 minutes. Turn the skewers over and grill for an additional 3 minutes. Serve warm.

Makes 2 servings.

One serving: 86 calories, 1g protein, 23g carbohydrate, 1g fat (0g saturated), 0mg cholesterol, 3mg sodium, 2g fibre

shopping list

TO BUY:

275g (10oz) top loin steak

1 tin or jar artichoke hearts

225g (8oz) portobello mushrooms

1 small head red lettuce leaves

1 container fresh pineapple cubes

STAPLES:

Garlic

Red onion

Olive oil spray

No-sugar-added oil and vinegar dressing

Fat-free, low-salt chicken stock

Ground cinnamon

Artificial sweetener

Salt

Black peppercorns

whisky pork chops

Whisky lends an intriguing flavour to this simple French pork dish. This is a hearty meal and takes about 30–40 minutes to make from start to finish. ● *Enjoy it with full-flavoured rosemary lentils and beetroot salad, followed by a refreshing cinnamon grapefruit.*

whisky pork chops

2 teaspoons olive oil
2 x 150g (5oz) boneless, centre loin pork chops, visible fat removed
125ml (4fl oz) whisky
125ml (4fl oz) fat-free, low-sodium chicken stock
2 tablespoons Dijon mustard
Salt and freshly ground black pepper to taste

Heat the oil in a medium-sized non-stick frying pan over a medium-high heat. Add the pork chops and brown for 2 minutes on both sides. Pour off excess fat. Add the whisky and flambé: if cooking over gas, warm the whisky in the pan for a few seconds and then tip the pan to let the flame ignite the liquid. Immediately remove from the heat and let the flame burn down. If you cook with electric heat, then throw a lighted match into the warmed whisky. Be sure to remove the match before serving.

Stir in the stock, cover and lower the heat. Cook over a low heat for 3 minutes, or until the chops are cooked through and a meat thermometer registers 70°C/160°F. Remove the chops to a plate and cover with foil to keep warm. Add the mustard and blend in with the sauce. Cook for 1–2 minutes to reduce and slightly thicken. Season with salt and pepper to taste. Remove the chops to 2 plates, spoon the sauce over them and serve.
Makes 2 servings.

One serving: 448 calories, 42g protein, 1g carbohydrate, 12g fat (3g saturated), 133mg cholesterol, 596mg sodium, 0g fibre

rosemary lentils

225ml (8fl oz) fat-free, low-sodium
   chicken stock
225ml (8fl oz) water
110g (4oz) red lentils
110g (4oz) yellow onion, diced
2 teaspoons fresh rosemary or
   1 teaspoon dried
2 medium-sized garlic cloves,
   crushed
Salt and freshly ground black
   pepper to taste
10g (1/2oz) chopped fresh parsley

Bring the stock and water to a rolling boil in a
medium-sized pot. Add the lentils, onion,
rosemary and garlic slowly, so that the water
does not stop boiling. Reduce the heat to
medium, cover with a lid and simmer for 20
minutes. Remove the lid and continue to cook
over a high heat, until any remaining liquid has
been absorbed. Season, sprinkle with fresh
parsley and serve with the pork.
Makes 2 servings.

One serving: 85 calories, 7g protein,
15g carbohydrate, 0.5g fat (0g saturated),
0mg cholesterol, 285mg sodium, 2g fibre

beetroot salad

450g (1lb) cooked beetroots,
   sliced
2 tablespoons distilled white
   vinegar
2g (1/16oz) artificial sweetener

Place the sliced beetroot on 2 salad plates.
Combine the vinegar and sweetener, spoon over
the beetroot and serve.
Makes 2 servings.

One serving: 58 calories, 2g protein,
15g carbohydrate, 0g fat (0g saturated),
0mg cholesterol, 285mg sodium, 0g fibre

cinnamon grapefruit

1 grapefruit
1/2 teaspoon cinnamon
2g (1/16oz) artificial sweetener

Preheat the grill. Line a baking tray with foil or
use a small oven-to-table dish. Peel the
grapefruit over a bowl to catch the juice. With a
serrated knife, cut the grapefruit into 1cm (1/2in)
slices (as you would slice a tomato). Place in a
single layer in the dish. Sprinkle with the
cinnamon and grill for 3 minutes. Mix the
sweetener into the grapefruit juice and spoon
over the grilled grapefruit before serving.
Makes 2 servings.

One serving: 40 calories, 1g protein,
11g carbohydrate, 0g fat (0g saturated),
0mg cholesterol, 0mg sodium, 1g fibre

shopping list

TO BUY:
   2 x 150g (5oz) boneless,
      centre loin pork chops
   1 small bottle whisky
   1 packet cooked beetroots
   1 small packet red lentils
   1 small bunch fresh parsley
   1 small bunch fresh rosemary
      or 1 jar dried
   1 grapefruit
STAPLES:
   Yellow onion
   Garlic
   Olive oil
   Distilled white vinegar
   Fat free, low-sodium chicken
      stock
   Dijon mustard
   Ground cinnamon
   Artificial sweetener
   Salt
   Black peppercorns

seared sesame tuna

Seared tuna with black and white sesame seeds is served in many restaurants, but you can make it at home in minutes. ● Flavour can vary considerably among the species of tuna. The yellowfin tuna is more delicately flavoured and particularly worth looking for. ● Black sesame seeds are available in some supermarkets and many health food shops. You can use either all white sesame seeds, all black or a combination of both. ● A side dish of bok choy and shiitake noodles completes this Oriental-style meal.

helpful hints

● *To chop fresh ginger quickly, cut it into small cubes and press through a garlic press with large holes. If using a press with small holes, just capture the juice that is squeezed out; it will give enough flavour for the recipe.*

● *To save clean-up time, cook the tuna first, then remove and stir-fry the bok choy and pasta in the same wok.*

● *To keep from having to look back at the recipe as you stir-fry the ingredients, line them up on a chopping board or plate in the order of use so you know which ingredient comes next.*

● *For crisp, not steamed, stir-fried vegetables, start with a very hot wok or frying pan. Let the vegetables sit a minute before tossing to allow the wok to regain its heat.*

seared sesame tuna

275g (10oz) fresh tuna steak
3 tablespoons sesame seeds
4 teaspoons olive oil
Salt and freshly ground black pepper to taste

Rinse the tuna and pat dry with kitchen paper. Spoon the sesame seeds over both sides of the tuna, pressing the seeds into the fish with the back of a spoon. Heat the oil in a wok or non-stick frying pan over a high heat. When the oil begins to smoke, add the tuna. Brown for 1 minute, then turn. Brown for another minute, then lower the heat to medium-high. Cook for another 3–4 minutes. Season with salt and pepper to taste. The tuna should be seared outside and just barely warm inside. Immediately remove from the pan to slow the cooking process. Cut the tuna in half, divide between 2 plates and serve.
Makes 2 servings.

One serving: 353 calories, 36g protein, 1g carbohydrate, 23g fat (4g saturated), 53mg cholesterol, 60mg sodium, 0g fibre

grilled scallops parmigiana p118

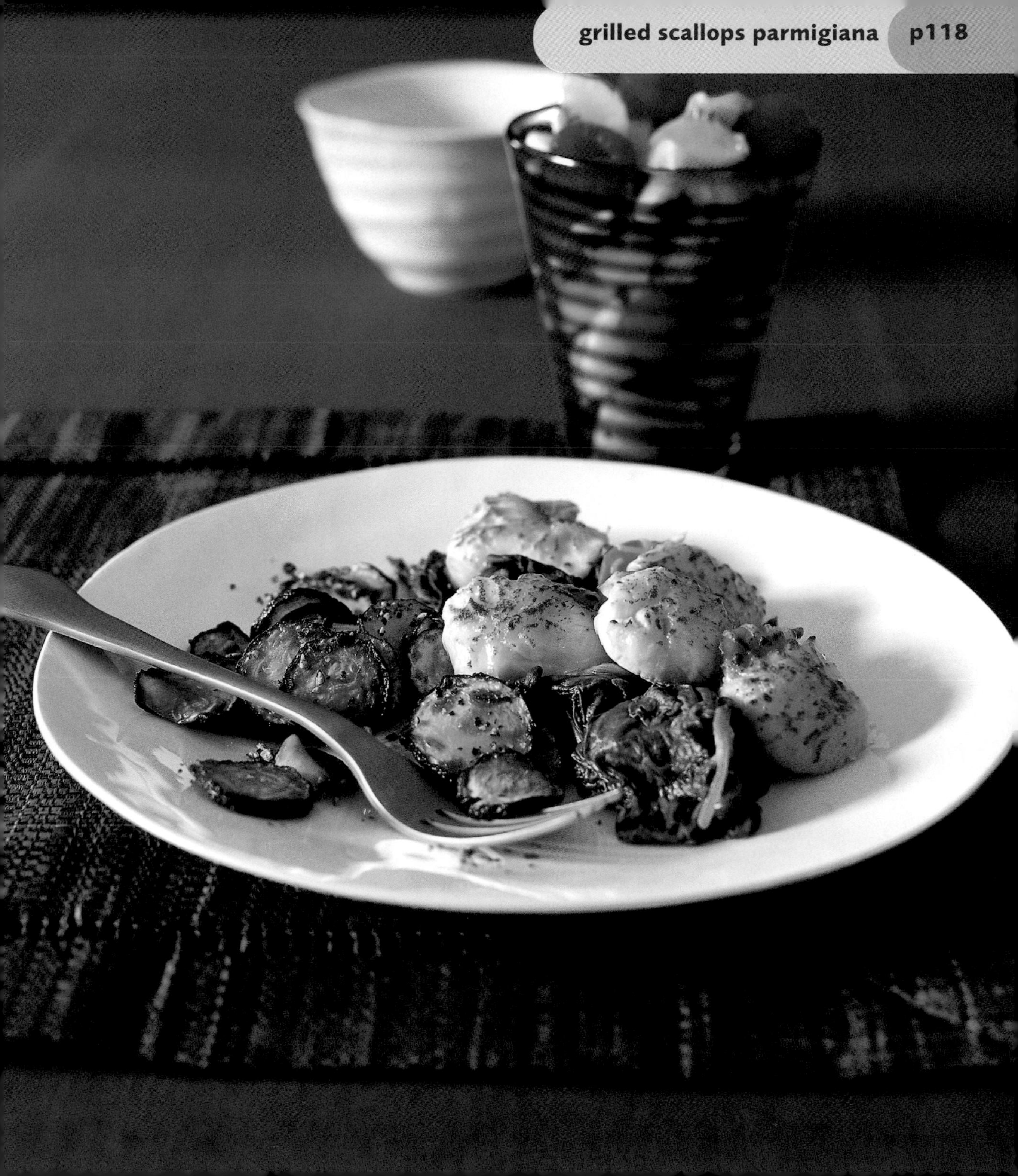

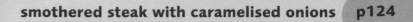
smothered steak with caramelised onions   p124

stir-fry bok choy with shiitake noodles

50g (2oz) wholemeal thin
    spaghetti
2 tablespoons low-sodium soy
    sauce
2 tablespoons dry sherry
2 tablespoons water
4 medium-sized garlic cloves,
    crushed
5cm (2in) piece fresh ginger,
    peeled and chopped
    (2 tablespoons)
2 teaspoons olive oil
110g (4oz) bok choy, sliced
110g (4oz) shiitake mushrooms,
    sliced
4 spring onions, sliced
Salt and freshly ground black
    pepper to taste

Bring a large saucepan filled with water to a boil.
Add the spaghetti and boil for 5 minutes, or
according to the packet's instructions. Do not
overcook. Drain.

Combine the soy sauce, sherry, water, garlic
and ginger in a small bowl. Make sure all
ingredients are prepared and ready for the wok.

Heat the oil until smoking in the same wok or
frying pan used for tuna. Add the spaghetti, bok
choy and mushrooms. Stir-fry for 2 minutes.
Draw to the sides of the wok, leaving a well in
the middle. Add the sauce and toss with the
vegetables for 2 minutes. Add the spring onions
and season with salt and pepper to taste. Toss
well. Spoon onto plates with the tuna.
Makes 2 servings.

One serving: 273 calories, 10g protein,
38g carbohydrate, 6g fat (1g saturated),
0mg cholesterol, 629mg sodium, 6g fibre

countdown

● *Prepare all ingredients.*
● *Boil pasta.*
● *Make tuna in wok and
remove.*
● *Stir-fry bok choy and
pasta.*

shopping list

TO BUY:
    275g (10oz) fresh tuna steak
    1 packet sesame seeds
        (white, black or
        combination)
    1 packet wholemeal thin
        spaghetti (50g/2oz
        needed)
    1 small bottle dry sherry
    1 small bok choy (110g/4oz
        needed)
    1 packet shiitake mushrooms
        (110g/4oz needed)
    1 small bunch spring onions
        (4 needed)
    5cm (2in) piece fresh ginger
STAPLES:
    Garlic
    Olive oil
    Low-sodium soy sauce
    Salt
    Black peppercorns

chicken provençal

helpful hints

- *Fresh thyme gives the dish a sweet flavour, though dried can be used.*
- *If using dried spices, make sure they are less than 6 months old.*
- *Any type of tomatoes can be substituted for plum tomatoes.*
- *The quickest way to wash watercress is to place it head first into a bowl of water. Leave for a minute, then lift out and shake dry, leaving dirt and grit behind.*
- *To give chicken a crisp texture, make sure the frying pan is very hot before browning.*
- *I call for regular brown rice instead of quick-cooking brown rice because it contains more nutrients. If you're really pressed for time, the quick-cooking brown rice works fine.*
- *I like to cook my rice like pasta, using a pan of boiling water that's large enough for the rice to roll freely. Use the method given here or follow the directions on the packet.*

The mild, warm climate and bright sun of the South of France nurture the colourful array of Provençal ingredients. Ripe tomatoes, garlic, olives and fresh herbs delicately spice the cuisine of this region. Memories of meals we had in Provence inspired this dinner.
- *Anchovies are used as a base for the chicken sauce. They practically melt to nothing when sautéed, yet give the sauce a rich flavour. Be sure to rinse them well before cooking to remove most of the salt.* ● *Serve with brown rice and a salad of chicory and watercress.*

chicken provençal

350g (12oz) boneless, skinless chicken breast
1/2 medium-sized red onion, diced
4 anchovy fillets packed in olive oil, rinsed
4 medium plum tomatoes, diced
2 medium-sized garlic cloves, crushed
2 tablespoons fresh thyme leaves or 2 teaspoons dried
1 teaspoon balsamic vinegar
2 teaspoons olive oil
8 stoned black olives, halved
Freshly ground black pepper to taste

Remove any visible fat from the chicken. Set a non-stick frying pan over a medium-high heat. Add the chicken and onion. Brown the chicken for 2 minutes on each side. While the chicken browns, add the anchovies and mash them with the back of your cooking spoon. Lower the heat and add the tomatoes, garlic and thyme. Cover and simmer for 5 minutes. Divide the chicken between 2 plates. Stir the sauce and add the vinegar, oil and black olives. Season with pepper to taste. Spoon the sauce over the chicken. Makes 2 servings.

One serving: 416 calories, 62g protein, 31g carbohydrate, 16g fat (3g saturated), 144mg cholesterol, 585mg sodium, 2g fibre

brown rice

75g (3oz) brown rice
Salt and freshly ground black pepper to taste

Rinse the rice and place in a large saucepan. Fill with water and bring to a boil. Boil for 30 minutes. Drain and season to taste. Divide between 2 plates and place the chicken and sauce on top.
Makes 2 servings.

One serving: 85 calories, 3g protein, 18g carbohydrate, 1g fat (0g saturated), 0mg cholesterol, 0mg sodium, 1g fibre

chicory and watercress salad

2 small heads chicory

1 small bunch fresh watercress, stemmed and washed

2 tablespoons no-sugar-added oil and vinegar dressing

Salt and freshly ground black pepper to taste

Wipe the chicory with damp kitchen paper. Remove 2.5cm (1in) from the bases. Cut the leaves crosswise into 2.5cm (1in) slices. Place in a small bowl. Break the watercress into smaller pieces and add to the bowl. Drizzle dressing over the top and season with salt and pepper to taste. Serve.

Makes 2 servings.

One serving: 87 calories, 1g protein, 2g carbohydrate, 9g fat (2g saturated), 0mg cholesterol, 101mg sodium, 0g fibre

countdown

- *Make rice.*
- *Make chicken.*
- *Make salad.*

shopping list

TO BUY:

  350g (12oz) boneless, skinless chicken breast

  1 container stoned black olives

  1 small packet brown rice

  1 tin anchovy fillets packed in olive oil

  4 medium plum tomatoes

  1 bunch fresh thyme or 1 jar dried

  2 small heads chicory

  1 small bunch watercress

STAPLES:

  Red onion

  Garlic

  Olive oil

  Balsamic vinegar

  No-sugar-added oil and vinegar dressing

  Salt

  Black peppercorns

mussels marinière

Imagine eating on the quay in Deauville, France, watching the fishing boats come in, breathing the fresh sea air and drinking a glass of chilled white wine. What a treat! Moules à la Marinière, or Mussels in White Wine, is a French dish normally enjoyed in these quaint surroundings. If you can't go to France, prepare this dish for an experience almost as satisfying! It takes less than 15 minutes to prepare, never mind the fabulous taste. ● Store mussels in the refrigerator. When ready for use, carefully scrub them with a vegetable brush under cold water. Scrape off the beard or thin hairs along the shell. Their shells should be tightly closed or snap shut when tapped. Discard any that do not close. ● Serve the mussels in large soup bowls with the reduced stock.

helpful hint

● The onion, celery and carrots can be sautéed ahead of time. Cook the mussels in wine just before serving.

countdown

● *Prepare ingredients.*
● *Cook vegetables.*
● *Add mussels.*

shopping list

TO BUY:
  900g (2lb) mussels
  1 small bottle dry white wine
  1 small bunch fresh parsley
  1 bag washed, ready-to-eat
    young salad leaves
STAPLES:
  Celery
  Yellow onion
  Carrots
  Olive oil
  No-sugar-added oil and
    vinegar dressing
  Multi-grain bread
  Black peppercorns

mussels marinière

2 teaspoons olive oil
110g (4oz) sliced yellow onion
2 celery stalks, sliced
2 medium carrots, sliced
125ml (4fl oz) dry white wine
Freshly ground black pepper to
  taste
900g (2lb) mussels
10g (½oz) fresh parsley, chopped
2 slices multi-grain bread

Heat the oil in a large saucepan over a medium-high heat. Sauté the onion, celery and carrots until they start to cook but not colour, about 5 minutes. Add the wine and freshly ground pepper to taste. Add the mussels and cover tightly with a lid. Bring to a boil and let boil for about 3 more minutes. The wine will boil up over the mussels causing them to open. As soon as they open, remove the pan from the heat. Do not over cook.

Lift the mussels out of the pan with a slotted spoon and divide between 2 large soup bowls. Discard any closed mussels – do not try to force them open. Sprinkle with parsley and serve. Meanwhile, bring the liquid to the boil and reduce rapidly by half. Ladle out the reduced stock to serve, leaving ½cm (¼in) of the stock in the pan – it may have some sand from the mussels in it. Serve with bread to dip in the stock. *Makes 2 servings.*

One serving: 374 calories, 33g protein, 31g carbohydrate, 11g fat (1g saturated), 64mg cholesterol, 861mg sodium, 5g fibre

young salad leaves

2 large handfuls washed, ready-to-
  eat young salad leaves
2 tablespoons no-sugar-added oil
  and vinegar dressing

Toss the salad leaves with the dressing. *Makes 2 servings.*

8g fat (1g saturated), 0mg cholesterol, 81mg sodium, 0g fibre

spicy crab and vegetable stir-fry

Oriental spices give this crab a zesty tang. In Vietnam this dish is normally made with whole crab claws in the shell. I have simplified the shopping and cooking by using tinned or frozen crab. ● *This entire meal is made in a wok. A non-stick frying pan can also be used and you will still achieve a good result.* ● *Lemon grass has long, thin, green-grey leaves with a spring onion-like base. Slice the end off the bulb and cut slices up to the woody part of the stem. Grated lemon rind can be substituted.* ● *Follow with an indulgent-tasting parfait for dessert.*

spicy crab and vegetable stir-fry

375g (13oz) crabmeat, drained
50g (2oz) tomato purée
½ teaspoon hot pepper sauce
125ml (4fl oz) water
2g (¹⁄₁₆oz) artificial sweetener
4 teaspoons rapeseed oil
50g (2oz) chopped shallots
2 medium-sized garlic cloves, crushed
2 tablespoons chopped fresh ginger or 2 teaspoons ground ginger
4 stalks lemon grass, sliced, or grated rind from 2 lemons
225g (8oz) fresh bean sprouts
225g (8oz) mange tout, trimmed
2 tablespoons unsalted, roasted peanuts, chopped

Flake the crabmeat with a fork into a medium-sized bowl, looking carefully for any shell or cartilage that might remain. Combine the tomato purée, hot pepper sauce, water and artificial sweetener in a small bowl and set aside. Make sure all ingredients are prepared and ready for stir-frying. Heat the oil in a wok or frying pan over a high heat until smoking. Add the shallots, garlic, ginger and lemon grass and stir-fry for 2 minutes. Add the bean sprouts and mange tout. Stir-fry for another 2 minutes. Add the crab and stir-fry for 3 more minutes.

Push the ingredients to the sides of pan leaving a well in the centre. Add the sauce and toss with the ingredients for an additional minute. Remove to 2 plates, sprinkle with peanuts and serve.
Makes 2 servings.

One serving: 493 calories, 52g protein, 25g carbohydrate, 23g fat (3g saturated), 144mg cholesterol, 694mg sodium, 4g fibre

helpful hints

● *Use a food processor to chop the shallots and peanuts.*

● *To chop fresh ginger quickly, cut it into small cubes and press through a garlic press with large holes. If using a press with small holes, just capture the juice that is squeezed out; it will give enough flavour for the recipe.*

● *If using ground ginger instead of fresh, add it to the sauce.*

● *To keep from having to look back at the recipe as you stir-fry the ingredients, line them up on a chopping board or plate in the order of use so you know which ingredient comes next.*

● *For crisp, not steamed, stir-fried vegetables, start with a very hot wok or frying pan. Let the vegetables sit a minute before tossing to allow the wok to regain its heat.*

● *Any type of berries can be used.*

● *Any flavour of light yoghurt can be used.*

● *Be careful toasting the pecans, as they burn easily.*

spicy crab and vegetable stir-fry continued

continued

countdown

- Prepare all ingredients
- Stir-fry crab dish.
- Prepare parfait.

shopping list

TO BUY:

1 pot light white
    chocolate–strawberry
    flavoured yoghurt

375g (13oz) tinned or frozen
    sweet crabmeat

1 tube tomato purée

1 small packet roasted
    peanuts (25g/1oz needed)

1 small packet pecans
    (10g/¹⁄₂oz needed)

2 large shallots

1 small piece fresh ginger
    or 1 jar ground

1 small bunch lemon grass
    (4 stalks needed)

225g (8oz) fresh bean
    sprouts

225g (8oz) mange tout

1 punnet fresh raspberries

STAPLES:

Garlic

Rapeseed oil

Hot pepper sauce

Artificial sweetener

raspberry parfait

110g (4oz) fresh raspberries

2g (¹⁄₁₆oz) artificial sweetener
    (optional)

225ml (8fl oz) light, white
    chocolate–strawberry yoghurt

6 pecan pieces, toasted
    (1 tablespoon)

Purée the raspberries in a food processor and blend in the artificial sweetener. Scoop half the yoghurt into 2 bowls or parfait glasses. Pour in half the sauce and top with the remaining yoghurt. Pour the remaining sauce over the yoghurt and top with the toasted pecans.

Refrigerate until ready to serve.

Makes 2 servings.

One serving: 110 calories, 5g protein, 15g carbohydrate, 4g fat (0.5g saturated), 3mg cholesterol, 58mg sodium, 2g fibre

neapolitan steak

The Italian city of Naples claims pizza as its symbol. The same earthy flavours they use in their popular topping go with steak. Here is a quick version of the zesty, tomato-based sauce that can be made in 20 minutes for a great, quick, mid-week supper. ● Continue the Italian theme with side dishes of Parmesan linguine and Italian greens.

neapolitan steak

225g (8oz) flank or skirt steak, visible fat removed
225g (8oz) no-sugar-added tinned, peeled plum tomatoes
50g (2oz) yellow onion, diced
2 medium-sized garlic cloves, crushed
2 teaspoons dried oregano
1 teaspoon balsamic vinegar
2 teaspoons olive oil
8 stoned black olives, halved
2g (¹⁄₁₆oz) artificial sweetener
Salt and freshly ground black pepper to taste

Set a medium-sized non-stick frying pan over a medium-high heat. Brown the steak for 2 minutes on each side. Lower the heat and continue to cook for 3–4 minutes. Remove the steak to a plate and cover with foil or another plate to keep warm. Lower the heat and add the tomatoes, onion, garlic and oregano. Cover and simmer for 5 minutes. Stir in the vinegar, oil, black olives and artificial sweetener. Season with salt and pepper to taste. Remove from the heat, slice the steak and serve with the sauce on top. *Makes 2 servings.*

> One serving: 336 calories, 42g protein, 10g carbohydrate, 16g fat (6g saturated), 101mg cholesterol, 240mg sodium, 4g fibre

parmesan linguine

50g (2oz) wholemeal linguine or spaghetti
2 teaspoons olive oil
Salt and freshly ground black pepper to taste
2 tablespoons freshly grated Parmesan cheese

Bring a large saucepan filled with water to the boil. Add the pasta and cook for 8 minutes, or according to the packet's instructions. Do not overcook. Drain, leaving 3 tablespoons of water on the pasta, and toss with oil. Season with salt and pepper to taste and sprinkle with Parmesan cheese. Serve with the steak. *Makes 2 servings.*

> One serving: 208 calories, 9g protein, 26g carbohydrate, 6g fat (2g saturated), 4mg cholesterol, 113mg sodium, 5g fibre

helpful hints

● *Make sure the dried oregano is less than 6 months old.*
● *Any type of washed, ready-to-eat salad leaves can be used.*
● *Buy good quality Parmesan cheese and grate it yourself. Freeze extra for quick use later – simply spoon out what you need and leave the rest frozen.*

countdown

● *Begin boiling water for pasta.*
● *Make salad.*
● *Make steak.*
● *Make pasta.*

neapolitan steak continued

shopping list

TO BUY:

225g (8oz) flank or skirt steak, visible fat removed

1 packet wholemeal linguine or spaghetti (50g/2oz needed)

1 container stoned black olives (8 needed)

1 tin no-sugar-added, peeled plum tomatoes (225g/8oz needed)

1 bag washed, ready-to-eat, Italian-style salad leaves

STAPLES:

Yellow onion

Garlic

Olive oil

Balsamic vinegar

Parmesan cheese

Dried oregano

Artificial sweetener

Salt

Black peppercorns

italian greens

2 large handfuls washed, ready-to-eat, Italian-style salad leaves

4 teaspoons balsamic vinegar

Salt and freshly ground black pepper to taste

Place the salad leaves in a bowl and sprinkle with balsamic vinegar. Add salt and pepper to taste and toss before serving.

Makes 2 servings.

One serving: 10 calories, 1g protein, 2g carbohydrate, 0g fat (0g saturated), 0mg cholesterol, 6mg sodium, 0g fibre

spicy chicken legs

Aromatic flavours of Chinese 5-spice powder make this dish a winner. It takes a little longer to cook this dish – about 30 minutes – but the flavour is worth it.
● Boneless, skinless chicken legs and thighs are now available. With the skin removed, the fat content is greatly reduced. Their richer-flavoured meat make a nice alternative to boneless, skinless chicken breasts. ● This dish tastes great the second day. Make extra for another quick meal. ● Serve with a simple Chinese side dish or garlic bean sprouts and rice.

spicy chicken legs

125ml (4fl oz) fat-free, low-sodium chicken stock

50ml (2fl oz) rice vinegar

1 teaspoon Chinese 5-spice powder

6 large garlic cloves

2 tablespoons low-sodium soy sauce

125ml (4fl oz) water

2 teaspoons sesame oil

275g (10oz) boneless, skinless chicken legs or thighs, visible fat removed

110g (4oz) broccoli florets

225g (8oz) sliced button mushrooms

Combine the chicken stock, vinegar, Chinese 5-spice, whole garlic cloves, soy sauce and water in a small bowl. Make sure all ingredients are prepped and ready for stir-frying. Heat the oil in a wok or frying pan over a high heat until smoking. Brown the chicken on all sides, about 2 minutes. Add the chicken stock mixture and reduce the heat to medium-low. Simmer gently for 15 minutes, turning the chicken several times. The liquid should be just at the bubbling stage. Add the broccoli and mushrooms and continue cooking for 5 minutes. The sauce will boil down to a glaze as the chicken cooks. Remove the garlic cloves. Spoon the completed dish into a bowl and cover with foil to keep warm.

Makes 2 servings.

One serving: 419 calories, 45g protein, 13g carbohydrate, 20g fat (4g saturated), 130mg cholesterol, 897mg sodium, 1g fibre

helpful hints

● *To save clean-up time, use the same wok or frying pan for the chicken and the rice with bean sprouts.*

● *If Chinese 5-spice powder is unavailable you can make it at home by mixing equal measures of ground cinnamon, cloves, fennel seeds, star anise and peppercorns.*

● *Distilled white vinegar diluted with a little water can be used instead of rice vinegar.*

● *To keep from having to look back at the recipe as you stir-fry the ingredients, line them up on a chopping board or plate in the order of use so you know which ingredient comes next.*

● *For crisp, not steamed, stir-fried vegetables, start with a very hot wok or frying pan. Let the vegetables sit for a minute before tossing to allow the wok to regain its heat.*

countdown

● *Start rice.*

● *Place chicken on to cook.*

● *Complete bean sprouts and rice.*

spicy chicken legs continued

continued

shopping list

TO BUY:

275g (10oz) boneless, skinless
chicken legs or thighs

1 small packet brown rice

1 small bottle rice vinegar

1 small bottle sesame oil

1 jar Chinese 5-spice powder

1 small packet broccoli florets
(110g/4oz needed)

225g (8oz) sliced button
mushrooms

1 small container fresh bean
sprouts

STAPLES:

Garlic

Fat-free, low-sodium chicken
stock

Low-sodium soy sauce

Salt

Black peppercorns

garlic bean sprouts and rice

75g (3oz) brown rice

Salt and freshly ground black
pepper to taste

2 teaspoons sesame oil

110g (4oz) fresh bean sprouts

2 medium-sized garlic cloves,
crushed

Rinse the rice and place in a large saucepan filled with water. Bring to a boil and cook for 30 minutes. Drain and season with salt and pepper to taste.

Again, make sure all ingredients are prepared and ready for stir-frying. Place the wok over a high heat and add the oil. Add the rice, bean sprouts and garlic and sauté for 2–3 minutes. Season with salt and pepper to taste. Place on 2 plates and spoon the stir-fried chicken and vegetables on top.

Makes 2 servings.

One serving: 207 calories, 11g protein,
25g carbohydrate, 9g fat (1g saturated),
0mg cholesterol, 10mg sodium, 1g fibre

right carbs

introduction

You're now entering the third and permanent phase of the low-carb lifestyle: great food that's good for you, too. This balanced approach to eating incorporates high-fibre carbohydrates into breakfast, lunch and dinner menus.

As with the other sections, I have organised the menus into a meal-at-a-glance chart with some easy and quick meals mid-week, alongside more elaborate ones for the weekends. They are arranged to give variety throughout the day and over the course of the week. The meals appear in the same order within the chapter. Just follow the meals in the order given for an easy two-week plan.

breakfast

The French Toast with Ham and the Ranchero Burrito are 2 of the 14 savoury breakfasts you can choose from. Try them all to add variety to your morning repertoire.

lunch

Choose from the wide selection to fit any appetite. When you're in a hurry, grab a Baby Spinach, Mushroom and Gammon Salad. Most restaurant menus will have a prawn or tuna salad, or a pasta salad with turkey (or chicken). Make the recipe provided here and use it as a guide for proportions when eating out. When you have more time, enjoy Tomatoes Stuffed with Anchovies and Capers or Ham and Mushroom Pitta Pizza.

dinner

Enjoy these meals in the proportions given, and you won't have to count calories and carbs or question what you eat. Dishes like Beef Stir-Fry with Oyster Sauce, Roasted Pork and Peach Salsa or Country Minestrone with Meatballs will entice you to stick to this low-carbohydrate, balanced style of eating.

Following the Right Carb 14-day plan, you will consume an average of 125 to 135 grams of carbohydrates per day. Carbohydrate percentage is based on carbohydrates less fibre consumed – the standard way to calculate carbohydrate consumption. The balance of these meals is 38 per cent of calories from carbohydrates, 30 per cent of calories from lean protein, 22 per cent of calories from monounsaturated fat, and 7 per cent of calories from saturated fat.[1]

[1] The Right Carb phase approximates a 40-30-30 dietary profile. While there are differences of opinion, it is generally agreed that fat levels (primarily mono-unsaturated) should make up to 30 per cent of one's diet. Carbohydrate intake should be restricted to 30 per cent more than protein intake. So if the calories from protein are 30 per cent of diet, the correct carbohydrate level should be 40%.

right carbs 14-day menu plan

week 1	breakfast	lunch	dinner
sunday	Smoked Salmon Omelettes 143	Layered Crab Salad 158–159	Japanese Beef Sukiyaki 175
monday	Grilled Ham and Cheddar Sandwich 144	Tomatoes Stuffed with Anchovies and Capers 160–161	Aromatic Poached Sole 176
tuesday	Spinach and Parmesan Omelette 145	Prawn Caesar Wrap 162	Chicken with Parmesan, and Tomato Sauce 177–178
wednesday	Ranchero Burrito 146	Turkey-avocado Pitta 163	Cioppino (Seafood Stew) 179–180
thursday	Western Omelette . . .147	Fresh Salmon Burgers 164	Pork Souvlaki 181
friday	Mediterranean Platter 148	Chicken Tostadas 165	Mediterranean Veal and Olives 182
saturday	Vietnamese Pancakes 149	Caribbean Prawn Salad 166	Country Minestrone with Meatballs 183–184

week 2	breakfast	lunch	dinner
sunday	French Toast with Ham 150	Ham and Mushroom Pitta Pizza 167	Curried Prawns and Vegetables 185–186
monday	Shiitake and Swiss Scramble 151	Fresh Tuna Salad 168	Chicken Fajitas 187
tuesday	Goat's Cheese and Palm Hearts Omelette 152	Spinach, Mushroom and Gammon Salad 169	Roast Beef and Shiitake Hash . . .189–190
wednesday	Cottage Cheese and Cucumber Sandwich 153	Turkey and Asparagus Penne Salad 170	Bahamian Fish Boil 191–192
thursday	Warm Turkey Sandwich 154	Waldorf Salad with Roast Beef Sandwich 171	Summer-to-winter Chicken Casserole 193
friday	Egg-in-toast 155	Fish and Cheese on Toast 172	Beef Stir-fry with Oyster Sauce 194–195
saturday	Frittata Primavera 156	Chicken Sandwich with Sun-dried Tomato Sauce 173	Roasted Pork and Peach Salsa 196

right carbs
breakfasts

smoked salmon omelettes

This is perfect for a weekend breakfast or parties.

smoked salmon omelettes

2 whole eggs

4 egg whites

25g (1oz) snipped fresh dill or 3 tablespoons dried

Salt and freshly ground black pepper to taste

Olive oil spray

110g (4oz) sliced smoked salmon

1 medium tomato, sliced

2 tablespoons reduced-fat soured cream

Several sprigs fresh dill for garnish (optional)

Preheat the grill. Whisk the eggs, egg whites and dill in a medium-sized bowl. Season with salt and pepper to taste. Set a 20.5–23cm (8–9in) non-stick frying pan over a medium-high heat. Spray with olive oil. Add half the egg mixture and swirl in the pan to form a thin layer. Cook for 1 minute and place under the grill for 1 minute, or until the omelette is cooked on top. Remove from the grill. Slide the omelette onto a plate and repeat for the second one. Place the smoked salmon and tomato slices on one half of each omelette, letting some of the salmon peek out from the edge. Spoon soured cream over the salmon and add sprigs of dill, again letting them peek out from the omelettes. Fold the omelettes in half once and then in half again to form a triangle. Serve hot.

Makes 2 servings.

bran cereal

50g (2oz) high-fibre, no-sugar-added bran cereal

225ml (8fl oz) skimmed milk

1 sliced banana

Divide the cereal between 2 bowls and add the milk and banana to each.

Makes 2 servings.

> **Total breakfast one serving: 428 calories, 33g protein, 61g carbohydrate, 15g fat (4g saturated), 237mg cholesterol, 832mg sodium, 15g fibre**

helpful hint

● *If using dried dill, make sure the herb is less than 6 months old. The leaves should be green, not grey.*

countdown

● *Preheat grill.*
● *Make omelettes and fill.*
● *Assemble cereal.*

shopping list

TO BUY:

1 small pot reduced-fat soured cream

110g (4oz) sliced smoked salmon

1 medium tomato

1 small bunch fresh dill or 1 jar dried

1 banana

STAPLES:

Eggs

Olive oil spray

High-fibre, no-sugar-added bran cereal

Skimmed milk

Salt

Black peppercorns

helpful hints

- *Any type of whole-grain bread can be used.*

countdown

- *Preheat grill.*
- *Make sandwich.*
- *Assemble cereal.*

shopping list

TO BUY:

1 small packet grated, reduced-fat mature Cheddar cheese

225g (8oz) sliced lean ham

2 small tomatoes

STAPLES:

Oatmeal

Skimmed milk

Wholemeal bread

Olive oil spray

Artificial sweetener

grilled ham and cheddar sandwich

This is a simple breakfast that can be made in 5 minutes and taken with you for breakfast-on-the-run.

grilled ham and cheddar sandwich

4 slices wholemeal bread

Olive oil spray

225g (8oz) sliced lean ham (about 4 slices)

25g (1oz) grated, reduced-fat mature Cheddar cheese

2 small tomatoes, sliced

Preheat the grill. Line a baking tray with foil. Place the bread on the tray and spray with olive oil. Place under the grill for 1 minute. Turn each slice, top with ham and sprinkle with cheese. Return to the grill for 2 minutes, or until the cheese melts. Serve as an open-faced sandwich with a sliced tomato on the side. Or, if taking it with you, place the tomato slices on one slice and cover with another slice to make a complete sandwich.

Makes 2 servings.

oatmeal

110g (4oz) oatmeal

450ml (16fl oz) water

225ml (8fl oz) skimmed milk

2g (1/16oz) artificial sweetener (optional)

To prepare in the microwave, combine the oatmeal and water in a microwave-safe bowl. Microwave on high for 4 minutes. Stir in the milk and artificial sweetener, divide between 2 bowls and serve warm.

Alternatively, to prepare on the hob, combine the oatmeal and water in a small saucepan over a medium-high heat, and bring to a boil. Reduce the heat to medium and cook for about 5 more minutes, stirring occasionally. Stir in the milk and sweetener, divide between 2 bowls and serve warm.

Makes 2 servings.

Total breakfast one serving: 488 calories, 39g protein, 60g carbohydrate, 14g fat (5g saturated), 52mg cholesterol, 116mg sodium, 10g fibre

whisky pork chops p126

frittata primavera p156

spinach and parmesan omelette

My husband made this breakfast one very hurried morning before going to work. His comment? 'I can't believe it took me only 15 minutes – start to finish!'

spinach and parmesan omelette

2 whole eggs

4 egg whites

Salt and freshly ground black
    pepper to taste

2 large handfuls washed, ready-to-
    eat fresh spinach

2 teaspoons olive oil

2 tablespoons freshly grated
    Parmesan cheese

Preheat the oven to 200°C/400°F/gas mark 6. Lightly beat the whole eggs and egg whites together in a medium-sized bowl. Season with salt and pepper to taste. Set a medium-sized non-stick ovenproof frying pan over a medium heat. Add the spinach and sauté for 3 minutes, or until wilted. Stir the cooked spinach into the egg mixture. In the same pan, heat the oil over a medium heat. Pour the egg mixture into pan and let set for 1 minute. Sprinkle with Parmesan and place in the oven for 3 minutes, or until eggs are set to desired consistency. Serve immediately. *Makes 2 servings.*

bran-yoghurt parfait

275g (10oz) blueberries

2g (¹/₁₆oz) artificial sweetener

225g (8oz) light blueberry-
    flavoured yoghurt

50g (2oz) high-fibre, no-sugar-
    added bran cereal

Purée blueberries in a food processor or press through a sieve. Stir in the sweetener. Divide half of the yoghurt between 2 bowls or parfait glasses and sprinkle each with bran. Pour some blueberry purée over the bran in each bowl. Spoon the remaining yoghurt over the purée and drizzle with the remaining blueberry purée before serving. *Makes 2 servings.*

Total breakfast one serving: 366 calories,
26g protein, 53g carbohydrate, 14g fat (3g saturated),
220mg cholesterol, 564mg sodium, 20g fibre

helpful hints

● *Buy good quality Parmesan cheese grate it yourself. Freeze extra for quick use later – simply spoon out what you need and leave the rest frozen.*

● *Washed, ready-to-eat fresh spinach is available in most supermarkets. It makes using fresh spinach a dream.*

countdown

● *Preheat oven to 200°C/400°F/gas mark 6.*

● *Prepare all ingredients.*

● *Make omelette.*

● *Assemble cereal.*

shopping list

TO BUY:

1 pot light blueberry-
    flavoured yoghurt

1 bag washed, ready-to-eat
    fresh spinach

1 small punnet blueberries

STAPLES:

Eggs

Olive oil

Parmesan cheese

Artificial sweetener

High-fibre, no-sugar-added
    bran cereal

Salt

Black peppercorns

ranchero burrito

This burrito is quick to make and easy to eat. Black bean pâté, grated Cheddar cheese and smoked turkey breast – all supermarket products designed to make our life easier – make this a 5-minute meal. ● Black bean pâté is usually found in the snack section near the nachos and dips in the supermarket. You can choose hot, medium or mild. Look for one that does not have added sugar.

helpful hints

- *If black bean pâté is unavailable, use reduced-fat refried beans instead.*
- *If you like your food hot and spicy, buy a hot black bean pâté and a spiced cheese that melts.*

countdown

- Preheat grill.
- Make burrito.
- Slice tomato.
- Prepare bran cereal and juice.

shopping list

TO BUY:
- 1 small packet grated, reduced-fat Cheddar cheese
- 110g (4oz) sliced smoked turkey breast
- 1 packet wholemeal tortillas
- 1 jar black bean pâté
- 1 medium tomato

STAPLES:
- Low-sodium tomato juice
- High-fibre, no-sugar-added bran cereal
- Skimmed milk

ranchero burrito

2 x 15cm (6in) wholemeal tortillas
50g (2oz) black bean pâté
110g (4oz) sliced smoked turkey breast
50g (2oz) grated, reduced-fat Cheddar cheese
1 medium tomato, sliced

Warm the tortillas in a microwave oven for 10 seconds, or in a warm oven for 15–20 seconds, to make them easier to roll. Spread the warmed tortillas with the black bean pâté, top with turkey and sprinkle with Cheddar cheese. Roll up and microwave for 45 seconds on high, or until the cheese melts. Or, place in a warm oven for 2 minutes. Cut in half crosswise and serve with tomato slices on the side.
Makes 2 servings.

bran cereal

50g (2oz) high-fibre, no-sugar-added bran cereal
225ml (8fl oz) skimmed milk

Divide the cereal and milk between 2 bowls.
Makes 2 servings.

tomato juice

225ml (8fl oz) low-sodium tomato juice

Divide between 2 glasses.
Makes 2 servings.

> Total breakfast one serving: 353 calories, 34g protein, 51g carbohydrate, 9g fat (4g saturated), 52mg cholesterol, 939mg sodium, 14g fibre

western omelette

Also known as a Denver omelette, this dish was created in kitchen wagons on the cattle trail in the Wild West. Apparently they used plenty of onions to disguise old eggs. This is a modern version that takes about 10 minutes to make.

western omelette

225ml (8fl oz) egg substitute
1/4 teaspoon cayenne pepper
Salt to taste
2 teaspoons olive oil
110g (4oz) diced onion
450g (1lb) green pepper, diced
175g (6oz) tinned roasted red
　　pepper, drained and diced
110g (4oz) sliced lean ham, diced

Preheat the grill. Season the egg substitute with cayenne and salt to taste. Heat the oil in a medium-sized non-stick frying pan over a medium-high heat. Add the onion and green pepper and sauté for 2 minutes. Add the roasted red pepper and ham and sauté for another minute. Add the egg mixture and let set for 2 minutes. Place under the grill for 5 minutes, or until set to the desired consistency. Slide out of the pan and serve.
Makes 2 servings.

oatmeal

110g (4oz) oatmeal
450ml (16fl oz) water
225ml (8fl oz) skimmed milk
2g (1/16oz) artificial sweetener
　　(optional)

To prepare in the microwave, combine the oatmeal and water in a microwave-safe bowl. Microwave on high for 4 minutes. Stir in the milk and sweetener, divide between 2 bowls and serve warm.

Alternatively, to prepare on the hob, combine the oatmeal and water in a small saucepan over a medium-high heat and bring to a boil. Reduce the heat to medium and cook for about 5 more minutes, stirring occasionally. Stir in the milk and sweetener, divide between 2 bowls and serve warm.
Makes 2 servings.

Total breakfast one serving: 385 calories,
31g protein, 54g carbohydrate, 12g fat (4g saturated),
93mg cholesterol, 782mg sodium, 16g fibre

helpful hints

● *Use a frying pan with an ovenproof handle.*
● *2 whole eggs and 4 egg whites can be used instead of egg substitute.*

countdown

● *Preheat grill.*
● *Make oatmeal.*
● *Make omelette.*

shopping list

TO BUY:
　110g (4oz) sliced lean ham
　1 jar or tin roasted red
　　pepper (175g/6oz needed)
STAPLES:
　Olive oil
　Egg substitute
　Frozen, diced onion
　Frozen, diced green bell
　　pepper
　Cayenne pepper
　Artificial sweetener
　Oatmeal
　Skimmed milk
　Salt

mediterranean platter

Sun-dried tomatoes, oranges and strawberries bring thoughts of a sunny Mediterranean morning. Better yet, it takes only a few minutes to assemble this breakfast.

countdown

- *Make platter.*
- *Assemble cereal.*

shopping list

TO BUY:

1 pot low-fat ricotta cheese

110g (4oz) sliced roasted boneless chicken breast

1 small jar sun-dried tomatoes

half a cucumber

1 small punnet strawberries

2 medium oranges

STAPLES:

High-fibre, no-sugar-added bran cereal

Skimmed milk

Low-carbohydrate wholemeal bread

mediterranean platter

110g (4oz) low-fat ricotta cheese

35g (1½oz) sun-dried tomatoes, drained and sliced

half a cucumber, peeled and sliced

2 medium oranges, peeled and sliced

110g (4oz) sliced roasted boneless chicken breast

2 slices low-carbohydrate wholemeal bread

Combine the ricotta cheese with the sun-dried tomatoes. Place on 2 plates. Arrange the cucumber, oranges and chicken slices around the ricotta mixture. Toast the bread and serve on the side.

Makes 2 servings.

bran cereal and fresh berries

50g (2oz) high-fibre, no-sugar-added bran cereal

225ml (8fl oz) skimmed milk

2 good handfuls strawberries, sliced

Divide the cereal between 2 bowls and add milk to each. Sprinkle with the strawberries.

Makes 2 servings.

Total breakfast one serving: 428 calories, 40g protein, 69g carbohydrate, 13g fat (5g saturated), 80mg cholesterol, 443mg sodium, 22g fibre

vietnamese pancakes

This paper-thin crêpe is topped with mushrooms, onion, smoked bacon joint and bean sprouts. When you are looking for a delicious variation from more traditional omelettes and frittatas, this version will fit the bill. It takes about 10 minutes to make and is worth every minute.

vietnamese pancakes

2 eggs
4 egg whites
2 tablespoons wholemeal flour
2 tablespoons low-sodium soy
    sauce
4 spring onions, thinly sliced
2 teaspoons rapeseed oil
110g (4oz) lean smoked pork joint,
    cut into thin strips
225g (8oz) portobello mushrooms,
    sliced
110g (4oz) yellow onion, diced
110g (4oz) bean sprouts

With a wire whisk, mix the eggs, egg whites, wholemeal flour and soy sauce together in a small bowl until smooth. Add the spring onions and set aside. Heat the oil in 23–25.5cm (9–10in) non-stick frying pan over a medium heat Add the pork, mushrooms, onion and bean sprouts. Sauté until the onion turns golden, about 4 minutes. Remove to a bowl and add half the egg mixture to the hot pan. Swirl the mixture around the pan to form a thin crêpe. Cook for 3 minutes, or until the centre is cooked and the sides of the pancake start to curl up. Slide onto a plate. Repeat with the second half of the mixture. Divide the pork and vegetable mixture between both crêpes and serve.
Makes 2 servings.

bran cereal

50g (2oz) high-fibre, no-sugar-
    added bran cereal
225ml (8fl oz) skimmed milk

Divide cereal between 2 bowls and add milk to each.
Makes 2 servings.

Total breakfast one serving: 349 calories, 29g protein, 50g carbohydrate, 9g fat (2g saturated), 55mg cholesterol, 851mg sodium, 15g fibre

helpful hints

- *If pressed for time, use pre-sliced mushrooms and onion.*
- *Lean ham can be substituted if smoked bacon joint is unavailable.*

countdown

- *Prepare ingredients.*
- *Make pancakes.*
- *Assemble cereal.*

shopping list

TO BUY:
    110g (4oz) lean smoked
        bacon joint
    225g (8oz) portobello
        mushrooms
    1 container bean sprouts
    1 bunch spring onions
        (4 needed)
STAPLES:
    Eggs
    Yellow onion
    Skimmed milk
    Wholemeal flour
    High-fibre, no-sugar-added
        bran cereal
    Rapeseed oil
    Low-sodium soy sauce

french toast with ham

For a change from scrambled eggs or omelettes, try this delicious French Toast. You can cook it with cheese or meat to vary the flavour, and it takes only minutes to make.

french toast with ham

125ml (4fl oz) egg substitute

Salt and freshly ground black pepper to taste

2 slices low-carbohydrate wholemeal bread

2 teaspoons olive oil

110g (4oz) sliced lean ham, cubed

Pour the egg substitute into a small bowl and season with salt and pepper to taste. Add the bread and let soak.

Heat the olive oil in a small frying pan over a medium heat. Remove the bread from the egg substitute and add to the pan. Cook for 1 minute, then turn. Add the ham to the cooked sides, cover with a lid and cook for 2 more minutes before serving.

Makes 2 servings.

bran cereal

50g (2oz) high-fibre, no-sugar-added bran cereal

225ml (8fl oz) skimmed milk

Divide the cereal and milk between 2 bowls.

Makes 2 servings.

vegetable juice

350ml (12fl oz) low-sodium, no-sugar-added tomato juice

Divide between 2 glasses.

Makes 2 servings.

Total breakfast one serving: 340 calories, 28g protein, 49g carbohydrate, 10g fat (2g saturated), 29mg cholesterol, 1019mg sodium, 17g fibre

shiitake and swiss scramble

Shiitake mushrooms and sautéed onions form the base for these scrambled eggs.
Although originally from Japan and Korea, shiitakes are now available in most supermarkets.
● *If possible, buy ready-diced onion to save preparation time, or keep diced onion in*
your freezer.

shiitake and swiss scramble

2 teaspoons olive oil
110g (4oz) onion, diced
50g (2oz) shiitake mushrooms,
    sliced
2 eggs
4 egg whites
Salt and freshly ground black
    pepper to taste
25g (1oz) grated, reduced-fat
    Swiss or Gruyère cheese
2 slices low-carbohydrate
    wholemeal bread

Heat the oil in a medium-sized non-stick frying pan over a medium heat. Add the onion and mushrooms and sauté for 3 minutes. Whisk the eggs and egg whites together lightly and season with salt and pepper to taste. Add the eggs to the pan and scramble with the vegetables, about 1 minute. Sprinkle with the cheese, cover and allow to sit until the cheese melts, about 30 seconds. Toast the bread and place on 2 plates. Top each piece of toast with the scrambled eggs and serve immediately.
Makes 2 servings.

spiced oatmeal

110g (4oz) oatmeal
450ml (16fl oz) water
2g (¹⁄₁₆oz) artificial sweetener
    (optional)
½ teaspoon ground ginger
225ml (8fl oz) skimmed or semi-
    skimmed milk

To prepare in the microwave, combine the oatmeal and water in a microwave-safe bowl. Microwave on high for 4 minutes. Stir in the sweetener and ginger. Stir in the milk, divide between 2 bowls and serve warm.

  Alternatively, to prepare on the hob, combine the oatmeal and water in a small saucepan over a medium-high heat and bring to a boil. Reduce the heat to medium and cook for about 5 more minutes, stirring occasionally. Stir in the sweetener and ginger. Stir in the milk, divide between 2 bowls and serve warm.
Makes 2 servings.

> Total breakfast one serving: 446 calories,
> 33g protein, 49g carbohydrate, 17g fat (4g saturated),
> 223mg cholesterol, 377mg sodium, 7g fibre

helpful hint

● *Any type of mushroom*
can be substituted.

countdown

● *Make oatmeal.*
● *Make eggs.*

shopping list

TO BUY:
  1 small packet grated,
    reduced-fat Swiss or
    gruyère cheese
  1 small packet shiitake
    mushrooms (25g/1oz
    needed)
STAPLES:
  Diced onion
  Eggs
  Olive oil
  Oatmeal
  Skimmed milk
  Low-carbohydrate
    wholemeal bread
  Ground ginger
  Artificial sweetener
  Salt
  Black peppercorns

goat's cheese and palm hearts omelette

helpful hint

- *2 whole eggs and 4 egg whites can be used instead of egg substitute.*
- *Any type of goat's cheese can be used.*
- *Artichoke hearts can be used instead of palm hearts.*

countdown

- *Make oatmeal.*
- *Make omelette.*

shopping list

TO BUY:

1 packet herbed goat's cheese (50g/2oz needed)

1 large tin or jar of palm hearts (350g/12oz needed)

STAPLES:

Egg substitute

Olive oil spray

Artificial sweetener

Oatmeal

Skim milk

Wholemeal bread

Salt

Black peppercorns

goat's cheese and palm hearts omelette

Palm hearts are the tender heart of the Sabal palm tree. If you can find fresh palm hearts, they're really a treat. Otherwise, they are sold in cans or jars in the supermarket.

goat's cheese and palm hearts omelette

Olive oil spray
350g (12oz) sliced palm hearts
225ml (8fl oz) egg substitute
50g (2oz) herbed goat's cheese, broken into small pieces
Salt and freshly ground black pepper to taste
2 slices wholemeal bread

Set a medium-sized non-stick frying pan over a medium-high heat and spray with olive oil. Add the palm hearts. Combine the egg substitute with the goat's cheese. Pour into the pan, cover with a lid and cook for 3–4 minutes. Sprinkle with salt and pepper to taste. Cut the omelette in half and slide onto 2 plates with a spatula. Serve with toasted wholemeal bread.
Makes 2 servings.

oatmeal

110g (4oz) oatmeal
450ml (16fl oz) water
225ml (8fl oz) skimmed milk
2g (1/16oz) artificial sweetener, (optional)

To prepare in the microwave, combine the oatmeal and water in a microwave-safe bowl. Microwave on high for 4 minutes. Stir in the milk and sweetener, divide between 2 bowls and serve warm.

Alternatively, to prepare on the hob, combine the oatmeal and water in a small saucepan over a medium-high heat and bring to a boil. Reduce the heat to medium and cook for about 5 more minutes, stirring occasionally. Stir in the milk and artificial sweetener, divide between 2 bowls and serve warm.
Makes 2 servings.

Total breakfast one serving: 461 calories, 35g protein, 53g carbohydrate, 15g fat (7g saturated), 24mg cholesterol, 1166mg sodium, 11g fibre

cottage cheese and cucumber sandwich

This is a quick and simple breakfast to make. Be sure to read the label on the cottage cheese, making sure it is low-fat with no sugar added.

cottage cheese and cucumber sandwich

2 slices rye bread
Olive oil spray
225ml (8fl oz) low-fat cottage cheese
half a cucumber, sliced

Toast the bread. Spray with olive oil. Place the toast on 2 plates, spread each toast with cottage cheese and top with cucumber slices. Serve the remaining cucumber slices on the side.
Makes 2 servings.

yoghurt crunch

225ml (8fl oz) light fruit-flavoured yoghurt
50g (2oz) high-fibre, no-sugar-added bran cereal

Divide the yoghurt between 2 bowls. Sprinkle with the bran cereal and stir together.
Makes 2 servings.

> Total breakfast one serving: 285 calories, 24g protein, 51g carbohydrate, 6g fat (2g saturated), 13mg cholesterol, 651mg sodium, 17g fibre

helpful hint

- *Any type of wholemeal bread can be used.*

countdown

- *Make sandwich.*
- *Assemble cereal.*

shopping list

TO BUY:
  1 small pot light fruit-flavoured yoghurt
  1 small pot low-fat cottage cheese
  half a cucumber
STAPLES:
  Olive oil spray
  High-fibre, no-sugar-added bran cereal
  Rye bread

countdown

- Preheat grill.
- Prepare grapefruit.
- Make sandwich.
- Assemble cereal.

shopping list

TO BUY:

1 small packet reduced-fat
   cream cheese

110g (4oz) sliced lean smoked
   turkey breast

1 medium tomato

1 medium grapefruit

STAPLES:

Olive oil spray

Low-carbohydrate wholemeal
   bread

High-fibre, no-sugar-added
   bran cereal

Skimmed milk

Salt

Black peppercorns

warm turkey sandwich

Sliced smoked turkey, tomato and cream cheese on toast make a quick, 10-minute breakfast.

warm turkey sandwich

2 slices low-carbohydrate
   wholemeal bread

Olive oil spray

2 tablespoons reduced-fat cream
   cheese

110g (4oz) sliced lean smoked
   turkey breast

1 medium tomato, sliced

Salt and freshly ground black
   pepper to taste

Preheat the grill. Spray the bread with olive oil and toast until golden brown. Spread the toast with cream cheese and top with the turkey and tomato slices. Season with salt and pepper to taste. Serve on 2 plates.

Makes 2 servings.

grapefruit

1 medium grapefruit, halved

With a serrated knife, cut around the edge of the grapefruit to separate the flesh from the skin. Cut between the segments and serve on 2 plates.

Makes 2 servings.

bran cereal

50g (2oz) high-fibre, no-sugar-
   added bran cereal

225ml (8fl oz) skimmed milk

Divide the cereal between 2 bowls and add milk to each.

Makes 2 servings.

Total breakfast one serving: 338 calories, 29g protein, 53g carbohydrate, 9g fat (3g saturated), 53mg cholesterol, 411mg sodium, 17g fibre

egg-in-toast

We used to call it 'Hole-in-the-Middle'. Some call it 'Egg-in-the-Hole'. Regardless, it's an old American favourite. I remember my father making this for breakfast; my job was to tear the hole out of the bread. Somehow I never got the hole to be the same size as the egg, but it was still very delicious. Whether the egg neatly fits the hole or runs over the bread, this is a quick and easy and fun breakfast.

egg-in-toast

2 slices low-carbohydrate wholemeal bread
Olive oil spray
2 eggs
35g (1½oz) reduced-fat Swiss or Gruyère cheese, sliced
Salt and freshly ground black pepper to taste

Tear a hole in each slice of bread about 5cm (2in) in diameter. Heat a non-stick frying pan over a low heat and spray with olive oil. Add the bread and the cutout pieces to the pan. Cook until golden, about 2 minutes. Turn the bread and cutouts over and break one egg into each hole. Cook for 1 minute, turn over and place the cheese slices over the eggs. Season with salt and pepper to taste. Cover with a lid and cook for 2–3 minutes, or until the eggs have set to the desired consistency.
Makes 2 servings.

bran cereal

50g (2oz) high-fibre, no-sugar-added bran cereal
225ml (8fl oz) skimmed milk

Divide the cereal and milk between 2 bowls.
Makes 2 servings.

grapefruit

1 medium grapefruit, halved

With a serrated knife, cut around the edge of the grapefruit to separate the flesh from the skin. Cut between the segments and serve on 2 plates.
Makes 2 servings.

> Total breakfast one serving: 340 calories, 25g protein, 51g carbohydrate, 13g fat (4g saturated), 226mg cholesterol, 414mg sodium, 17g fibre

helpful hints

● *It doesn't matter if the egg spills over onto the bread or pan.*
● *To determine the weight of each slice of cheese, divide the packet weight by the number of slices.*
● *If you like your egg yolk firm, gently flip the bread and egg over before adding the cheese. Place the cheese on the top side.*

countdown

Prepare grapefruit.
Make egg.
Assemble cereal.

shopping list

TO BUY:
1 small packet sliced, reduced-fat Swiss or gruyère cheese (35g/1½oz needed)
1 grapefruit
STAPLES:
Olive oil spray
Eggs
High-fibre, no-sugar-added bran cereal
Skim milk
Low-carbohydrate wholemeal bread
Salt
Black peppercorns

frittata primavera

A frittata is an Italian omelette that is cooked slowly so that it becomes thick, more like a quiche than an omelette.

frittata primavera

225ml (8fl oz) egg substitute

50g (2oz) fresh purple basil leaves

Salt and freshly ground black pepper to taste

8 large spears asparagus or 16 thin (50g/2oz)

4 teaspoons olive oil

150g (5oz) yellow courgettes, sliced

110g (4oz) sliced red onion

225g (8oz) whole portobello mushrooms, sliced thinly

25g (1oz) grated, reduced-fat, mature Cheddar cheese

Combine the egg substitute and basil in a medium-sized bowl. Season with salt and pepper to taste. Cut or snap off the 2.5cm (1in) fibrous stem on the asparagus and discard. Slice the remaining asparagus into 2.5cm (1in) pieces. Heat the oil in a medium-sized non-stick frying pan over a medium-high heat and add the courgettes, onion, mushrooms and asparagus. Sauté for 5 minutes. Pour the egg mixture into the pan, and swirl around the vegetables. Sprinkle the frittata with cheese. Cover, reduce the heat to low and cook for 10 minutes more before serving.

Makes 2 servings.

bran cereal

50g (2oz) high-fibre, no-sugar-added bran cereal

225ml (8fl oz) skimmed milk

Divide the cereal and milk between 2 bowls.
Makes 2 servings.

Total breakfast one serving: 359 calories,
25g protein, 45g carbohydrate, 14g fat (3g saturated),
12mg cholesterol, 542mg sodium, 15g fibre

right carbs
lunches

layered crab salad

Layering sweet crabmeat with fresh vegetables and light vinaigrette dressing makes a delicious and colourful salad. It's perfect for a weekend lunch or entertaining. There is no cooking required, so this meal can be assembled in mere minutes. Cooked crabmeat is sold frozen or in tins. The meat should be white with a little pink colouring. There are many brands and qualities available. Try different ones to find one that suits your palate. This salad is also great for any type of leftover cooked seafood. ● Sherry wine vinegar has a very subtle flavour that perfectly complements the crab. ● The Italians like to cover sliced bread with leftover cheese or vegetables and heat it in a wood fire. The resulting crostini or 'little crusts' are used to garnish salads and starters. My version uses freshly grated Parmesan cheese.

layered crab salad

2 tablespoons sherry vinegar
4 teaspoons Dijon mustard
4 teaspoons olive oil
2 tablespoons water
110g (4oz) red onion, chopped
2 tablespoons fresh tarragon or
    2 teaspoons dried tarragon
Salt and freshly ground black
    pepper to taste
110g (4oz) cooked crabmeat
1 bag ready-to-eat mixed young
    salad leaves
half a cucumber, peeled and sliced
2 medium tomatoes, sliced

Whisk the sherry wine vinegar and mustard together in a medium-sized bowl. Whisk in the olive oil and water until smooth. Add the onion and tarragon, and season with salt and pepper to taste. Mix half the dressing with the crabmeat. Arrange the salad greens in the bottom of a glass salad bowl. Layer the cucumber slices on top. Drizzle the remaining dressing over the salad. Spoon the crabmeat over the cucumber. Arrange the sliced tomatoes around the edge of the bowl, sprinkle with salt and pepper to taste and serve.
Makes 2 servings.

One serving: 259 calories, 25g protein, 15g carbohydrate, 11g fat (1g saturated), 88mg cholesterol, 592mg sodium, 1g fibre

helpful hints

● Bottled, no-sugar-added oil and vinegar dressing can be used instead of the recipe provided. Add tarragon and onion to the bottled dressing.
● Buy good quality Parmesan cheese and grate it yourself. Freeze extra for quick use later – simply spoon out what you need and leave the rest frozen.
● Any type of salad leaves can be used.
● If using dried tarragon, make sure the herb is less than 6 months old.
● Red wine or balsamic vinegar can be used.

countdown

● Preheat grill.
● Make dressing.
● Make crab salad.
● Make crostini.

parmesan crostini

Olive oil spray
2 slices multi-grain bread
2 tablespoons freshly grated
*   Parmesan cheese*

Preheat the grill. Spray olive oil over the bread. Sprinkle with Parmesan cheese. Place under the grill about 15cm (6in) from the heat for 2–3 minutes, or until the cheese starts to melt. Serve with the salad.
Makes 2 servings.

One serving: 83 calories, 6g protein,
10g carbohydrate, 4g fat (1g saturated),
4mg cholesterol, 221mg sodium, 3g fibre

grapes and yoghurt

225ml (8fl oz) light fruit-flavoured
*   yoghurt*
30 grapes

Spoon the yoghurt into 2 dessert bowls and sprinkle with grapes.
Makes 2 servings.

One serving: 79 calories, 4g protein,
16g carbohydrate, 0g fat (0g saturated),
3mg cholesterol, 59mg sodium, 0g fibre

shopping list

TO BUY:
*   1 pot light fruit-flavoured*
*   yoghurt*
*   110g (4oz) cooked crabmeat*
*   (fresh, tinned or frozen)*
*   1 small bottle sherry wine*
*   vinegar*
*   1 small bunch fresh tarragon*
*   or 1 jar dried*
*   half a cucumber*
*   2 medium tomatoes*
*   1 bag ready-to-eat, young*
*   salad leaves*
*   1 small bunch grapes*
*   (30 needed)*
STAPLES:
*   Olive oil*
*   Olive oil spray*
*   Red onion*
*   Multi-grain bread*
*   Parmesan cheese*
*   Dijon mustard*
*   Salt*
*   Black peppercorns*

tomatoes stuffed with anchovies and capers

This recipe was given to me by a friend from Tuscany. It always reminds me of sitting on her terrace looking out on the rolling green hills and heavily laden olive trees. This light lunch can be made in minutes and enjoyed in your own backyard. ● Serve this lunch on the weekend or when you're having friends for lunch. ● Bruschetta is a Roman garlic bread. When testing the season's first pressing of olive oil, the Romans would taste it on a slice of bread that was sometimes rubbed with fresh garlic. If you like a lot of garlic, crush the garlic clove onto the bread instead of rubbing. ● A fresh strawberry smoothie completes this summery meal.

helpful hints

- *To save time, chop the parsley in the food processor.*
- *Try not to overprocess the filling: coarsely chop using the pulse button.*
- *Keep hard-boiled eggs on hand for a quick breakfast, snack or lunch.*
- *Frozen strawberries can be used for the smoothie. Make sure they are not packed in a sugar syrup.*

countdown

- *Hard boil the eggs.*
- *Assemble bruschetta.*
- *Make tomatoes.*
- *Toast bruschetta.*

tomatoes stuffed with anchovies and capers

6 eggs (only the whites are used)
2 ripe tomatoes, stemmed and halved crosswise
2 anchovy fillets, drained and rinsed
4 teaspoons capers, drained
2 tablespoons bread crumbs (wholemeal if possible)
2 tablespoons balsamic vinegar
25g (1oz) chopped fresh parsley, divided into 2 piles
4 teaspoons olive oil
Salt and freshly ground black pepper to taste

Place the eggs in a small saucepan and cover with cold water. Bring to a boil, then reduce the heat to a very gentle simmer. Cook for 12 minutes. Drain and rinse eggs under cold water. When cool enough to handle, peel the eggs, cut in half and remove and discard the yolks.

Hollow out the tomatoes with a spoon, reserving the pulp. Mash the anchovy fillets with a fork and place in the bowl of a food processor. Add the capers, tomato pulp and egg whites, then coarsely chop. If you don't have a food processor, chop by hand. In a small bowl, soak the bread crumbs in the vinegar. Set aside half of the parsley for garnish. Add the remaining parsley and egg white mixture to the bread crumbs. Stir in the olive oil and season with salt and pepper to taste. Combine well. Fill the tomatoes with the mixture, sprinkle with the reserved parsley and serve.
Makes 2 servings.

One serving: 173 calories, 16g protein, 8g carbohydrate, 10g fat (1g saturated), 0mg cholesterol, 489mg sodium, 0g fibre

garlic bruschetta

Olive oil spray
1 small garlic clove, halved
2 slices crusty country multi-grain
   bread

Spray the bread with olive oil and rub the cut side of the garlic on the bread. Toast the bread and serve with the tomatoes.
Makes 2 servings.

> One serving: 61 calories, 4g protein,
> 11g carbohydrate, 2g fat (0g saturated),
> 0mg cholesterol, 115mg sodium, 3g fibre

strawberry smoothie

3 good handfuls strawberries
225ml (8fl oz) light strawberry-
   flavoured yoghurt
2 teaspoons vanilla essence
2g (¹⁄₁₆oz) artificial sweetener
1¹⁄₂ pint glasses full of ice cubes

Place the strawberries, yoghurt, vanilla essence and sweetener in a blender. Blend until smooth. Add the ice cubes and blend until thick. Pour into 2 glasses.
Makes 2 servings.

> One serving: 96 calories, 5g protein,
> 18g carbohydrate, 0.5g fat (0g saturated),
> 3mg cholesterol, 59mg sodium, 2g fibre

shopping list

TO BUY:

   1 pot light strawberry-
      flavoured yoghurt
   1 small tin anchovies packed
      in olive oil
   1 small jar capers
   1 small container bread
      crumbs
   2 ripe tomatoes
   1 small bunch fresh parsley
   1 punnet fresh strawberries

STAPLES:

   Eggs
   Garlic
   Olive oil
   Olive oil spray
   Balsamic vinegar
   Multi-grain bread
   Vanilla essence
   Artificial sweetener
   Salt
   Black peppercorns

prawn caesar wrap

Caesar Salad, one of America's most popular salads, is said to have been created in 1924 in Tijuana, Mexico, by a restaurateur named Caesar Cardini. I don't think he ever dreamed that 70 years later, his combination of anchovies, garlic, lemon juice, croûtons and lettuce would be on nearly every restaurant menu in the United States.

helpful hints

● *1 tablespoon low-sugar (less than 0.5g per 2 tablespoons) Caesar salad dressing can be substituted for this homemade one.*
● *Buy peeled prawns.*
● *Any type of lettuce can be used.*
● *Buy good quality Parmesan cheese and grate it yourself. Freeze extra for quick use later – simply spoon out what you need and leave the rest frozen.*

countdown

● *Make dressing.*
● *Make wrap.*
● *Assemble yoghurt and pear.*

shopping list

TO BUY:
1 pot light fruit-flavoured yoghurt
225g (8oz) large raw prawns
1 small tin anchovies packed in olive oil
1 packet 30cm (12in) wholemeal tortillas
1 small head cos lettuce
1 lemon
2 medium pears
STAPLES:
Garlic
Olive oil
Worcestershire sauce
Parmesan cheese
Black peppercorns

prawn caesar wrap

8 anchovies, rinsed
2 small garlic cloves, crushed
2 tablespoons freshly squeezed lemon juice
4 teaspoons olive oil, divided
4 teaspoons Worcestershire sauce
225g (8oz) large raw prawns, peeled and deveined
2 x 32cm (12in) wholemeal tortillas
6 large cos lettuce leaves, torn into bite-sized pieces
2 tablespoons freshly grated Parmesan cheese
Freshly ground black pepper to taste

To make the dressing, put the anchovies, garlic, lemon juice, 2 teaspoons of the olive oil and the Worcestershire sauce in a food processor and blend thoroughly, or mix and mash together well by hand. Heat the remaining 2 teaspoons of olive oil in a small non-stick frying pan over a medium-high heat. Add the prawns and sauté for 2 minutes. Remove the pan from the heat, leaving the prawns in the pan to finish cooking.

Wrap the tortillas in kitchen paper and microwave on high for 20 seconds to soften. Remove from the microwave, discard the kitchen paper and place the tortillas on a work surface. Spread the dressing over each tortilla. Place lettuce evenly over the dressing and sprinkle with Parmesan cheese. Cut the prawns in half and place on the lettuce, making sure to add any juices from the pan. Season with black pepper to taste. Fold up the top and bottom edges of the tortilla, then roll up tightly to make a neat parcel. Slice in half and serve.

Makes 2 servings.

One serving: 333 calories, 33g protein, 18g carbohydrate, 15g fat (3g saturated), 178mg cholesterol, 1076mg sodium, 5g fibre

pears and yoghurt

225ml (8fl oz) light fruit-flavoured yoghurt
2 medium pears, cored and sliced

Spoon the yoghurt into 2 dessert bowls and top with the pear slices.

Makes 2 servings

One serving: 148 calories, 5g protein, 34g carbohydrate, 1g fat (0g saturated), 3mg cholesterol, 59mg sodium, 4g fibre

turkey-avocado pitta

Turkey, crunchy alfalfa sprouts and nutty avocado blend together for a fresh taste in this pitta sandwich. It's sometimes hard to find a ripe avocado, but you can ripen one quickly by removing the small stem and storing in a paper bag in a warm spot until soft to the touch.

turkey-avocado pitta

1 wholemeal pitta bread, halved

110g (4oz) sliced smoked turkey breast, cut into 1cm (½in) strips

Half a small ripe avocado, stoned, peeled and sliced

2 handfuls alfalfa sprouts, tops only

1 small tomato, sliced

1 tablespoon no-sugar-added oil and vinegar dressing

Grill or toast the pitta halves for 1 minute, or until the bread is warm. Place the turkey, avocado slices, alfalfa sprouts and tomato slices in the pockets of the pitta bread and spoon dressing over the turkey and vegetables before serving.

Makes 2 servings.

> **One serving:** 339 calories, 25g protein, 29g carbohydrate, 15g fat (3g saturated), 40mg cholesterol, 154mg sodium, 6g fibre

fresh berries yoghurt

225ml (8fl oz) light mixed berry-flavoured yoghurt

3 good handfuls fresh raspberries

Place the yoghurt in 2 small dessert dishes and sprinkle with the berries.

Makes 2 servings.

> **One serving:** 81 calories, 5g protein, 16g carbohydrate, 0.5g fat (0g saturated), 3mg cholesterol, 58mg sodium, 3g fibre

helpful hints

- *Any type of sprouts can be used.*
- *Any flavour of light yoghurt can be used.*

countdown

- *Preheat grill.*
- *Peel avocado.*
- *Make sandwich.*
- *Assemble yoghurt.*

shopping list

TO BUY:

1 pot light mixed berry-flavoured yoghurt

110g (4oz) sliced smoked turkey breast

1 small packet wholemeal pitta bread

1 small ripe avocado

1 punnet alfalfa sprouts

1 small tomato

1 small punnet fresh raspberries

STAPLES:

No-sugar-added oil and vinegar dressing

fresh salmon burgers

countdown

- Make salmon burgers.
- Assemble cantaloupe and yoghurt cup.

shopping list

TO BUY:

1 pot light fruit-flavoured
   yoghurt

175g (6oz) salmon fillet

1 small container wholemeal
   bread crumbs

1 tube no-salt-added tomato
   purée

1 small bunch spring onions
   (8 needed)

1 small tomato

1 small cantaloupe

STAPLES:

Eggs

Multi-grain bread

Mayonnaise made with olive
   or soya bean oil

Salt

Black peppercorns

My sons have given me a strong warning, 'Don't mess with my burgers.' The fact is that this all-American dish is changing. I've recently noticed salmon burgers on several menus and decided to create this quick lunch. The flavourful salmon meat requires very little fish for a rich-tasting burger. ● The salmon can be chopped in a food processor. However, it is very soft and takes only a few minutes to chop by hand if you don't have a food processor.

fresh salmon burgers

175g (6oz) salmon fillet

8 spring onions, sliced

25g (1oz) wholemeal bread
   crumbs

1 tablespoon no-salt-added
   tomato purée

2 egg whites

Salt and freshly ground black
   pepper to taste

2 tablespoons mayonnaise made
   with olive or soya bean oil

2 slices multi-grain bread

1 small tomato, sliced

Remove any fat or dark meat from the salmon. Cut the pink meat into 5cm (2in) cubes and chop in food processor or by hand. Add half the spring onions to the salmon along with the bread crumbs, tomato purée and egg whites. Season with salt and pepper to taste. Form into 2 burgers about 10cm (4in) in diameter and 1cm ($\frac{1}{2}$in) thick. Set a non-stick frying pan over a medium-high heat and brown the burgers on one side, about 1 minute. Reduce the heat to medium and cook for 3 minutes. Turn over, raise the heat to medium-high and cook for another 2 minutes. Meanwhile, mix the mayonnaise and remaining spring onions together in a small bowl. Season with salt and pepper to taste. Toast the bread. To serve, place the salmon burgers on the toasted bread and top with mayonnaise. Serve tomato slices alongside the salmon burger.

Makes 2 servings.

One serving: 350 calories, 31g protein, 19g carbohydrate, 17g fat (3g saturated), 65mg cholesterol, 1341mg sodium, 3g fibre

cantaloupe yoghurt

225ml (8fl oz) light fruit-flavoured
   yoghurt

1 cantaloupe, cubed

Spoon the yoghurt into 2 dessert bowls and top with the cantaloupe.

Makes 2 servings.

One serving: 127 calories, 6g protein, 27g carbohydrate, 1g fat (0g saturated), 3mg cholesterol, 77mg sodium, 3g fibre

chicken tostadas

Crisp tortillas, smooth beans, hot flavours and cool tomatoes make this recipe a favourite quick meal. A tostada is simply a crisp tortilla. Here it is topped with chicken and vegetables, but the variations are endless. ● To save washing the processor bowl during preparation, chop all of the vegetables first and then mash the beans. If you don't have a food processor, simply chop the vegetables by hand and mash the beans with a fork.

chicken tostadas

2 x 20.5cm (8in) wholemeal
    tortillas
Olive oil spray
2 tablespoons no-sugar-added oil
    and vinegar dressing
2 teaspoons ground cumin
2 medium-sized jalapeño peppers,
    seeded and sliced
110g (4oz) sliced roasted chicken
    breast, skinned cut into 1cm
    (½in) strips
110g (4oz) red onion, chopped
2 medium-sized garlic cloves,
    crushed
75g (3oz) tinned dark red kidney
    beans, rinsed and drained
4 tablespoons water
Salt and freshly ground black
    pepper to taste
175g (6oz) washed, ready-to-eat
    lettuce, shredded

Preheat the oven to 200°C/400°F/gas mark 6. Line a baking tray with foil. Place the tortillas on the tray and spray both sides of the tortillas with olive oil. Bake for 5 minutes in the oven. Remove from the oven, turn and bake for 5 more minutes.

Combine the dressing with 1 teaspoon cumin and 1 tablespoon chopped jalapeño and toss with the chicken.

If using a food processor, chop the onion and reserve 2 tablespoons for the garnish. Add the garlic and remaining jalapeños to the onion in the processor bowl. Add the beans, remaining teaspoon of ground cumin and water. Purée to a smooth paste. Season with salt and pepper to taste.

Spread the tortillas with the bean paste. Place the chicken on top of the beans and top with the lettuce. Sprinkle with the remaining chopped red onion and serve.

Makes 2 servings.

One serving: 332 calories, 25g protein, 33g carbohydrate, 14g fat (2g saturated), 48mg cholesterol, 402mg sodium, 1g fibre

coriander tomatoes

2 medium tomatoes, diced
4 tablespoons chopped fresh
    coriander leaves
Salt and freshly ground black
    pepper to taste

Combine the tomatoes and coriander and season with salt and pepper to taste. Serve with the tostadas.
Makes 2 servings.

One serving: 31 calories, 2g protein, 6g carbohydrate, 0g fat (0g saturated), 0mg cholesterol, 13mg sodium, 0g fibre

helpful hints
● Red onion is used for the beans and as a garnish. Chop it all at one time and divide accordingly.
● For optimum flavour, make sure the ground cumin is less than 6 months old.

countdown
● Preheat oven to 200°C/400°F/gas mark 6.
● Bake tortilla.
● Prepare tomatoes.

shopping list
TO BUY:
110g (4oz) sliced roasted chicken breast
1 packet 20.5cm (8in) wholemeal tortillas
1 tin dark red kidney beans (110g/4oz needed)
2 medium tomatoes
1 small bunch coriander
2 medium jalapeño peppers
1 bag washed, ready-to-eat shredded lettuce
STAPLES:
Red onion
Garlic
Olive oil spray
No-sugar-added oil and vinegar dressing
Ground cumin
Salt
Black peppercorns

caribbean prawn salad

helpful hint

- *Any type of bean, such as haricot or kidney beans can be used.*

countdown

- *Make yoghurt cup.*
- *Make prawn salad.*

shopping list

TO BUY:

1 pot light tropical fruit-flavoured yoghurt

225g (8oz) cooked prawns

1 tin black beans (225g/8oz needed)

1 medium-sized green pepper

1 small tomato

1 small head lettuce

1 mango

2 limes

STAPLES:

Red onion

Celery

Mayonnaise made with olive or soya bean oil

Hot pepper sauce

Salt

Black peppercorns

Emerald waters and crystal-clear blue skies create the backdrop for this tropical lunch. Prawns, hot pepper sauce and black beans are staples throughout the Caribbean. ● *Based on total worldwide consumption, mangoes are second in popularity only to bananas. They can be found in many supermarkets. They can be messy to cube, but I offer an easy method below.*

caribbean prawn salad

2 tablespoons mayonnaise made with olive or soya bean oil

2 tablespoons warm water

Several drops hot pepper sauce

2 tablespoons freshly squeezed lime juice

75g (3oz) tinned black beans, rinsed and drained

1 medium-sized green pepper, diced

2 celery stalks, diced

110g (4oz) red onion, diced

1 small tomato, diced

225g (8oz) cooked prawns, cubed

Salt and freshly ground black pepper to taste

Several lettuce leaves, washed and torn into bite-sized pieces

Combine the mayonnaise, water, hot pepper sauce and lime juice in a medium-sized bowl. Add the black beans, green pepper, celery, onion, tomato and prawns. Toss well. Season with salt and pepper to taste. Place the lettuce leaves on a plate and spoon the prawn salad on top of the lettuce to serve.

Makes 2 servings.

One serving: 346 calories, 31g protein, 27g carbohydrate, 14g fat (2g saturated), 178mg cholesterol, 341mg sodium, 3g fibre

mango yoghurt

1 mango

125ml (4fl oz) light tropical fruit-flavoured yoghurt

Slice off each side of the mango as close to the stone as possible. Take the mango half in your hand, skin- side down. Score the fruit in a cross-hatch pattern through to the skin. Bend the skin backwards so that the cubes pop up like a porcupine. Slice the cubes off the skin. Score and slice any fruit left on the stone.

Divide the yoghurt between 2 cups and top with the mango cubes.

Makes 2 servings.

One serving: 117 calories, 5g protein, 26g carbohydrate, 0.3g fat (0g saturated), 3mg cholesterol, 60mg sodium, 1g fibre

ham and mushroom pitta pizza

This dish is covered with onion, mushrooms, peppers and ham – and it can be made faster than ordering out pizza. ● A secret to cooking the pizza fast is to preheat the baking tray.

ham and mushroom pitta pizza

Olive oil spray
1 medium-sized green pepper, sliced
4 slices red onion
2 small portobello mushrooms, sliced
1 wholemeal pitta bread
1 medium tomato sliced
110g (4oz) sliced lean ham, torn into bite-sized pieces
110g (4oz) reduced-fat mozzarella cheese, sliced

Preheat the grill. Line a baking tray with foil and place under the grill. Set a non-stick frying pan over a medium-high heat and spray with olive oil. Add the pepper, onion and mushrooms and sauté for 5 minutes. Slice open the pitta bread so that you have 2 round pizza bases. Remove the baking tray from the grill and place the pitta halves on the foil, cut-side up. Spray the pitta bread with olive oil and place the tomato slices on top. Spoon the pepper mixture over the tomatoes and top with the ham and cheese. Grill for 3 minutes, or until the cheese is bubbly. Serve hot. Makes 2 servings.

One serving: 354 calories, 36g protein, 35g carbohydrate, 8g fat (3g saturated), 35mg cholesterol, 1009mg sodium, 5g fibre

fennel salad

1 small fennel bulb, sliced
1 tablespoon no-sugar-added oil and vinegar dressing
Salt and freshly ground black pepper to taste

Remove the stem and fern-like leaves from the fennel. Wash and reserve the leaves. Thinly slice the fennel. Toss the fennel with the dressing. Snip small pieces from the fennel leaves with scissors (about 4 tablespoons) and sprinkle on top as a garnish. Season with salt and pepper to taste. Serve with the pizza. Makes 2 servings.

One serving: 53 calories, 0g protein, 0g carbohydrate, 4g fat (1g saturated), 0mg cholesterol, 38mg sodium, 0g fibre

banana

1 medium banana

Slice the banana in half and serve. Makes 2 servings.

One serving: 70 calories, 1g protein, 18g carbohydrate, 0.5g fat (0g saturated), 0mg cholesterol, 1mg sodium, 1g fibre

helpful hint

● Any type of washed, ready-to-eat salad can be substituted for the fennel salad.
● The fennel bulb can be sliced with a mandolin or in a food processor fitted with a thin-slicing blade.

countdown

● Preheat grill.
● Prepare all ingredients.
● Make pizza.
● While pizza bakes, make salad.

shopping list

TO BUY:
1 ball reduced-fat mozzarella cheese (110g/4oz needed)
110g (4oz) lean ham
1 small packet wholemeal pitta bread
1 medium-sized green pepper
2 portobello mushrooms (50g/2oz needed)
1 medium tomato
1 small fennel bulb
1 medium banana
STAPLES:
Olive oil spray
Red onion
No-sugar-added oil and vinegar dressing
Salt
Black peppercorns

fresh tuna salad

A salad made from fresh tuna rather than tinned is a treat. In fact, if you have any leftover cooked fish, it can be used in this salad. ● *Fish seasoning is a mixture of herbs and spices that is added to water to flavour fish. It usually includes bay leaves, peppercorns, mustard seeds, allspice, cloves and dried ginger (see hints).*

fresh tuna salad

175g (6oz) fresh tuna
2 teaspoons fish seasoning
   (optional)
2 celery stalks, diced
2 medium tomatoes, chopped
110g (4oz) chopped yellow onion
10g (1/2oz) chopped fresh parsley
2 tablespoons mayonnaise made
   with olive or soya bean oil
Salt and freshly ground black
   pepper to taste
175g (6oz) washed, ready-to-eat
   mixed salad leaves
2 slices rye bread
Olive oil spray

Place the tuna in a medium saucepan and cover with cold water. Add the fish seasoning. Bring to a simmer and gently cook until the tuna turns opaque or white, about 3–5 minutes. Reserve 2 tablespoons of the poaching liquid. Drain the fish and pat dry with kitchen paper. Gently combine the celery, tomatoes, onion, parsley, mayonnaise and poaching liquid in a medium-sized bowl. Flake in the tuna. Season with salt and pepper to taste and stir to incorporate the tuna and seasoning. Place the salad leaves on 2 plates and top with the tuna salad. Spray the bread with olive oil and toast. Serve with the salad.
Makes 2 servings.

One serving: 339 calories, 28g protein, 23g carbohydrate, 18g fat (3g saturated), 37mg cholesterol, 318mg sodium, 4g fibre

fresh peach yoghurt

225ml (8fl oz) light fruit-flavoured
   yoghurt
2 medium peaches, stoned and
   sliced

Divide the yoghurt between 2 dessert bowls and top with the peach slices.
Makes 2 servings.

One serving: 87 calories, 5g protein, 18g carbohydrate, 0g fat (0g saturated), 3mg cholesterol, 58mg sodium, 1g fibre

spinach, mushroom and gammon salad

Baby spinach leaves and mushrooms topped with gammon is a flavourful lunchtime salad. This version takes only minutes to make. ● Gammon can vary considerably in fat content, so look for the leanest gammon available. ● A warm dessert of pineapple and pine nuts rounds off this delightfully crunchy meal.

spinach, mushroom and gammon salad

175g (6oz) sliced lean gammon, cut into thin strips

150g (5oz) cooked chickpeas

2 tablespoons no-sugar-added oil and vinegar dressing

8 spring onions, sliced

Salt and freshly ground black pepper to taste

110g (4oz) button mushrooms, sliced

350g (12oz) washed, ready-to-eat fresh spinach, torn into bite-sized pieces

50g (2oz) fresh bean sprouts, rinsed and drained

Place the gammon and chickpeas on a foil-lined baking tray and grill for 10 minutes, or until crisp. Combine the dressing and spring onions together in a medium-sized bowl. Season with salt and pepper to taste. Add mushrooms, spinach and sprouts. Toss well. Sprinkle with the gammon strips and chickpeas and serve.
Makes 2 servings.

One serving: 387 calories, 29g protein, 35g carbohydrate, 15g fat (3g saturated), 40mg cholesterol, 911mg sodium, 9g fibre

pineapple and toasted pine nuts

2 tablespoons pine nuts

150g (5oz) fresh pineapple cubes

Place the pine nuts on a foil-lined tray under the grill for 1 minute. Toss the pineapple and pine nuts together and divide between 2 dessert bowls.
Makes 2 servings.

One serving: 72 calories, 0.5g protein, 10g carbohydrate, 0.5g fat (0g saturated), 0mg cholesterol, 1mg sodium, 1g fibre

helpful hints

● The pine nuts can be toasted at the same time as the gammon and chickpeas. Watch them carefully, as they burn easily.

● To clean whole mushrooms, wipe them gently with damp kitchen paper.

● Buy fresh pineapple cubes in the fruit and veg section of the supermarket.

countdown

● Preheat grill.
● Cook gammon.
● Toast pine nuts.
● Make salad.
● Toss pineapple and pine nuts together.

shopping list

TO BUY:
175g (6oz) sliced lean gammon
1 tin chickpeas (150g/5oz needed)
1 small packet pine nuts
1 small bunch spring onions (8 needed)
1 small packet button mushrooms (110g/4oz needed)
1 bag washed, ready-to-eat fresh spinach
1 packet fresh bean sprouts
1 small packet fresh pineapple cubes
STAPLES:
No-sugar-added oil and vinegar dressing
Salt
Black peppercorns

turkey and asparagus penne salad

This turkey, asparagus, tomato and basil penne salad can be assembled in the time it takes to boil water and cook the penne. My first experience with wholemeal pasta was a surprise. It has a nutty flavour, very good texture and can be used like regular pasta.

turkey and asparagus penne salad

50g (2oz) wholemeal penne or macaroni

110g (4oz) asparagus

75g (3oz) sliced carrots

1 medium tomato, cut into 2.5cm (1in) cubes

110g (4oz) sliced smoked turkey breast

25g (1oz) fresh basil, snipped with scissors

3 tablespoons no-sugar-added oil and vinegar dressing

Salt and freshly ground black pepper to taste

Bring a large saucepan filled with water to the boil. Add the pasta and cook for 10 minutes, or according to the packet's instructions. Do not overcook. While the pasta is cooking, cut or snap off the 2.5cm (1in) fibrous stem on the asparagus and discard. Slice the remaining asparagus into 2.5cm (1in) pieces. Add the asparagus and carrots for the last 2 minutes of cooking time. Drain. Place the pasta, asparagus, carrots, tomato, turkey and basil in a bowl. Add the dressing and toss well. Season with salt and pepper if needed and serve warm.
Makes 2 servings.

One serving: 334 calories, 23g protein, 26g carbohydrate, 15g fat (3g saturated), 40mg cholesterol, 170mg sodium, 5g fibre

clementine and orange yoghurt

225ml (8fl oz) light orange-flavoured yoghurt

2 medium clementines, peeled and segmented

Divide the yoghurt into 2 dessert bowls and top with clementine slices.
Makes 2 servings.

One serving: 87 calories, 5g protein, 18g carbohydrate, 0.2g fat (0g saturated), 3mg cholesterol, 59mg sodium, 0g fibre

waldorf salad and roast beef sandwich

Salad greens with crisp apples and nuts were first served at the Waldorf Astoria Hotel in Manhattan in 1893 and has been a standard on menus ever since. Add an open-faced roast beef sandwich to the spread and enjoy an all-American lunch.

waldorf salad

1 tablespoon mayonnaise made with olive or soya bean oil

1 tablespoon freshly squeezed lemon juice (about ½ lemon)

Salt and freshly ground black pepper to taste

4 pecan halves, broken into pieces (1 tablespoon)

2 celery stalks, sliced

1 small red apple, cored and cut into 1cm (½ in) cubes

Several cos lettuce leaves, washed and dried

Combine the mayonnaise and lemon juice in a medium-sized bowl. Season with salt and pepper to taste. Toast the pecans under the grill for 1 minute, or until brown, to bring out their flavour (optional). Be careful: they burn easily. Toss the celery, apple and pecans in the mayonnaise mixture. Place the lettuce leaves on 2 plates and spoon the salad onto the leaves to serve.
Makes 2 servings.

> One serving: 151 calories, 2g protein, 16g carbohydrate, 10g fat (1g saturated), 3mg cholesterol, 116mg sodium, 4g fibre

roast beef sandwich

2 slices rye bread

1 tablespoon Dijon mustard

110g (4oz) sliced lean roast beef, sliced

1 small tomato, sliced

Spread the bread with mustard. Divide the roast beef between each slice of bread. Top with the tomato slices. Serve any extra tomato slices on the side.
Makes 2 servings.

> One serving: 179 calories, 22g protein, 13g carbohydrate, 6g fat (2g saturated), 46mg cholesterol, 337mg sodium, 3g fibre

yoghurt

225ml (8fl oz) light fruit-flavoured yoghurt

Divide the yoghurt between 2 dessert bowls.
Makes 2 servings.

> One serving: 50 calories, 4g protein, 9g carbohydrate, 0g fat (0g saturated), 51mg cholesterol, 511mg sodium, 6g fibre

helpful hints

● *Any type of lettuce can be used.*

● *Toasting pecans can be tricky, as they burn quickly. Watch them carefully.*

countdown

● *Make salad.*
● *Make sandwich.*
● *Assemble yoghurt.*

shopping list

TO BUY:

1 pot light fruit-flavoured yoghurt

110g (4oz) sliced lean roast beef

1 small packet pecan halves (10g/½oz needed)

1 small tomato

1 small head cos lettuce

1 lemon

1 small red apple

STAPLES:

Celery

Mayonnaise made with olive or soya bean oil

Dijon mustard

Rye bread

Salt

Black peppercorns

fish and cheese on toast

helpful hints

- *Any type of firm, non-oily white fish can be used, for example turbot, halibut or monkfish.*
- *To determine the weight of each slice of cheese, divide the packet weight by the number of slices.*

countdown

- *Make tomato tapenade.*
- *Make fish.*

shopping list

TO BUY:

1 pot light vanilla-flavoured yoghurt

1 small packet sliced, reduced-fat Cheddar cheese (35g/1½oz needed)

175g (6oz) fish fillet

1 small bottle capers

1 small jar or tin stoned green olives

1 medium tomato

2 medium oranges

STAPLES:

Garlic

Red onion

Olive oil

Balsamic vinegar

Wholemeal bread

Salt

Black peppercorns

This dish of fresh fish sautéed with onions and served over cheese on toast reminds me of the lunches we have while sitting on the docks and watching the boats come in with their fresh catch. ● A tapenade is a thick paste usually made from capers, olives, oil and vinegar. It is a great hors d'oeuvre or topping, in this case, to dress fresh sliced tomatoes.

fish and cheese on toast

175g (6oz) fish fillet

2 teaspoons olive oil

Salt and freshly ground black pepper to taste

110g (4oz) red onion, diced

2 slices wholemeal bread2 slices reduced-fat Cheddar cheese (35g/1½oz)

Rinse the fillet and pat dry with kitchen paper. Heat the oil in a small non-stick frying pan over a medium-high heat. Add the fillet and sauté for 5 minutes. Turn and season the cooked side. Add the onion to the pan and sauté for 3 more minutes. Toast the bread on one side, turn, cover with cheese and return to the grill until the cheese melts. Divide the fish in half, place on top of the melted cheese and spoon the onion over the fillet to serve.

Makes 2 servings.

One serving: 249 calories, 26g protein, 13g carbohydrate, 11g fat (4g saturated), 46mg cholesterol, 341mg sodium, 3g fibre

tomato tapenade salad

2 medium-sized garlic cloves, crushed

2 tablespoons drained capers

4 stoned green olives

2 teaspoons balsamic vinegar

1 medium tomato, sliced

Salt and freshly ground black pepper to taste

Place garlic, capers, olives and balsamic vinegar in a food processor and purée. Alternatively, finely chop by hand. Divide the tomato slices between 2 plates. Sprinkle with salt and pepper to taste and spoon the tapenade on top. Serve at room temperature.

Makes 2 servings.

One serving: 27 calories, 1g protein, 4g carbohydrate, 1g fat (0g saturated), 0mg cholesterol, 410mg sodium, 0g fibre

orange-vanilla yoghurt

2 medium-sized oranges

225ml (8fl oz) light vanilla-flavoured yoghurt

Peel and segment the oranges. Divide the yoghurt between 2 dessert bowls and top with the orange segments.

One serving: 174 calories, 6g protein, 39g carbohydrate, 0.5g fat (0g saturated), 3mg cholesterol, 0mg sodium, 6g fibre

chicken sandwich with sun-dried tomato sauce

Sun-dried tomatoes and capers make a great sauce for chicken breasts. The chicken can be sautéed in minutes in garlic and lemon juice, or buy roasted chicken to save time. ● People often ask me what a caper is. Capers are small, unopened flowers from a bush that grows in the Mediterranean region. Capers are picked, dried and pickled in a vinegar brine. There are many types of capers in the supermarket. They vary from the small, nonpareil type from southern France to larger versions. The flavour depends largely on the brining and pickling process. Buy a good-quality, well-known brand for the best results.

chicken sandwich with sun-dried tomato sauce

2 x 75g (3oz) boneless, skinless chicken breasts

2 teaspoons freshly squeezed lemon juice (½ small lemon)

4 medium-sized garlic cloves, crushed

¼ teaspoon freshly ground black pepper

2 slices multi-grain bread

2 tablespoons sun-dried tomatoes, drained and diced

3 tablespoons capers, drained

2 tablespoons mayonnaise made with olive or soya bean oil

Several leaves red-leaf lettuce

Remove any visible fat from the chicken and pound it flat to about ½cm (¼in) with a meat mallet or the bottom of a sturdy frying pan. Combine the lemon juice, garlic and black pepper in a small bowl. Set a medium-sized non-stick frying pan over a medium-high heat. Add the lemon mixture and chicken. Cook for 3 minutes. Turn and cook for 3 more minutes. Toast the bread. Combine the sun-dried tomatoes and capers with the mayonnaise. (Use the same bowl as for the lemon mixture.) Place the bread on 2 plates, cover with lettuce, top with chicken and spread with sauce to serve. *Makes 2 servings.*

One serving: 327 calories, 32g protein, 16g carbohydrate, 17g fat (2g saturated), 77mg cholesterol, 596mg sodium, 4g fibre

apple yoghurt

225ml (8fl oz) light fruit-flavoured yoghurt

2 apples, cored and sliced

Divide the yoghurt between 2 bowls and top with the apple slices.

One serving: 131 calories, 4g protein, 30g carbohydrate, 0.5g fat (0g saturated), 3mg cholesterol, 58mg sodium, 4g fibre

helpful hint

● The sauce can be made several days ahead and refrigerated.

countdown

● Make chicken.
● Assemble dessert.

shopping list

TO BUY:

1 pot light fruit-flavoured yoghurt

2 x 75g (3oz) boneless, skinless chicken breasts

1 small jar sun-dried tomatoes in olive oil

1 small jar capers

1 small loaf multi-grain bread

1 small head red-leaf lettuce

1 lemon

2 apples

STAPLES:

Garlic

Mayonnaise made with olive or soya bean oil

Salt

Black peppercorns

right carbs

dinners

japanese beef sukiyaki

This is a fun beef dish that's cooked at the table with an electric frying pan or wok. Alternatively, you can cook the entire meal in the kitchen and bring it to the table. The recipe for beef sukiyaki is for two servings, but can easily be doubled or tripled.

japanese beef sukiyaki

50g (2oz) vermicelli or thin wholemeal spaghetti

50ml (2fl oz) fat-free, low-sodium chicken stock

50ml (2fl oz) low-sodium soy sauce

125ml (4fl oz) dry sherry

2g (1/16oz) artificial sweetener

4 teaspoons sesame oil

225g (8oz) yellow onion, sliced

4 celery stalks, sliced

175g (6oz) beef sirloin, cut into strips about 10cm (4in) long and 2.5cm (1in) wide

110g (4oz) mushrooms, sliced

150g (5oz) washed, ready-to-eat fresh spinach

175g (6oz) sliced water chestnuts drained

8 spring onions, sliced

Freshly ground black pepper to taste

Bring a large saucepan filled with water to a boil. When the water boils, add the noodles and boil for 5 minutes, or according to the packet's instructions. Do not overcook. Drain and divide between 2 plates.

Combine the chicken stock, soy sauce, sherry and sweetener in a small bowl. Make sure all ingredients are prepared and ready for stir-frying. Heat the sesame oil in non-stick frying pan or wok. Add the onion and celery and cook for 3 minutes. Add the beef and cook for 1 minute, tossing constantly. Add half of the sauce and stir. Add the mushrooms and cook for 30 seconds. Add the spinach, water chestnuts and spring onions and cook for 1 minute. Add the remaining sauce and cook for 30 seconds more, continuing to stir. Season with black pepper to taste. Remove immediately from the pan and serve over the noodles. Spoon the sauce on top.
Makes 2 servings.

One serving: 666 calories, 46g protein, 68g carbohydrate, 18g fat (6g saturated), 76mg cholesterol, 1604mg sodium, 14g fibre

fresh peaches in kirsch

2 medium peaches, stoned and sliced

2 tablespoons kirsch

Divide the peach slices between 2 dessert bowls and sprinkle with kirsch.
Makes 2 servings.

One serving: 69 calories, 1g protein, 10g carbohydrate, 0g fat (0g saturated), 0mg cholesterol, 0mg sodium, 1g fibre

helpful hints

● *Any type of liqueur or brandy can be substituted for the kirsch*

● *To keep from having to look back at the recipe as you stir-fry the ingredients, line them up on a chopping board or plate in the order of use so you know which ingredient comes next.*

countdown

● *Cook noodles.*
● *Prepare remaining ingredients.*
● *Bring to table and cook.*

shopping list

TO BUY:

175g (6oz) beef sirloin

1 tin sliced water chestnuts

1 bottle sesame oil

1 small packet wholemeal vermicelli or thin spaghetti (50g/2oz needed)

1 small bottle dry sherry

1 small bottle kirsch

1 packet sliced mushrooms (110g/4oz needed)

1 bunch spring onions (8 needed)

1 bag washed, ready-to-eat fresh spinach (150g/5oz needed)

2 medium peaches

STAPLES:

Celery

Yellow onion

Fat-free, low-sodium chicken stock

Low-sodium soy sauce

Artificial sweetener

Black peppercorns

aromatic poached sole

The ingredients are folded in a piece of foil. The natural juices are sealed in as the fish steams, and a burst of aroma escapes when you open the foil parcel. You can assemble the parcel about an hour in advance and then place it in the oven when needed. ● *There's a large variety of flavoured or infused olive oils available. Using them is an easy way to add flavour to a dish.*

helpful hints

● *Use snapper or bream instead of sole if you prefer.*
● *If possible, buy diced sun-dried tomatoes to save the time spent dicing whole ones.*
● *Olive oil with a small crushed garlic clove works fine as a substitute for garlic-infused oil.*
● *For optimum flavour, make sure the dried thyme is less than 6 months old.*
● *Fat-free, low-sodium chicken stock can be substituted for the dry white wine.*

countdown

● *Preheat grill.*
● *Make fish.*
● *While fish cooks, make couscous.*

shopping list

TO BUY:
  2 x 150g (5oz) thin fish fillet
  1 jar diced sun-dried tomatoes
  1 small bottle dry white wine (if you do not have chicken stock)
  1 packet couscous
  1 bottle garlic-infused olive oil
  1 small packet sliced mushrooms, (75g/3oz needed)
  225g (8oz) courgettes
  1 small bunch grapes
STAPLES:
  Dried thyme
  Foil
  Salt
  Black peppercorns

aromatic poached sole

2 x 150g (5oz) fillets of sole, skinned
2 x 2.5cm (10in) squares foil
Salt and freshly ground black pepper to taste
75g (3oz) sliced mushrooms
75g (3oz) diced and drained sun-dried tomatoes
½ teaspoon dried thyme
50ml (2fl oz) dry white wine or fat-free, low-sodium chicken stock

Preheat the grill. Line a baking tray with foil and place under the grill about 12.5cm (5in) from the heat. Centre the fish on the foil squares. Season with salt and pepper. Spread the mushrooms and sun-dried tomatoes over the fish. Sprinkle with the thyme and pour the wine or chicken stock on top. Fold the edges of foil together, sealing tightly to prevent them from leaking. Place the parcels on the baking tray and grill for 15 minutes. Serve the fish in the pouch or remove to plates and spoon the sauce and vegetables on top.
Makes 2 servings.

One serving: 213 calories, 31g protein, 6g carbohydrate, 6g fat (0g saturated), 52mg cholesterol, 169mg sodium, 2g fibre

garlic-courgette couscous

225ml (8fl oz) water
225g (8oz) courgettes, sliced
110g (4oz) couscous
4 teaspoons garlic-infused olive oil
Salt and freshly ground black pepper to taste

Combine the water and courgette in a medium saucepan, and bring to the boil over a high heat. Remove from the heat, add the couscous, cover and set aside for 5 minutes. Add the infused oil and toss with a fork. Season to taste and serve.
Makes 2 servings.

One serving: 263 calories, 8g protein, 38g carbohydrate, 10g fat (1g saturated), 0mg cholesterol, 8mg sodium, 2g fibre

grapes

30 grapes

Divide the grapes between 2 dessert plates.
Makes 2 servings.

One serving: 58 calories, 1g protein, 16g carbohydrate, 0g fat (0g saturated), 0mg cholesterol, 2mg sodium, 0g fibre

ham and mushroom pitta pizza **p167**

chicken sandwich with sun-dried tomato sauce   p173

chicken with parmesan and tomato sauce

This quick dinner takes only 20 minutes to make. The pasta and broccoli are cooked in the same saucepan to save washing an extra pan.

chicken with parmesan and tomato sauce

Olive oil spray

225g (8oz) boneless, skinless chicken breast, visible fat removed

Salt and freshly ground pepper to taste

125ml (4fl oz) low-sugar, low-fat tomato sauce for pasta

2 tablespoons freshly grated Parmesan cheese

Set a medium-sized non-stick frying pan over a medium-high heat. Spray with olive oil and brown the chicken for 2 minutes on each side. Season each cooked side with salt and pepper to taste. Add the pasta sauce and simmer for 4 minutes. Sprinkle with Parmesan cheese, cover with a lid and set aside for 1 minute. Divide between 2 plates and serve with the pasta and broccoli.

Makes 2 servings.

One serving: 248 calories, 39g protein, 4g carbohydrate, 9g fat (3g saturated), 100mg cholesterol, 390mg sodium, 1g fibre

pasta and broccoli

50g (2oz) wholemeal spaghetti

110g (4oz) broccoli florets

2 teaspoons olive oil

Salt and freshly ground black pepper to taste

Bring a large pan of water to the boil and add the pasta. Cook for 5 minutes, add the broccoli and continue to cook for 4 minutes. Drain and toss with the olive oil. Season with salt and pepper to taste.

Makes 2 servings.

One serving: 206 calories, 9g protein, 30g carbohydrate, 6g fat (1g saturated), 0mg cholesterol, 28mg sodium, 6g fibre

helpful hints

● *Buy good quality Parmesan cheese and grate it yourself. Freeze extra for quick use later – simply spoon out what you need and leave the rest frozen.*

● *When draining pasta, leave a little water on the pasta for added sauce.*

● *If pressed for time, omit the poached spiced pears and serve 1 medium pear per person.*

countdown

● *Place water for pasta on the hob to boil.*

● *Make poached spiced pears.*

● *Make pasta and broccoli.*

● *Make chicken.*

shopping list

TO BUY:

  225g (8oz) boneless, skinless
    chicken breast
  1 jar whole cloves
  1 small bottle low-sugar, low-
    fat, tomato pasta sauce
    (110g/4oz needed)
  1 small packet wholemeal
    spaghetti (50g/2oz needed)
  1 small bag frozen sweetcorn
  1 small packet broccoli florets
    (110g/4oz needed)
  1 bag washed, ready-to-eat,
    Italian-style salad leaves
  1 small bunch fresh mint
  2 ripe pears
  1 lemon
STAPLES:
  Olive oil spray
  Olive oil
  No-sugar-added salad
    dressing
  Parmesan cheese
  Artificial sweetener
  Salt
  Black peppercorns

chicken with parmesan and tomato sauce continued

italian-style salad

350g (12oz) washed, ready-to-eat,
  Italian-style salad leaves
175g (6oz) frozen sweetcorn
2 tablespoons no-sugar-added
  salad dressing

Toss the salad and corn with the dressing.
Makes 2 servings.

> One serving: 151 calories, 3g protein,
> 19g carbohydrate, 9g fat (1g saturated),
> 0mg cholesterol, 85mg sodium, 2g fibre

poached spiced pears

450ml (16fl oz) water
2g (¹/₁₆oz) artificial sweetener
8 whole cloves
8 strips lemon peel from 1 lemon
2 ripe pears
2 sprigs fresh mint

Place the water, sweetener, cloves and lemon peel in a medium-sized saucepan. Peel the pears over the pan to catch the juice. Core and slice the pears. Add the pear slices to the saucepan. Bring to a simmer and poach gently for 10 minutes. Remove the pear slices and arrange in a circle on 2 dessert plates. Place a sprig of mint in the centre of each plate.
Makes 2 servings.

> One serving: 98 calories, 1g protein,
> 26g carbohydrate, 1g fat (0g saturated),
> 0mg cholesterol, 1mg sodium, 4g fibre

cioppino (seafood stew)

Cioppino is a 20-minute, one-pot meal that is great in winter or summer. Italian immigrants are credited with bringing this soup – a hearty combination of seafood and vegetables – to San Francisco.

cioppino

225g (8oz) fresh sea scallops

175g (6oz) fish fillet

3 teaspoons olive oil

Salt and freshly ground black pepper to taste

225g (8oz) red onion, sliced

2 medium-sized green peppers, sliced

5 medium-sized garlic cloves, crushed

110g (4oz) unpeeled red potatoes, washed, halved and sliced

450ml (16fl oz) low-sodium, no-sugar-added tinned whole tomatoes (including juice)

450ml (16fl oz) bottled clam juice

¼ teaspoon red pepper flakes

2 tablespoons balsamic vinegar

25g (1oz) chopped fresh basil

2 slices multi-grain bread

Olive oil spray

Wash the scallops and fish and pat dry with kitchen paper. Cut the fish into 2.5cm (1in) pieces about the same size as the scallops. Heat the olive oil in a medium-sized non-stick frying pan over a high heat. Add the fish and scallops and sauté for 2 minutes. Remove to a large soup bowl and season with salt and pepper to taste. In the same frying pan and sauté the onion, pepper and 4 garlic cloves over a high heat for 3 minutes. Add the potatoes, tomatoes, clam juice and red pepper flakes, breaking up the whole tomatoes with a spoon. Bring to a simmer, cover and simmer for 15 minutes. Add the balsamic vinegar and season with salt and pepper to taste. Spoon the mixture over the fish and sprinkle with the basil.

Spray the bread with olive oil. Cut the remaining garlic clove in half and rub the bread with the cut sides of the garlic. Toast beneath the grill and serve with the cioppino.
Makes 2 servings.

One serving: 502 calories, 46g protein, 50g carbohydrate, 14g fat (2g saturated), 67mg cholesterol, 966mg sodium, 8g fibre

helpful hints

● *Any type of firm, non-oily white fish can be used, for example turbot, halibut or monkfish.*

● *If clam juice is unavailable, use fish stock instead.*

● *Several drops hot pepper sauce can be substituted for red pepper flakes.*

● *Look for watermelon cut into cubes in the fruit and veg section of the supermarket.*

● *If pressed for time, omit the Watermelon Spritzer and just serve the watermelon cubes.*

countdown

● *Make stew.*

● *While stew simmers, make salad.*

● *Make watermelon spritzer.*

cioppino (seafood stew) continued

beetroot and onion salad

shopping list

TO BUY:

225g (8oz) fresh sea scallops

175g (6oz) fish fillet

*1 bottle no-sugar-added
lemon-lime or citrus-
flavoured sparkling water*

*1 small bottle red pepper
flakes*

*1 tin no-sugar-added whole
tomatoes*

*2 bottles clam juice
(500ml/18fl oz needed)*

*1 packet cooked beetroots
(450g/1lb needed)*

*2 medium-sized green
peppers*

110g (4oz) red potatoes

1 small bunch fresh basil

*1 packet watermelon cubes
or 1/4 whole watermelon
(275g/10oz needed)*

2 limes

STAPLES:

Red onion

Garlic

Olive oil

Olive oil spray

Balsamic vinegar

*No-sugar-added oil and
vinegar dressing*

Multi-grain bread

Artificial sweetener

Salt

Black peppercorns

*450g (1lb) cooked beetroots,
sliced*

110g (4oz) sliced red onion

*2 tablespoons no-sugar-added oil
and vinegar dressing*

*Salt and freshly ground black
pepper to taste*

Divide the sliced beetroot between 2 plates.
Sprinkle with the onion and drizzle with the
dressing. Season with salt and pepper to taste
and serve with the cioppino.

Makes 2 servings.

One serving: 129 calories, 2g protein,
13g carbohydrate, 9g fat (1g saturated),
0mg cholesterol, 159mg sodium, 0g fibre

watermelon spritzer

*450ml (16fl oz) no-sugar-added
lemon-lime or citrus-flavoured
sparkling water, chilled*

*2 tablespoons freshly squeezed
lime juice*

2g (1/16oz) artificial sweetener

275g (10oz) watermelon cubes

Place the sparkling water, lime juice, sweetener
and watermelon cubes in a blender. Blend until
smooth. Pour into 2 glasses and serve
immediately.

Makes 2 servings.

One serving: 53 calories, 1g protein,
13g carbohydrate, 0.6g fat (0g saturated),
0mg cholesterol, 3mg sodium, 1g fibre

pork souvlaki

Barbecued, skewered meats called souvlaki are sold as a quick meal on many street corners in Athens. A simple Greek marinade of lemon juice, olive oil, oregano and garlic flavours the meat. ● Bulghur is wheat kernels that have been steamed, dried and crushed. It has a chewy texture and tastes delicious in salads.

pork souvlaki

50ml (2fl oz) freshly squeezed lemon juice (2 lemons)

2 teaspoons olive oil

2 teaspoons dried oregano

2 medium-sized garlic cloves, crushed

225g (8oz) pork tenderloin, visible fat removed and meat cut into 4cm (1½in) cubes

2 small green peppers, cut into 5cm (2in) square pieces

half a small yellow onion, cut into pieces 1cm (½in) wide and 5cm (2in) long

2 kebab skewers

Preheat the grill. Combine the lemon juice, oil, oregano and garlic in a medium-sized bowl or large freezer bag. Add the pork and marinate for 15 minutes. Remove the pork from the marinade and thread onto skewers, alternating with the green pepper and onion pieces. Line a baking tray with foil and place the souvlaki on the tray. Place beneath the pre-heated grill and grill for 5 minutes. Turn and cook for 5 more minutes. Serve over the bulghur wheat.
Makes 2 servings.

One serving: 299 calories, 36g protein, 16g carbohydrate, 10g fat (3g saturated), 106mg cholesterol, 82mg sodium, 1g fibre

bulghur wheat salad

225ml (8fl oz) fat-free, low-sodium chicken stock

75g (3oz) coarse bulghur or cracked wheat

Salt and freshly ground black pepper to taste

50g (2oz) raisins

25g (1oz) pine nuts

2 teaspoons olive oil

Pour the stock into a small saucepan and bring to the boil over a high heat. Add the bulghur wheat and a pinch of salt and pepper. Lower the heat, stir and cover with a lid. Gently simmer for 10 minutes, or until the liquid is absorbed. Stir the raisins, pine nuts and olive oil into the cooked bulghur. Season with additional salt and pepper to taste.
Makes 2 servings.

One serving: 245 calories, 5g protein, 32g carbohydrate, 5g fat (1g saturated), 0mg cholesterol, 553mg sodium, 4g fibre

apricots

8 medium-sized fresh apricots

Divide between 2 plates.
Makes 2 servings.

One serving: 67 calories, 2g protein, 16g carbohydrate, 0.5g fat (0g saturated), 0mg cholesterol, 1mg sodium, 3g fibre

helpful hints

● If using wooden skewers, soak in water before using.

● To make marinating the pork easier, place it in self-seal freezer bags. You only need to flip the bag over to turn the meat in the marinade – and there's no bowl to wash.

countdown

● Preheat grill
● Marinate pork.
● Make salad.
● Cook souvlaki.

shopping list

TO BUY:

225g (8oz) pork tenderloin

1 packet bulghur or cracked wheat

1 small packet pine nuts

1 small packet raisins

2 small green peppers

2 lemons

8 medium-sized fresh apricots

STAPLES:

Yellow onion

Garlic

Olive oil

Dried oregano

Fat free, low-salt chicken stock

Salt

Black peppercorns

mediterranean veal and olives

Olives and pine nuts give this 20-minute veal stew a rich Mediterranean flavour. ● *Warm, bright sunshine, rolling hills touched with varying shades of green from the rows of olive trees, good food, thoughts of Italy and Greece... these memories inspired this quick, veal dinner and accompanying dish of orange-flavoured Ebly.*

helpful hints

● *Buy lean veal, or remove as much fat from the meat as possible before you cook it.*
● *Veal stewing meat can be ordered from your butcher.*
● *Pork tenderloin can be used instead of veal.*
● *Store any leftover pine nuts in your freezer.*

countdown

● *Prepare veal.*
● *While veal cooks, make Ebly.*

shopping list

TO BUY:
225g (8oz) veal stewing meat
1 tin low-sodium, no-sugar-added crushed tomatoes (225ml/8fl oz needed)
1 small jar stoned black olives
1 small packet pine nuts
1 small packet Ebly
1 small bottle dry white wine
1 small carton orange juice
225g (8oz) broccoli florets
1 small bunch fresh basil
1 orange
STAPLES:
Yellow onion
Garlic
Olive oil
Olive oil spray
Fat free, low-sodium chicken stock
Salt
Black peppercorns

mediterranean veal and olives

Olive oil spray
225g (8oz) veal stewing meat, visible fat trimmed and meat cut into 2.5cm (1in) cubes
225g (8oz) diced yellow onion
2 medium-sized garlic cloves, crushed
125ml (4fl oz) dry white wine
225g (8fl oz) low-salt, no-sugar-added tinned crushed tomatoes
225g (8oz) broccoli florets
8 black olives, stoned and halved
2 tablespoons pine nuts
25g (1oz) fresh basil, torn into bite-sized pieces
Salt and freshly ground black pepper to taste

Set a non-stick frying pan over a medium-high heat and spray with olive oil. Brown the veal on all sides for 3 minutes. Remove the veal, add the onion and garlic to the pan and cook for 2 minutes. Add the wine and cook for another minute. Add the tomatoes and broccoli. Reduce the heat to medium-low and return the veal to the pan. Cover and simmer for 15 minutes. Add the olives and pine nuts. Cook for 5 more minutes. Add the basil, season with salt and pepper to taste and serve.
Makes 2 servings.

One serving: 409 calories, 38g protein, 22g carbohydrate, 13g fat (4g saturated), 100mg cholesterol, 497mg sodium, 5g fibre

orange ebly

125ml (4fl oz) fat-free, low-sodium chicken stock
35g (1½oz) Ebly
2 teaspoons olive oil
1 tablespoon orange juice
1 orange, peeled and split into segments
Salt and freshly ground black pepper to taste

Bring the stock to the boil in a medium saucepan and add the Ebly. Boil for 10 minutes, uncovered. Drain and add the oil, orange juice and orange segments. Season with salt and pepper to taste and serve with the veal.
Makes 2 servings.

One serving: 222 calories, 5g protein, 41g carbohydrate, 5g fat (1g saturated), 0mg cholesterol, 142mg sodium, 0g fibre

country minestrone with meatballs

'Minestra' is Italian for soup, and minestrone is a hearty vegetable soup. This meatball minestrone is a complete meal in one pot. The recipe can be doubled easily so, if you have time, make extra to use another time. ● *Spices can add exciting flavours with very little effort. Fennel seeds are oval, green-brown seeds that come from the common fennel plant. They have an anise taste and are used in many liqueurs. They can be found in health food shops or the spice section of your supermarket, and they will keep for 6 months. Here, combined with oregano, they give the meatballs a unique flavour.* ● *Follow this comforting main course with a second helping of soul food – ginger-spiced apple sauce.*

country minestrone with herbed meatballs

2 teaspoons fennel seeds

1 teaspoon dried oregano

110g (4oz) lean minced beef sirloin

Salt and freshly ground black pepper to taste

2 teaspoons olive oil

110g (4oz) yellow onion, sliced

2 celery stalks, sliced

4 medium-sized garlic cloves, crushed

225ml (8fl oz) tinned low-sodium, no-sugar-added diced tomatoes

450ml (16fl oz) fat-free, low-sodium chicken stock

450ml (16fl oz) water

50g (2oz) wholemeal spaghetti or linguine, broken into small pieces

275g (10oz) washed, ready-to-eat fresh spinach

110g (4oz) tinned small haricot beans, rinsed and drained

2 tablespoons freshly grated Parmesan cheese

Mix the fennel seeds and oregano into the minced beef. Add a little salt and pepper to taste. Form into meatballs about 4–5cm (1½–2in) in diameter. Heat the oil in a medium-sized non-stick saucepan over a medium-high heat. Brown the meatballs on all sides, about 5 minutes, or until cooked through. Remove to a plate. Add the onion and celery to the saucepan. Sauté for 3 minutes without letting them brown. Add the garlic, tomatoes, chicken stock and water. Bring to a boil. Add the pasta and cook gently for 8–9 minutes, stirring once or twice to make sure the pasta rolls freely in the liquid. Add the spinach and beans to the cooking pasta. Return the meatballs to the soup and cook until heated through, about 2 minutes. Season to taste and serve in 2 large soup bowls with Parmesan cheese sprinkled on top.
Makes 2 servings.

One serving: 510 calories, 45g protein, 62g carbohydrate, 14g fat (5g saturated), 55mg cholesterol, 965mg sodium, 21g fibre

helpful hints

● *If you are not serving the soup immediately or are making some to freeze later, cook the pasta in a separate pan of water for 10 minutes. Drain, reserving 3 tablespoons of the cooking liquid. Add ½ teaspoon olive oil to the liquid and toss with the pasta to keep it from sticking. Add the pasta to the soup a few minutes before serving to warm through. The pasta will absorb the soup liquid if left to sit for any length of time.*

● *Cannellini beans or chickpeas can be substituted for haricot beans.*

● *Frozen spinach can be used instead of fresh. Defrost and squeeze dry before using.*

● *Buy good quality Parmesan cheese and grate it yourself. Freeze extra for quick use later – simply spoon out what you need and leave the rest frozen.*

● *If pressed for time, omit the Ginger-spiced Apple Sauce and serve 1 medium apple per person.*

countdown

● *Make minestrone.*

● *Core, peel and cook apples.*

● *Assemble salad.*

● *Complete apple sauce.*

shopping list

TO BUY:

110g (4oz) lean minced beef
  sirloin
1 tin low-sodium, no-sugar-
  added diced tomatoes
  (225ml/4fl oz needed)
1 small tin haricot beans
  (110g/4oz needed)
1 jar fennel seeds
1 packet wholemeal spaghetti
  or linguine (50g/2oz
  needed)
1 bag washed, ready-to-eat
  fresh spinach (275g/10oz
  needed)
1 bag washed, ready-to-eat,
  Italian-style salad leaves
2.5cm (1in) piece fresh ginger
2 Granny Smith apples
1 lemon

STAPLES:

Celery
Yellow onion
Garlic
Parmesan cheese
Olive oil
No-sugar-added oil and
  vinegar dressing
Dried oregano
Fat-free, low-salt chicken
  stock
Ground cinnamon
Artificial sweetener
Salt
Black peppercorns

country minestrone with meatballs continued

italian salad

150g (5oz) washed, ready-to-eat,
  Italian-style salad leaves
2 tablespoons no-sugar-added oil
  and vinegar dressing

Toss the salad with the dressing and serve.
Makes 2 servings.

One serving: 79 calories, 0g protein,
1g carbohydrate, 8g fat (1g saturated),
0mg cholesterol, 78mg sodium, 0g fibre

ginger-spiced apple sauce

2 Granny Smith apples, cored and
  cut into eighths
125ml (4fl oz) water
2 tablespoons freshly squeezed
  lemon juice (1 lemon)
2g (1/16oz) artificial sweetener
2 tablespoons grated fresh ginger
1/2 teaspoon ground cinnamon

Place the apples and water in a medium
saucepan. Cover with a lid and bring to a boil.
Cook for 10 minutes. Alternatively, place the
apples and water in a microwave-safe bowl.
Cover and microwave on high for 5 minutes. Let
stand for 2 to 3 minutes.

Place the cooked apples and water in the bowl
of a food processor and add the lemon juice and
sweetener. Grate the ginger over the bowl,
making sure to catch any ginger juice. Process
until thoroughly mixed. Spoon into 2 dessert
bowls. Sprinkle the apple sauce with a little
cinnamon and serve.
Makes 2 servings.

One serving: 90 calories, 0.5g protein,
24g carbohydrate, 0.5g fat (0g saturated),
0mg cholesterol, 1mg sodium, 4g fibre

curried prawns and vegetables

This meal takes a little more time, about 30 minutes, but is very much worth the effort. Juicy prawns cooked in a light curry sauce produce a flavour-packed, ethnic meal – try it when you want something with a zing. ● Authentic curries are made with a blend of about 15 spices. I have used shop-bought curry powder to shorten the preparation time for this meal. This type of powder loses its flavour quickly and should be not used if more than 3–4 months old.

curried prawns and vegetables

1 tablespoon olive oil

2 medium-sized garlic cloves, crushed

2.5cm (1in) piece fresh ginger, chopped (2 tablespoons)

2 tablespoons wholemeal flour

2 teaspoons ground cumin

1½ tablespoons curry powder

225ml (8fl oz) fat-free, low-sodium chicken stock

225g (8oz) broccoli florets

110g (4oz) sliced red onion

50g (2oz) raisins

350g (12oz) large raw prawns, peeled and deveined

Salt and freshly ground black pepper to taste

2 tablespoons crème fraîche

Heat the olive oil in a non-stick frying pan over a medium heat. Add the garlic, ginger, wholemeal flour, cumin and curry, stirring to blend well. Add the chicken stock. Cook until the sauce begins to thicken, about 1 minute. Add the broccoli florets, onion and raisins. Cover and simmer for 5 minutes. Add the raw prawns and cook uncovered for 2 minutes, or until the prawns are cooked. Season with salt and pepper to taste. Remove from the heat and blend in the crème fraîche. Divide between 2 plates and serve.
Makes 2 servings.

One serving: 451 calories, 42g protein, 36g carbohydrate, 17g fat (5g saturated), 281mg cholesterol, 564mg sodium, 1g fibre

helpful hints

● Buy peeled raw prawns – it is well worth the time otherwise spent shelling them yourself.

● If only cooked prawns are available, add them to at the end of the cooking time, just long enough to heat them through.

● To chop fresh ginger quickly, cut it into small cubes and press through a garlic press with large holes. If using a press with small holes, just capture the juice that is squeezed out; it will give enough flavour for the recipe.

● Lentil salad can be made a day ahead and served warm or at room temperature. Make extra if you have time for a great lunch or snack

● To shorten preparation time for this meal, omit the lentil salad and serve a quick-cooking brown rice instead.

countdown

● Start lentil salad.

● Prepare ingredients for curried prawns.

● Cook curried prawns.

● Finish lentil salad.

curried prawns and vegetables continued

lentil salad

225ml (8fl oz) fat-free, low-sodium
    chicken stock

225ml (8fl oz) water

110g (4oz) green lentils

2 whole garlic cloves

4 spring onions, thinly sliced

2 tablespoons no-sugar-added oil
    and vinegar dressing

Salt and freshly ground black
    pepper to taste

Bring the stock and water to the boil in a medium saucepan. Rinse the lentils and slowly pour into the boiling stock, so that the stock continues to boil. Add the garlic and reduce the heat to medium-low. Simmer for 20 minutes, or until lentils are cooked through but still firm. Meanwhile, mix the spring onions with the dressing. Add salt and pepper to taste. Drain the lentils and remove the garlic cloves. Mix the dressing with the lentils while still warm.

Makes 2 servings.

One serving: 147 calories, 6g protein,
13g carbohydrate, 9g fat (1g saturated),
0mg cholesterol, 357mg sodium, 2g fibre

lychees

150g (5oz) tinned lychees, drained

Divide the lychees between 2 dessert bowls and serve.

Makes 2 servings.

One serving: 63 calories, 1g protein,
16g carbohydrate, 0.5g fat (0g saturated),
0mg cholesterol, 1mg sodium, 1g fibre

chicken fajitas

Fajitas make deliciously light meals. Served with an array of colourful vegetables and wrapped in warm tortillas, these little Mexican sandwiches are an entire meal in themselves.
- *Enjoy grapefruit with a kick for dessert.*

chicken fajitas

50ml (2fl oz) freshly squeezed lemon juice (2 lemons)

3 teaspoons rapeseed oil, divided

1 teaspoon ground cumin

Pinch ground cayenne

225g (8oz) boneless, skinless chicken breast, very thinly sliced

4 x 20.5cm (8in) wholemeal tortillas

225g (8oz) red onion, sliced

2 medium-sized red peppers, sliced

2 medium-sized green peppers, sliced

4 garlic cloves, crushed

2 medium tomatoes, diced

50g (2oz) grated, reduced-fat Cheddar cheese

25g (1oz) chopped fresh coriander leaves

Preheat the oven to 180°C/350°F/gas mark 4. Mix the lemon juice, 1 teaspoon of the oil, the cumin and cayenne together in a microwave-safe bowl. Microwave for 30 seconds on high. Alternatively, place in a small saucepan, bring to the boil and then immediately remove from the heat. Place the chicken in the warm marinade for 15 minutes, stirring to make sure all of the chicken is covered. Tightly wrap the tortillas in 2 foil parcels and place in the preheated oven for 10 minutes. Remove and leave wrapped in foil.

Heat the remaining 2 teaspoons of oil in a medium-sized non-stick frying pan until the oil begins to smoke. Remove the chicken from the marinade, saving any marinade that remains (most will be absorbed by the chicken), and sauté the chicken for about 1 minute. Add the onion, peppers and garlic. Sauté for 2 minutes. Add the marinade and toss with the chicken and vegetables for another minute, or until the sauce reduces and just coats the chicken.

To serve, arrange the diced tomatoes, grated cheese and chopped coriander in small bowls. Spoon the chicken and vegetables onto a warm serving dish along with the wrapped tortillas. Fill the tortillas with the chicken and vegetables, sprinkle with the tomatoes, grated cheese and coriander and fold to eat.

Makes 2 servings.

One serving: 630 calories, 63g protein, 56g carbohydrate, 23g fat (8g saturated), 116mg cholesterol, 614mg sodium, 2g fibre

helpful hints

- *Red, yellow and green peppers make this a colourful dish, but you can use one or any combination of peppers you like.*
- *Heating dried spices releases their oils, increasing their flavour.*
- *Triple Sec and other orange liqueurs can be bought in miniature bottles at many supermarkets and most off-licences.*

countdown

- *Preheat oven to 180°C/350°F/gas mark 4.*
- *Make fajitas.*
- *Make grapefruit.*

chicken fajitas continued

tipsy grapefruit

1 grapefruit
1 tablespoon Triple Sec or other
  orange liqueur

Separate the grapefruit segments with a serrated knife and scoop out onto 2 dessert plates. Sprinkle with the Triple Sec and serve.
Makes 2 servings.

One serving: 101 calories, 1g protein, 17g carbohydrate, 0g fat (0g saturated), 0mg cholesterol, 1mg sodium, 1g fibre

roast beef and shiitake hash

Roast beef, shiitake mushrooms and fresh thyme transform a 1950s-style American 'hash' to a modern version that takes only 20 minutes to make. I've shortened the cooking time by using lean roast beef from the deli and making a light gravy from chicken stock. The gravy just coats the hash. I've updated the flavour using shiitake mushrooms, pine nuts and fresh thyme. This hash keeps well, so make double if you have time.

roast beef and shiitake hash

2 teaspoons olive oil

110g (4oz) unpeeled red potatoes, washed and cut into 2.5cm (1in) cubes

110g (4oz) diced red onion

2 medium-sized red peppers, diced

110g (4oz) shiitake mushrooms, diced

225g (8oz) sliced lean roast beef, diced

2 tablespoons wholemeal flour

225ml (8fl oz) fat-free, low-sodium chicken stock

Salt and freshly ground black pepper to taste

Heat the oil in a non-stick frying pan over a medium-high heat. Add the potatoes and sauté for 5 minutes, tossing to turn halfway through. Add the onion, peppers and mushrooms. Sauté for 10 minutes, again tossing to turn halfway through. Add the roast beef and toss for 1 minute. Push the ingredients to the side of the pan, leaving a hole in the centre. Add the flour, then the stock and stir until the sauce thickens. Toss with the ingredients to lightly bind the hash. Season with salt and pepper to taste. Divide between 2 plates and serve.
Makes 2 servings.

> One serving: 409 calories, 39g protein, 29g carbohydrate, 14g fat (4g saturated), 93mg cholesterol, 364mg sodium, 1g fibre

green salad

350g (12oz) washed, ready-to-eat mixed salad leaves

75g (3oz) cannellini beans

2 tablespoons no-sugar-added oil and vinegar salad dressing

Salt and freshly ground black pepper to taste

Place the salad leaves and beans in a bowl and drizzle with the dressing. Season with salt and pepper to taste and toss. Serve with the hash.
Makes 2 servings.

> One serving: 136 calories, 4g protein, 14g carbohydrate, 9g fat (1g saturated), 0mg cholesterol, 82mg sodium, 3g fibre

helpful hints

- *Ask the deli to cut the roast beef in a single slice to make it easier to cube.*
- *Pecans or almonds can be substituted for the walnuts.*
- *If pressed for time, substitute 1 medium apple per person for the Cinnamon Walnut Baked Apples*

countdown

- *Make hash.*
- *While hash cooks, make salad.*
- *Make baked apples.*

shopping list

TO BUY:

225g (8oz) sliced lean roast beef

1 tin cannellini beans (110g/4oz needed)

1 small packet broken walnuts (about 25g/1oz needed)

110g (4oz) red potatoes

2 medium-sized red peppers

1 packet shiitake mushrooms (110g/4oz needed)

1 bag washed, ready-to-eat mixed salad leaves

2 Red Delicious apples

roast beef and shiitake hash continued

STAPLES:

Olive oil

Red onion

Wholemeal flour

*Fat-free, low-sodium chicken
    stock*

Ground cinnamon

Artificial sweetener

*No-sugar-added oil and
    vinegar salad dressing*

Salt

Black peppercorns

cinnamon-walnut baked apples

2 tablespoons broken walnuts
1 teaspoon ground cinnamon
2g (¹/₁₆oz) artificial sweetener
2 Red Delicious apples, cored

Chop the walnuts with the cinnamon and sweetener in a food processor. Place the apples in 2 small dessert bowls, and fill the core of each apple with the cinnamon-walnut mixture. (Some of the mixture may spill over the top. This is fine.) Cover each bowl with another bowl or microwave-safe cling film. Microwave on high 4 minutes. Remove and let stand, covered, 2 minutes. Serve in the dessert bowls.
Makes 2 servings.

One serving: 159 calories, 2g protein, 24g carbohydrate, 8g fat (0.8g saturated), 0mg cholesterol, 1mg sodium, 4g fibre

bahamian fish boil

With excellent fresh fish available all year round, the natives of the Bahamas are masters at cooking fish. ● This 20-minute meal is made in one pot. The fish should be cooked just long enough so that it is tender and juicy. Also, be sure to season the fish well before it cooks. ● For an interesting change, try this chayote salad. Chayote squash, also called 'mirliton' or 'christophene', looks like a gnarled pear. It has a flavour similar to courgettes, but retains its crisp texture when cooked.

bahamian fish boil

*110g (4oz) sweet potatoes or
  yams, peeled and cut into 1cm
  (¹/₂in) pieces
4 celery stalks, sliced
110g (4oz) sliced yellow onion
8 sprigs fresh thyme or 2
  teaspoons dried
675ml (24fl oz) cold water
350g (12oz) mahi mahi fillet cut
  into 2.5cm (1in) pieces
2 tablespoons freshly squeezed
  lemon juice (1 lemon)
Salt and freshly ground black
  pepper to taste
Several drops hot pepper sauce
1 tablespoon olive oil
2 slices multi-grain bread*

Place the potatoes, celery, onion, thyme and water in a saucepan. Cover and cook over a medium-high heat for 15 minutes. Meanwhile, season both sides of the fish with the lemon juice, salt and pepper, pressing the seasoning into the fillet. Lower the heat and add the fish to the saucepan. Cover and gently simmer for 5 minutes. Add the pepper sauce and olive oil, then season with additional salt and pepper to taste. Meanwhile, toast the bread. Serve the soup in large soup bowls with the toasted bread. *Makes 2 servings.*

One serving: 353 calories, 38g protein,
34g carbohydrate, 10g fat (1g saturated),
126mg cholesterol, 418mg sodium, 6g fibre

helpful hints

● *Fresh thyme works best in this dish. If using dried, make sure the herb is less than 6 months old.*
● *Any type of white fish can be used. A delicate, flaky fish such as sole will need only 2 minutes to cook.*
● *If chayote is unavailable use baby courgettes instead.*
● *Any type of hot pepper sauce can be used.*
● *Any type of washed, ready-to-eat lettuce can be used instead of the chayote salad.*

countdown

● *Start vegetables boiling in the stock.*
● *Season fish and add to stock.*
● *While fish cooks, make salad.*

shopping list

TO BUY:
  *350g (12oz) mahi mahi fillet
  110g (4oz) orange-fleshed
    sweet potatoes or yams
  1 bunch fresh thyme or
    1 jar dried
  2 small chayotes
  1 bag washed, ready-to-eat
    lettuce leaves
  1 medium mango
  1 lemon*

bahamian fish boil continued

STAPLES:
  Celery
  Yellow onion
  Garlic
  Hot pepper sauce
  Olive oil
  No-sugar-added oil and
    vinegar dressing
  Multi-grain bread
  Salt
  Black peppercorns

chayote salad

2 tablespoons no-sugar-added oil
  and vinegar dressing
2 medium-sized garlic cloves,
  crushed
2 small chayotes, peeled and
  sliced
Salt and freshly ground black
  pepper to taste
Several lettuce leaves, washed and
  dried

Heat the dressing in a medium-sized non-stick frying pan over a medium-high heat and add the garlic and chayote slices. Toss for 3–4 minutes. Season with salt and pepper to taste. Place the lettuce leaves on a plate and spoon the chayote on top before serving.

Makes 2 servings.

One serving: 126 calories, 2g protein,
11g carbohydrate, 9g fat (1g saturated),
0mg cholesterol, 83mg sodium, 0g fibre

mango

1 medium mango

Slice off each side of the mango as close to the stone as possible. Take the mango half in your hand, skin- side down. Score the fruit in a cross-hatch pattern. Bend the skin backwards so that the cubes pop up like a porcupine. Slice the cubes off the skin. Score and slice any fruit left on the stone.

   Divide the mango cubes between 2 dessert bowls.

Makes 2 servings.

One serving: 67 calories, 1g protein,
18g carbohydrate, 0g fat (0g saturated),
0mg cholesterol, 2mg sodium, 1g fibre

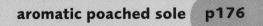
aromatic poached sole **p176**

mediterranean veal and olives   p182

summer-and-winter chicken casserole

This flavourful casserole takes only 30 minutes to make and is a meal in a bowl, but light enough to enjoy year-round.

summer-and-winter chicken casserole

675ml (24fl oz) fat-free, low-sodium chicken stock

450ml (16fl oz) low-sodium, no-sugar-added, tinned diced tomatoes (including juice)

225g (8oz) red onion, sliced

2 celery stalks, sliced

75g (3oz) white cabbage, sliced

50g (2oz) wholemeal fusilli pasta

1 tablespoon horseradish

1 tablespoon balsamic vinegar

275g (10oz) washed, ready-to-eat fresh spinach

2 slices wholemeal bread

50g (2oz) grated, reduced-fat Swiss or Gruyère cheese

Salt and freshly ground black pepper to taste

Bring the chicken stock and tomatoes to the boil in a large saucepan over a medium-high heat. Add the onion and celery. Cover, lower the heat to medium and cook on a slow boil for 10 minutes. Add the cabbage and fusilli. Boil uncovered for 10 minutes. Combine the horseradish and vinegar. Add to the pan and stir in the spinach. Simmer for 2 minutes, until the spinach is just wilted. Toast the bread. Add the cheese to the casserole. Season with salt and pepper to taste. Serve with the toasted bread. *Makes 2 servings.*

One serving: 434 calories, 36g protein, 66g carbohydrate, 7g fat (3g saturated), 15mg cholesterol, 1289mg sodium, 22g fibre

grilled cinnamon oranges

2 medium oranges

½ teaspoon ground cinnamon

2 tablespoons flaked almonds

2g (¹/₁₆oz) artificial sweetener

Preheat the grill. Line a baking tray with foil or use a small oven-to-table dish. Peel the oranges over a bowl to catch the juice. With a serrated knife, cut the oranges into circular 1cm (½in) slices over the bowl. Place the orange slices in a single layer in the baking dish. Sprinkle with the cinnamon and almonds and grill for 3 minutes. Combine the sweetener with the reserved orange juice. Pour the juice over the grilled oranges and serve. *Makes 2 servings.*

One serving: 129 calories, 4g protein, 19g carbohydrate, 6g fat (0.5g saturated), 0mg cholesterol, 0mg sodium, 4g fibre

helpful hints

● *Any type of short-cut wholemeal pasta can be used.*
● *If pressed for time, omit the grilled cinnamon oranges and serve 1 orange per person.*

countdown

● *Preheat grill.*
● *Prepare all ingredients.*
● *Make casserole.*
● *While casserole cooks, toast bread.*
● *Make grilled oranges.*

shopping list

TO BUY:
1 small packet grated, reduced-fat Swiss or Gruyère cheese (50g/2oz needed)
1 tin low-sodium, no-sugar-added, tinned diced tomatoes (450ml/16fl oz needed)
1 small jar horseradish
1 packet flaked almonds
1 packet wholemeal fusilli pasta (50g/2oz needed)
¼ head white cabbage
1 bag washed, ready-to-eat fresh spinach
2 medium oranges
STAPLES:
Celery
Red onion
Fat-free, low-sodium chicken stock
Balsamic vinegar
Wholemeal bread
Ground cinnamon
Artificial sweetener
Salt
Black peppercorns

beef stir-fry with oyster sauce

You can make a beef, broccoli and water chestnut stir-fry in less time than it takes to send out for Chinese food. The popularity of Chinese food in America has made this a classic 'American' dish.

beef stir-fry with oyster sauce

50ml (2fl oz) bottled oyster sauce
50ml (2fl oz) dry sherry or water
2 teaspoons sesame oil, divided
225g (8oz) broccoli florets
225g (8oz) lean beef (fillet, sirloin, flank or skirt) cut into 5 x 1cm (2 x ½ in) strips
250g (9oz) sliced water chestnuts
Salt and freshly ground black pepper to taste

Combine the oyster sauce, sherry and 1 teaspoon of the sesame oil in a small bowl. Make sure all ingredients are prepped and ready for stir-frying. Heat the remaining teaspoon of sesame oil in a non-stick wok or frying pan until smoking. Add the broccoli and stir-fry for 3 minutes. Add the beef, water chestnuts and sauce. Stir fry for 2 more minutes. Season with salt and pepper to taste and serve over brown rice.
Makes 2 servings.

One serving: 470 calories, 47g protein, 37g carbohydrate, 15g fat (5g saturated), 102mg cholesterol, 675mg sodium, 8g fibre

brown rice

75g (3oz) brown rice
8 spring onions, sliced
2 teaspoons sesame oil
Salt and freshly ground black pepper to taste

Fill a large saucepan with about 2–3 litres (4–5 pints) of water and bring to the boil. Place the rice in a strainer and rinse under cold water. Add to the saucepan, stir once or twice and boil for 30 minutes. Alternatively, follow the cooking instructions on the packet. Drain leaving about 3 tablespoons water on the rice. Toss the spring onions and sesame oil with the rice. Season with salt and pepper to taste.
Makes 2 servings.

One serving: 140 calories, 3g protein, 20g carbohydrate, 5g fat (1g saturated), 0mg cholesterol, 2mg sodium, 1g fibre

minted clementines

225ml (8fl oz) no-sugar-added
    lemon-lime or citrus-flavoured
    sparkling water, chilled
2 sprigs fresh mint
2g (¹/₁₆oz) artificial sweetener
2 medium clementines, peeled
    and divided into segments

Pour the sparkling water into a small bowl and add the mint sprigs, sweetener and clementine segments. Stir to dissolve the sweetener. Let the clementine segments marinate for 15 minutes, then remove and arrange on 2 small plates. Pour a little of the marinade over the segments and garnish with a sprig of mint before serving.
Makes 2 servings.

One serving: 37 calories, 0.5g protein,
10g carbohydrate, 0.2g fat (0g saturated),
0mg cholesterol, 1mg sodium, 0g fibre

countdown

- *Start rice.*
- *Marinate tangerines.*
- *Prepare beef ingredients.*
- *Stir-fry beef.*
- *Finish rice.*

shopping list

TO BUY:
    225g (8oz) lean beef (fillet,
        sirloin, flank, or skirt)
    1 tin sliced water chestnuts
        (350g/12oz needed)
    1 bottle oyster sauce
    1 small bottle sesame oil
    1 small packet brown rice
    1 small bottle no-sugar-
        added lemon-lime or citrus-
        flavoured sparkling water
        (225ml/8fl oz needed)
    1 small bottle dry sherry
    225g (8oz) broccoli florets
    1 small bunch spring onions
        (8 needed)
    1 small bunch fresh mint
    2 medium clementines
STAPLES:
    Artificial sweetener
    Salt
    Black peppercorns

roasted pork and peach salsa

helpful hints

- If peaches are not available, use fresh pear or papaya.
- Shop-bought salsa can be used instead of fresh peach salsa. Make sure there is no sugar added.

countdown

- Preheat oven to 200°C/400°F/gas mark 6.
- Start pork.
- Start pasta.
- Make salsa.
- Finish pasta.

shopping list

TO BUY:

225g (8oz) pork tenderloin

1 packet wholemeal fusilli or macaroni pasta (50g/2oz needed)

225g (8oz) courgettes

2 jalapeño peppers

1 small bunch fresh coriander

2 ripe peaches

1 lime

1 cantaloupe

STAPLES:

Carrots

Olive oil

Olive oil spray

Dried oregano

Ground cumin

Artificial sweetener

Salt

Black peppercorns

For best results, the peaches should be ripe. Look for tree-ripened peaches, which have more flavour. ● Both the pork and pasta salad can be served warm or at room temperature.

roasted pork and peach salsa

225g (8oz) pork tenderloin

Olive oil spray

½ teaspoon dried oregano

½ teaspoon ground cumin

2 ripe peaches, washed, halved and stoned

2 teaspoons freshly squeezed lime juice

2g (¹⁄₁₆oz) artificial sweetener

2 tablespoons chopped fresh coriander leaves

2 jalapeño peppers, deseeded and chopped (2 tablespoons)

Salt and freshly ground black pepper to taste

Preheat the oven to 200°C/400°F/gas mark 6. Line a baking tray with foil. Remove any visible fat from the pork, place on the foil and spray both sides with olive oil. Sprinkle the pork with the oregano and cumin. Place in the oven and roast for 25 minutes.

While the pork roasts, dice the peaches. Combine the lime juice and sweetener in a small bowl. Add the peaches, coriander and jalapeños. Toss well and season with salt and pepper to taste.

When the pork is cooked, slice and serve immediately, or let cool to room temperature and then slice. Serve with the salsa on the side.

Makes 2 servings.

One serving: 278 calories, 35g protein, 19g carbohydrate, 8g fat (3g saturated), 106mg cholesterol, 83mg sodium, 1g fibre

pasta salad

50g (2oz) wholemeal fusilli or macaroni pasta

225g (8oz) sliced carrots

275g (10oz) sliced courgettes

4 teaspoons olive oil

Salt and freshly ground black pepper to taste

Fill a large saucepan with water and bring to the boil. Add the pasta and boil for 7 minutes. Add the carrots and courgettes. Continue to boil for 2 minutes, or until the pasta is cooked through but firm. Drain the pasta and vegetables and toss with the olive oil. Season with salt and pepper to taste. Serve with the pork.

Makes 2 servings.

One serving: 285 calories, 9g protein, 40g carbohydrate, 10g fat (2g saturated), 0mg cholesterol, 51mg sodium, 7g fibre

melon

1 cantaloupe, cubed

Divide the cantaloupe between 2 dessert bowls.

Makes 2 servings.

One serving: 77 calories, 2g protein, 18g carbohydrate, 1g fat (0g saturated), 0mg cholesterol, 20mg sodium, 2g fibre

desserts

introduction

With this chapter to hand, there's no need to abandon your healthy eating lifestyle when you want a special treat or have guests for dinner.

Most desserts, unfortunately, are laden with carbohydrates. I created these recipes for those times when you want something sweet at the end of a meal, while staying within the guidelines of a low-carb lifestyle.

Desserts have not been included as part of the Quick Start section, but the Strawberry Pecan Whip and Coffee Latte Whip are two desserts that you can enjoy during the Quick Start phase (and subsequent phases). They're satisfying at the end of a meal and have limited carbohydrate content. A few desserts are included in the Which Carb section because they fit the nutritional guidelines for that menu. But most desserts have been included in the Right Carb meals.

I have created some additional temptations as alternatives to a simple fruit dessert. The Mocha Fudge Soufflé and the Raspberry Parfait are winners and can be served to guests with pride.

dessert index

helpful hints

- *Any fruit-flavoured, sugar-free jelly can be used.*
- *Be careful toasting pecans, as they burn easily.*

countdown

- *Set water to boil.*
- *Make recipe.*

shopping list

TO BUY:

1 packet sugar-free, low-calorie strawberry jelly

1 small pot semi-skimmed ricotta cheese

1 small packet pecan pieces

STAPLES:

Vanilla essence

strawberry pecan whip

'Whipped Jell-O' was a favourite of mine when I was young. Here is an updated version that fits perfectly into a low-carb lifestyle – and can be eaten in Quick Start, Which Carbs and Right Carbs.

strawberry pecan whip

125g (4½oz) sugar-free, low-calorie strawberry jelly

225ml (8fl oz) boiling water

225ml (8fl oz) cold water

1 teaspoon vanilla essence

2 tablespoons pecan pieces, toasted

50ml (2fl oz) semi-skimmed ricotta cheese

Dissolve the jelly in boiling water, stirring for 2 minutes. Add the cold water and place in the refrigerator to set for 1½ hours. Stir the vanilla essence and pecans into the ricotta cheese. Whip into the partially set jelly with an electric beater. Divide between 4 dessert bowls. Refrigerate to set once more before serving. *Makes 4 servings.*

One serving: 147 calories, 8g protein, 3g carbohydrate, 11g fat (3g saturated), 15mg cholesterol, 45mg sodium, 1g fibre

apricot almond custard

Good quality dried apricots add more flavour to this dish. Once reconstituted, they should look like fresh apricots. This dessert can be eaten during Right Carbs.

apricot almond custard

6 dried apricots
125ml (4fl oz) skimmed milk
2g (¹/₁₆oz) artificial sweetener
¼ teaspoon almond essence
1 egg
1 tablespoon flaked almonds

Preheat the oven to 180°C/350°F/gas mark 4. Bring a small saucepan of water to the boil and add the apricots. Boil for 3–4 minutes to reconstitute, then drain and coarsely chop. Combine the apricots, milk, sweetener, almond essence and egg in a small bowl. Divide between 2 ovenproof ramekins or a bowl 8 x 4.5cm (3 x 1¾ in) deep. Sprinkle the almonds on top. Bake for 30 minutes, or until the custard is firm.
Makes 2 servings.

One serving: 143 calories, 8g protein, 17g carbohydrate, 6g fat (1g saturated), 108mg cholesterol, 64mg sodium, 3g fibre

countdown

- *Preheat oven to 180°C/350°F/gas mark 4.*
- *Set a small saucepan of water to boil.*
- *Complete recipe.*

shopping list

TO BUY:
1 packet dried apricots (6 needed)
1 small bottle almond essence
1 small packet flaked almonds (about 10g/½oz needed)
STAPLES:
Skimmed milk
Artificial sweetener
Egg

coffee latte whip

This recipe was created for the Quick Start phase but can be used during any phase.

coffee latte whip

1 tablespoon gelatine (7g/¹/₂₄oz)
50ml (2fl oz) cold water
115ml (4fl oz) boiling water
4g (¹/₂₈oz) artificial sweetener
¹/₂ tablespoon unsweetened cocoa powder
50ml (2fl oz) strong, decaffeinated, black coffee
2 tablespoons whipping cream

Soak the gelatine in the cold water for 5 minutes. Pour the boiling water into the cold water-gelatine mixture to dissolve the gelatine. Stir in the sweetener, cocoa powder and coffee. Pour into a bowl and refrigerate for 1 hour to set. Remove the gelatine from the refrigerator and whip with an electric beater. Add the whipping cream and continue to whip until fluffy. Pour into 2 dessert dishes and refrigerate to set, about 15 minutes.

Makes 2 servings.

One serving: 74 calories, 4g protein, 3g carbohydrate, 6g fat (4g saturated), 21mg cholesterol, 12mg sodium, 0.5g fibre

mocha fudge cake

Melting the chocolate in a microwave takes only minutes.

mocha fudge cake

50g (2oz) bittersweet or plain chocolate

1 tablespoon strong, decaffeinated, black coffee

2g (1/16oz) artificial sweetener

4 egg whites

Preheat the oven to 180°C/350°F/gas mark 4. Place the chocolate in a microwave-safe bowl and microwave on high for 2 minutes to melt. Stir in the coffee and sweetener.

Beat the egg whites until stiff peaks form. Fold into the chocolate mixture. Spoon into 2 soufflé dishes 4cm (1½in) high and 10cm (4in) in diameter, or a single Pyrex bowl 8cm (3in) high and 15cm (6in) in diameter. Bake in the oven for 8 minutes and serve warm.

Makes 2 servings.

One serving: 169 calories, 11g protein, 9g carbohydrate, 15g fat (9g saturated), 0mg cholesterol, 111mg sodium, 0g fibre

helpful hints

- *Buy high-quality chocolate for best results.*
- *Instant coffee can be used.*

countdown

- *Preheat oven to 180°C/350°F/gas mark 4.*
- *Melt chocolate.*
- *Whip egg whites.*
- *Complete recipe.*

shopping list

TO BUY:

50g (2oz) bittersweet or plain chocolate

STAPLES:

Eggs

Decaffeinated coffee

Artificial sweetener

index

notes

acknowledgments

Many, many thanks go to my husband, Harold. He has been the main force behind this book. Since his decision five years ago to adopt a low-carb lifestyle, he has stood by my work and by my side. He encouraged me to create the recipes, helped to test and taste them and edited every word.

I'd like to thank my assistant, Jackie Murrill, for her patience and help in testing these recipes. She spent hours on her feet working with me – and always with a smile.

James Connolly, President and Publisher of Bay Books, deserves a big thank you. He supported this project and worked very hard to bring the US edition to print in what must be record time.

Many thanks go to Martha Hopkins, my editor, who worked night and day to meet our tight schedule.

I'd also like to thank my family who embraced the project and supported me through it. My son James, his wife Patty and their son Zachary, who all came for dinner with a smile knowing they would be recipe-tasting guinea pigs. My son Charles and his girlfriend Lori who tested recipes via email. My son John, his wife Jill and their son Jeffrey, who cheered me on. My sister Roberta and brother-in-law Robert, who helped to edit my thoughts and words.

Thanks go to Kathy Martin, my editor at the Miami Herald, who has been a friend and booster for my columns and books.

Producing and hosting a weekly radio program has been a delight as well as an enormous amount of work. Thanks to the management and staff at WLRN 91.3 FM, public radio for South Florida, for their friendship and help.

I'd like to thank the many readers and students who correspond with me from all over the US to say how much they enjoy the recipes and how much better they feel. This kind of encouragement makes the lonely time in front of the computer worthwhile.

Most importantly, I'd like to thank all of you who read this book and prepare the meals. I hope you enjoy them and reap the benefits as much as I've enjoyed creating the recipes and watching the wonderful results.